GOD's

GREAT LOVE STORY

FROM GARDEN TO GLORY
A 7-WEEK JOURNEY THROUGH THE BIBLE

RACHEL ROTERT

Book cover and interior typesetting: Vanessa Mendozzi

ISBN: 978-0-9600245-0-6 (paperback)
ISBN: 978-0-9600245-1-3 (ebook)

CONTENTS

INTRODUCTION

God's Great Love Story exists to help bring the Bible to life as a relevant, compelling love story.

Many folks carry around strong feelings about the Bible, but few people have actually read it. Some use out-of-context passages as weapons to condemn others. Some write off the Bible as an outdated group of texts with no relevance to modern society. Some feel so overwhelmed by the genealogies, prophecies, and hard-to-pronounce names that the very idea of picking up the Bible feels as painful as a root canal and as boring as golf on the radio.

As a person who loves the Bible and notices these common barriers between modern Christians and scripture, one of my deepest desires is to help others fall in love with these stories and better understand them. The Bible is not just some dusty collection of rules and antiquated legends. On the contrary, this is a collection of true love stories about imperfect people and a perfect God. These folks were ridiculously flawed, just like you and me, but time and time again, God went out of his way to rescue them, love them, and show them how to live amazing, full lives under his protection and grace.

Before we go on, you should know that unlike many Christian authors, I'm not actually a bonafide expert on all things Bible. I'm not a pastor, and I've never spent a day in seminary. However, I am the daughter and granddaughter of people who raised me to love God and explore the Bible at an early age. I've always been an avid reader, and from my early teen years, I have read the Bible in its entirety at least twice a year. I continually seek out new information and perspectives about faith and Biblical history, and I spend daily quiet time with God. I want you to know that I am highly aware that my lack of a religion degree makes me unqualified to write this book. In fact, this is one reason that I wrote a first draft of this book seven years ago and then got too scared to release it into the world. I felt unworthy and unqualified to tell this beautiful story.

Here's the thing though. We're all unworthy and unqualified. Anyone who thinks they have it all figured out is probably not actually great friends with Jesus. Because I know how unqualified I am, I have thoughtfully sought advice from actual experts to assist in my interpretation of each Biblical section. I have absorbed dozens of books about grace and dozens of sermons about Revelation. I have done my best to wrap my mind around complex theological concepts and put these concepts in words that reflect their simplest and most beautiful truths. I know that no human words exist that would fully explain the glory of God or the complexity of his plans. Nonetheless, I've done my best. I truly feel that through writing this book, I've grown to love and appreciate God even more, and I've become more motivated to share that love with others.

So here's what I've learned. From Genesis to Revelation, the Bible tells one cohesive story, and it's a lot simpler than you think. It's also a lot more complex and beautiful than you may realize.

It is a story of a family that was blessed, broken, restored, and set apart. It's a story of war and peace, of politics and scandal. It's a story of the ultimate superhero battling for the hearts of his children in a world that was broken by those very children. This story is certainly not always pretty. But it's beautiful. And it's bigger than all of us. The Bible is a story of God lifting up little imperfect perfectionists like us and equipping them to do great things.

Most of all, this is a love story. God's great love story.

I may not be qualified to tell it, but as God's imperfect and beloved daughter, I will do my best to do it anyway.

Why?

Because it's a story too amazing not to tell.

Since the goal of this book is to help increase your love, understanding, and connection to the Bible, I have constructed this book with that overarching goal in mind. My aim is to address and reduce any barriers that may have prevented you from reading and fully understanding the Bible in the past.

Barrier #1- The Bible is ridiculously long.

It's true. The Bible is 1200 pages, and our attention spans can typically only handle 140 characters or less. For a fairly slow reader like myself, it takes about six months to a year to get through the whole thing.

How I'll try to help - In rewriting each Biblical passage, I have tried to focus on big ideas. I've dramatically condensed things like genealogies, highly descriptive ceremony procedures, and repetitive passages that may be interesting but don't really contribute to God's overarching love story. I have condensed each Biblical chapter to a paragraph, which transforms each Biblical book into a few manageable pages.

Barrier #2- The Bible is super old.

Our understanding of the world has changed immeasurably in the past few millennia, so these ancient texts are chock full of customs that are difficult for us to understand in light of our modern culture. Human beings simply had a different understanding of science, medicine, mental health, women's rights, slavery, and many other topics back then, so it's tempting to discard these texts when we come across a verse that feels "off" in some way.

How I'll try to help - I'm quite a history nerd, and I've digested many sermons and books that have helped me understand how the more difficult Bible passages make sense in the context of ancient Middle Eastern cultures. Laws and passages that feel confusing or antiquated to us were actually quite useful and revolutionary when these passages were written. When we get to difficult passages that discuss ancient cultural assumptions, my aim will be to help these passages make sense in the context of our modern understanding of science and human rights. I will use literary choices to prevent these more antiquated cultural ideas from distracting from the timeless, relevant lessons in each story.

Barrier #3- All the old-fashioned language.

Many Bible translations were compiled decades or centuries ago, so few of them use vernacular that we would consider modern or conversational. If you read a passage written in a voice that feels much older than your own voice, it's understandably hard to see yourself in that passage, and it takes extra brain power to find personal meaning in it.

How I'll try to help- I've had a great deal of fun re-writing each Bible passage to include simple, contemporary, modern language that you and I actually use in our daily speech. I hope my writing style helps you more easily see yourself in these stories and more easily internalize the wisdom within the stories.

Barrier#4- Those prophecy books hurt my brain.

The Old Testament prophecy books and Revelation are full of easily misunderstood passages full of complex symbolism and expressions of God's anger. It's hard to unravel the symbols, and it's hard to understand that our loving God and the powerful Judge are the same being. It's easier to just skip over the tricky books and focus on the books that don't stress us out as much.

How I'll try to help- I spent many years with the same thoughts, and I truly understand this barrier to recognizing the Bible as a great love story. It took a lot of reading, digging, listening, and praying for me to be able to see my loving Father within the trickiest books of the Bible. But once I saw these passages in a fresh, new light, the Biblical books that once frustrated and confused me now bring me to a state of tearful gratitude for the Father who loves us too much to watch passively as we destroy ourselves. I will do my best to reveal God's ever-present love even in the darkest moments of Israel's history. He loves us enough to lift us out of the darkness we created for ourselves and pull us into his beautiful, warm, never-ending light.

What to Expect

As with any worthy learning experience, the Bible may be a bit difficult to digest all at once. This remarkable piece of literature is chock full of wisdom, history, and different perspectives, so it helps to divide this information into small, manageable chunks. To assist you in breaking it down and sticking with this journey, I have divided this book into thirty-five daily readings (seven weeks, five readings per week).

A typical daily reading should take around twenty minutes and will familiarize you with either one large book of the Bible or a handful of small books.

Each daily reading will include a brief introduction with the following elements:

- **Big Idea** - A one-sentence summary of the upcoming section.
- **Break-Down Bullets** - Some of these sections will familiarize you with the people you can expect to meet within the reading, and other introductions will summarize the

most prominent themes or lessons you may notice that day.

- **How God Shows Up** - A quick summary about where our loving, powerful Creator fits into the upcoming section. Challenge yourself to see God through this lens as you read.

My hope is that these introductions will help you discover the simple, beautiful truths that draw the 66 books together. Hopefully, this helps you understand each Bible story in a fresh light and discover how each Bible book fits into the larger story.

At the end of each weekly section, you will find a few resources to help you reflect on the readings, including:

- **Discussion Questions** - I highly encourage you to read this book alongside your family or a small group of friends. Set aside time each week to chat about what you learned during the latest readings, and use these questions to help facilitate your discussion. Please visit www.godsgreatlovestory.com for session plans and videos designed to help your group find personal meaning in these timeless stories.
- **Music Meditations** - These song listening suggestions pair each Biblical book with a song that may help you understand that text in a new light. I encourage you to incorporate a few of the music meditations into your individual quiet time each week, and prayerfully consider how the message in each song relates to the Biblical material. You may even choose to listen to some of these songs while you read. As a music therapist, I believe that music reveals emotions and insights

that words alone cannot reach. There is a growing body of research that supports the idea that spoken and written words stimulate a small part of our brain, while music activates many parts of the brain simultaneously. This means that when we include music in our learning and growth, we set ourselves up for a deeper level of insight, emotion, and connection.

- **Application Ideas** - These suggestions may help you take practical action steps and begin positive life changes in response to what you're learning.

I pray that this book helps you understand the Bible and fall in love with God more deeply than before. I hope these stories allow you see God's beauty and glory in a new way. As you begin to relate to the beautiful, imperfect characters in these stories, I hope this fresh perspective inspires you to apply Biblical lessons to your life like never before.

May the grace and peace of God be with you as you begin this journey.

WEEK ONE

Foundation

GENESIS-DEUTERONOMY

DAY ONE - CHOSEN FAMILY
GENESIS

BIG IDEA

The great Creator lifts up seemingly insignificant people to fulfill his higher plans.

CAST OF CHARACTERS

- **Adam and Eve-** Residents of a perfect garden who lose their home and their innocence by breaking God's only rule.
- **Noah-** Obediently goes against the grain to take on a project that requires significant patience and courage.
- **Abraham and Sarah-** Elderly nomads and unlikely ancestors of a nation.
- **Isaac and Rebecca-** Fall in love at first sight but have a house divided in their old age.
- **Jacob and Esau-** Twins who take sibling rivalry to a new level.
- **Leah and Rachel-** Sister wives who turn pregnancy into a competition.
- **Judah-** Ancestor of great kings who shows leadership and integrity among his brothers.
- **Joseph-** Resilient and scrappy young man who rises from prison to power against all odds.

HOW GOD SHOWS UP

God creates everything glorious and good. People choose to break the rules and ruin the perfect life God has handed them. As most of humanity falls into chaos, God nurtures and lifts up a handful of imperfect people with good hearts. When they dare to trust him, God sets them on a new path. God turns these ordinary nomads into the ancestors of a great nation.

GENESIS

1. At the start, the all-powerful, overwhelmingly big God looks at the dark, formless universe and speaks life into it. In six steps, God speaks everything into existence from the stars and the insects to the flowers and the birds. It is all beautiful, but his most prized creation is man.

2. The Lord rests on the seventh day to look with happiness on the beauty of his creation. The intimate, tender Yahweh shapes the first people like an artist molds a lump of clay, and he breathes life into these special children who bear his image. He creates a perfect, beautiful garden that contains plenty of delicious food and water for Adam and Eve, and he instructs them to take care of the garden, the animals, and each other as they enjoy a perfect, innocent life. God gives Adam and Eve only one rule, asking them to avoid eating from the tree of knowledge, in order to preserve their humility and childlike trust in God's provision.

3. Adam and Eve disobey God's only command to them,

giving birth to pride and causing them to fall into a cycle of playing God instead of trusting God. Even though these ancestors of humanity live in a perfect environment, they fall into sin by focusing on the one thing they do not have. They choose to listen to the snake's tempting voice instead of God's loving guidance. The Father sends his first children out of the garden to protect them from eating from the tree of life and living forever in their sinful state.

4. Adam and Eve raise their first two sons, Cain and Abel, in the wilderness. Cain kills Abel out of jealousy, and he is quickly banished to another land by God. Meanwhile, God blesses the grieving Adam and Eve with another son, Seth.

5. The author records a genealogy from Adam to Noah, listing the lifespan of each prominent ancestor of humanity. The fascinating thing about this is that most people live to be hundreds of years old during this time. For example, Methuselah (Noah's grandfather) lives to be a staggering 969 years old!

6. Every human being on earth falls into wickedness and corruption except a humble and good-hearted man named Noah. God looks with sadness upon his precious children and regrets creating them. God commands Noah to build an ark, which is an enormous and unusual task for one man to accomplish alone. Despite many challenges and possibly many strange looks from the neighbors, Noah is obedient to God.

7. God floods the land, destroying everyone and everything except Noah, his family, and all the animals on the ark. Noah and his family must co-exist on the ark for nearly

half a year before the waters even begin to recede.

8.   The flood ends at last, and the ark lands on top of a mountain, seven long months after the flood had first begun. Noah offers a sacrifice to express gratitude for the survival of his precious family, and God promises to never again destroy the entire earth as a punishment for human imperfection.

9.   God says to Noah and his family "My dear children, I will multiply your family and allow you to inhabit the whole earth, ruling over the other animals wherever you go. I will never again allow such a widespread flood to occur on earth, and I will place a rainbow in the sky after each thunderstorm as a sign of this promise." Later, Noah has a moment of drunken vulnerability after he enjoys the wine planted in his new vineyard. Noah's son Ham seeks to humiliate his father, while his other sons Shem and Japheth preserve Noah's dignity.

10. Noah's family multiplies and repopulates all nations. It's worth noting that the disrespectful Ham becomes the father of the nations that would later fall deeply into war and sin, while Shem's family tree would eventually lead to the nation of Israel and Jesus.

11. People become self-righteous in their planning, trying to build a tower to the heavens without the help of God. The Lord causes them to speak many different languages and scatters them all over the earth. This new separation proves to be an obstacle great enough that God's children stop their power-hungry pursuits for the time being. A genealogy links Shem (one of Noah's sons) to his descendant Abram.

12. God calls Abram to move to a new land with his wife, nephew, and servants to start a new nation, although he is already very old and without children. Abram obediently leaves everything familiar, and God shows him the land he promises to fill with Abram's descendants one day. Abram then continues south into Egypt and tells the king that his wife is his sister for fear that the king will kill him otherwise. This lie backfires, the truth comes out, and the king deports Abram and his family out of Egypt.

13. Abram separates from his nephew, Lot, after the family sets up camp in an area not quite big enough for the family's many animals. The close quarters leads the two **quarreling** men to a decision to separate, and Lot journeys east to the city of Sodom.

14. Four evil kings raid the city of Sodom, and a man escapes from the chaos to report this news to Abram. Abram organizes a small army to rescue Lot and many others from the raiders. In the wake of his victory, King Melchizedek blesses Abram, and the king of Sodom offers abundant gratitude and a monetary reward that Abram humbly turns down.

15. After a long and dangerous journey, God promises Abram his divine protection and as many descendants as the stars in the sky. He also reveals that his future family will be enslaved in a foreign land for 400 years but will eventually be freed and returned to the Promised Land.

16. Abram's wife, Sarai, is an old woman who has not been able to have children and does not trust in God's promise of a son. She takes matters into her own hands, offering her slave girl Hagar to Abram to produce an heir. Abram

impregnates Hagar, and although this was Sarai's idea in the first place, Sarai treats her cruelly due to overwhelming jealousy. Hagar runs away in fear, but an angel meets her in the wilderness to validate her pain and to encourage her to stay with the family a little while longer despite the injustice. God promises to bless this broken and abused slave girl with many descendants and promises to deliver her and her son to freedom when the time is right.

17. When Hagar's son Ishmael is thirteen, Abram and the males in his family circumcise each other as a sign of obedience and trust in God's promise to still give Abram a son through Sarai. Their names change to Abraham and Sarah as a sign of their transformative faith.

18. An angel informs Abraham that Sarah is pregnant in her old age, and this news causes Sarah to laugh in disbelief. Meanwhile, Abraham pleads for God to spare Sodom (Lot's new home) from his wrath and judgment. God promises to spare Sodom if only ten righteous people dwell within the entire city, but Sodom's sin is so widespread and pervasive that God cannot justify saving it.

19. Lot witnesses the wickedness within the hearts of Sodom's residents as they surround his house and threaten to abuse the two angels staying with him. The angel house guests warn Lot that God must soon destroy the city, and they give Lot and his family a chance to leave safely. They escape just in time, but Lot's wife is a bit too attached to Sodom. She looks back and is promptly turned into a pillar of salt.

20. Abraham and Sarah travel onward, and Abraham makes the mistake of lying to King Abimelech, falsely declaring

that Sarah is his sister. He does this for fear that the king will kill Abraham and take Sarah as his own. In this case, an unnecessary lie comes from Abraham's unnecessary lack of trust in God.

21. Sarah finally gives birth to her miracle child, Isaac, and her gratitude and amazement at this fulfilled promise brings her joy and laughter. Abraham sends Hagar and Ishmael into the wilderness, and when Ishmael is close to dying of thirst in the desert, Hagar surrenders her child to God in a spirit of desperation. God hears the child's cry and opens Hagar's eyes to a nearby well, which saves his life. God allows the boy to grow into a strong, capable hunter and the father of the Arab nation. Meanwhile, Abraham and King Abimelech agree to treat each other with respect and honesty, which allows Abraham to live peacefully in Abimelech's land for a long time.

22. God asks Abraham to offer his long-awaited son Isaac as a sacrifice in order to radically test Abraham's faith and dedication. God ultimately allows Isaac to live, and Abraham passes the test.

23. Sarah passes away, and a mournful Abraham buys a burial ground for her.

24. Abraham sends his most trusted servant to his old hometown to find a potential wife for Isaac more suitable than the sinful Canaanite women living near Abraham's family. A young, beautiful woman named Rebecca shows kindness and generosity to the servant at a well, and the servant praises God, knowing that she would be the perfect partner for Isaac. After gaining permission and a tender blessing

of good fortune from Rebecca's family, the servant and Rebecca journey home. Isaac and Rebecca are immediately smitten with each other, and she comforts him greatly as he mourns the recent loss of his mother.

25. Abraham dies at the age of 175 and is buried next to his wife. The author outlines a genealogy which includes Abraham's descendants as a result of his second marriage as well as a list of Ishmael's descendants. Isaac's wife Rebecca has twin sons named Jacob and Esau who prove to be opposites and rivals from the very beginning. Firstborn Esau gives up his birthright to Jacob for a meal, showing how little he cares about his inheritance.

26. God appears before Isaac and promises him many descendants, echoing his earlier covenant with Abraham. Unfortunately, Isaac makes the same mistake as his father, telling King Abimelech that Rebecca is his sister. Upon discovering their lie, the king banishes Isaac and Rebecca from his country. After a time of frustration and wandering, Abimelech forgives Isaac, and they share a meal to celebrate their peaceful restoration.

27. When Isaac is blind and on his death bed, he calls Esau to his side to ask for his favorite meal so that he might bestow his final blessing to this favored son. Rebecca eavesdrops at the door and instructs her preferred son Jacob to trick Isaac into blessing him instead. In this way, Jacob is granted the ability to become more powerful than his brother. Esau seeks murderous revenge upon Jacob, so Rebecca protects Jacob by sending her young son to his uncle's house in a different village until Esau's rage cools down.

28. Before Jacob journeys to his uncle Laban's village, Isaac encourages him to find a decent, respectable woman to marry while he's there, since the local Canaanite women who Esau married do not align with Isaac and Rebecca's values. Esau learns of his parents' disapproval of his wives and finds a slightly more respectable spouse from the family of Ishmael. In the solitude of Jacob's journey, he receives a profound vision of heaven in which God promises him many descendants. Jacob awakes with a new sense of reverence for God.

29. When Jacob arrives at the community well, he falls in love with Laban's daughter Rachel at first sight and excitedly hurries home with her to embrace Laban and ask for his daughter's hand. For seven years, Jacob works diligently for Rachel's father to earn the right to marry her. When wedding day finally arrives, Laban tricks Jacob into marrying Rachel's older sister Leah instead. The relentless Jacob agrees to work for Laban for seven additional years in order to finally marry his true love, Rachel. As Leah becomes the mother of Jacob's three eldest sons, this lesser-loved wife hopes that her ability to bear these children will finally earn her Jacob's love and affection. By the time she has her fourth child, Judah, she decides to surrender her marriage to God and simply praise Him.

30. Rachel has trouble getting pregnant and becomes jealous of her sister's fertility, so she gives up in despair and allows her slave woman, Bilhah, to have children with Jacob on her behalf. This leads Leah to offer her slave woman, Zilpah to Jacob, which of course deepens the sisters' competitive feud. God hears Rachel's desperate prayers at last and blesses her

with a son named Joseph. Meanwhile, Jacob reveals to his father-in-law that after many years, he is ready to return home with his family and his portion of Laban's flocks. God blesses Jacob's animals to make them healthier than those Laban would keep.

31. When Jacob becomes more successful than Laban, his in-laws turn on him, and Jacob decides it's time to secretly leave town with his wives and kids. Laban pursues them initially but soon comes to an agreement with Jacob, letting his daughters go freely with their husband.

32. Jacob sends generous gifts ahead of his caravan for his long-estranged brother, in an effort to smooth over old hurts and make peace with Esau before seeing him in person. The night before the brothers reunite, Jacob wrestles with God. After this uniquely intimate and strengthening interaction, God changes Jacob's name to Israel and blesses him. This name change points again to the fact that ordinary people can be radically transformed by knowing God.

33. Israel meets up with Esau, and the brothers treat each other with kindness, generosity and forgiveness. As young men, the brothers had hurt each other deeply through rivalry and deception, but after not speaking for over fourteen years, their relationship is finally restored.

34. Israel and Leah's daughter, Dinah, is tragically raped by a Canaanite leader named Shechem. Dinah's brothers furiously carry out revenge on the rapist and all the males in his town by deceiving, killing, and robbing them. Israel is of course upset that his daughter had been abused, but he is perhaps more disappointed that his sons rashly acted out

in a way that put the rest of the family in danger.

35. God gives Israel instructions to worship him as the one true God, ridding his life of foreign idols. Shortly after this reminder of priorities, Rebecca's nurse Deborah passes away. The family's time of mourning deepens when Israel's beloved Rachel dies in childbirth, and his father Isaac passes away in his old age. Perhaps God prepared Israel's heart for these losses by turning him toward righteousness and renewed faith just before.

36. The author records a genealogy of Esau and other families that eventually populate Edom.

37. As Israel's clear favorite child, Joseph predicts that God will bless him richly, so his older brothers jealously sell him as a slave to a group of men who are traveling to Egypt. The travelers sell Joseph to Potipher, one of the officers of the Egyptian king.

38. Judah, one of Israel's sons, is tricked into sleeping with his daughter-in-law Tamar after she disguises herself as a prostitute. After her husband dies and Judah ignores her desire to remarry, this act of deception is the only way Tamar feels she can start a family. When Tamar becomes pregnant with twins, Judah lets her live and takes responsibility for her despite cultural pressure to kill her. Strangely enough, King David and Jesus Christ are eventually born as a result of this scandal.

39. Joseph finds success and favor as Potipher's servant in the Egyptian palace. When Potipher's wife takes notice and tries to seduce him, Joseph refuses to betray his master this way. In her anger and embarrassment, she tells palace officials

that Joseph tried to rape her. This vengeful lie leads to the arrest of Joseph.

40. Joseph interprets the dream of a fellow prisoner, the king's wine steward, revealing that this man would be released three days later. When the dream comes true, the newly freed wine steward forgets all about Joseph for the time being.

41. When the king has a mysterious dream two years later, the wine steward suddenly remembers Joseph's gift of dream interpretation and suggests that the king speak to Joseph about it. Joseph predicts that the land will experience seven years of plenty followed by seven years of famine, and the impressed king hires Joseph to oversee the food storage process that would prepare Egypt to prosper during the famine. Talk about rags to riches! Joseph goes from slavery and imprisonment to a prominent government position in one short meeting.

42. During the predicted time of famine, Joseph's brothers travel to Egypt to buy corn. The brothers do not realize that the governor in charge of food distribution is actually Joseph, but Joseph recognizes them and notices that his youngest brother Benjamin is not with the group. Joseph deceives his brothers by holding his older brother Simeon hostage until the others agree to return home to retrieve Benjamin. When the brothers return home to share the news, Israel responds "First I lost my dear Joseph, and now Simeon. I can't lose Benjamin too; the grief would kill me."

43. When the famine worsens, the sons of Israel must return to Egypt for more food. Judah says "We can't show our face

in that palace without Benjamin, but don't worry, Father. I will guard my baby brother with my life." When Joseph gazes upon his younger brother, he is so emotional that he must leave the room to cry, but the brothers still haven't recognized Joseph as their long lost brother. Joseph invites his family to dinner, and the brothers are surprised to see they have been seated in order from oldest to youngest.

44. Joseph hides a silver cup in Benjamin's bag so that he can justify arresting his beloved baby brother to keep him in Egypt. Judah begs Joseph "Please sir! Take me in my brother's place. I could not live with myself if my father had to bear the loss of his baby son."

45. Judah's tender act of sacrifice causes Joseph to emotionally break down and say "My dear brothers, it's me. I'm Joseph. I want you to know I'm not mad at you for selling me into slavery because I think God sent me to this place to lift me up and save you from the famine. Here in Egypt, I have a ton of power and influence, and I want you to go get Dad and come back so that I can take care of you all and share the blessings God has given me." The mended family shares a tearful embrace, and the brothers gleefully return home to reveal to Israel that his beloved son Joseph is alive and well.

46. Israel and his family travel to Egypt to live near Joseph, and when the grateful father finally embraces his long lost son, he says "My dear son! You're alive! I can now die a happy man."

47. Joseph finds a place for his family to live, and he happily supports all of them financially. As the famine becomes even

more severe in neighboring lands, the family realizes that without Joseph's connections in Egypt, they likely would have starved, and God's promise for the exponential growth of the nation of Israel would have never been fulfilled. At the end of Israel's life, he asks his sons to eventually bury his body in their homeland instead of in Egypt.

48. In his final days, Israel calls Joseph and his two sons to his bedside, saying "My beloved son, God has promised to grow our family, and now here we are! I am so pleased that I get to meet these two precious grandsons before I die. Because your mother was so dear to me, I am filled with love for young Ephraim and Manasseh and would like to offer a special blessing on their lives. God, bless these sweet boys and lead them as you have led me. Protect them and make their families great." Interestingly, Israel blesses Joseph's younger son more than his older son, perhaps mirroring his own birth-right role reversal with Esau.

49. Israel gathers his twelve sons one last time and speaks his final words to each of them. "Gather round, my boys. Several of you have sinned against me and others, allowing greed and violence to infect your precious hearts. I hope you will humble yourselves and change. Judah, you will be a strong, respected leader among your brothers. My dear Joseph, you resiliently overcame slavery and rose up in this foreign land. I am so unbelievably proud of you, and I hope that God sets you apart and offers his richest blessings on your life."

50. All the brothers mourn the loss of Israel, but Joseph is especially broken. Joseph notices that his brothers still feel

guilty and self-conscious about the past, and he responds "When you sold me into slavery, you wished harm on me, but God brought good out of that circumstance, allowing our family to rise up and survive the famine. Please don't beat yourself up about the past. I forgive you, I love you, and I will continue to care for you and your kids." Joseph lives a long, peaceful life and even gets to meet a few of his great-grandchildren before dying at the age of 110.

DAY TWO - FREED FROM SLAVERY
EXODUS

BIG IDEA

Our superhero God conquers enemy armies and parts seas to protect his children.

CAST OF CHARACTERS

- **Moses-** Humble and reluctant leader who is adopted by Egyptian royalty and later equipped by God to do the impossible.
- **Pharaoh-** Hard-hearted king who stubbornly refuses to surrender to God.
- **Aaron-** Moses' well-spoken brother and right hand man.
- **Miriam-** Moses' protective big sister and leader of a freedom celebration song.
- **Jethro-** Wise father-in-law who encourages Moses to accept help.
- **Bezalel-** Talented artist who helps create a beautiful place to worship God.
- **The Wandering Nation-** These downtrodden slaves are fiercely protected by God, but they continuously fail to show proper respect and gratitude to their Deliverer. They quickly turn away from God to make a new idol to worship.

HOW GOD SHOWS UP

The fiercely protective Father notices his children being abused, oppressed, and overworked. He will not tolerate it anymore. God makes impossible and terrifying things happen to take down the stubborn Egyptian king and lead his people to safety. God lifts up an unlikely leader to build a new society dedicated to God. The Father offers peace and rest to his formerly enslaved children and encourages them to take care of themselves and each other.

EXODUS

1. God fulfills his promise by allowing the children and grand-children of Israel to grow incredibly quickly into a great, strong multitude. The king of Egypt feels threatened by the Israelites and crushes their spirits by allowing Egyptians to take them into slavery. The pharaoh issues a proclamation for Egyptian midwives to kill the newborn Israelite babies. Out of respect for God, the midwives refuse to follow this order, and the budding nation continues to grow. God notices the courageous mercy of the midwives and blesses their families.

2. Moses is born during this dangerous time and is sent adrift in a watertight basket by his birth mother to save his life. The pharaoh's daughter finds Moses on the shore of the Nile, and she adopts him, hiding the fact that he is a Hebrew baby. This is the first of many miraculous protections that

God would issue on Moses' life. As a young man, Moses recognizes Hebrews being overworked, abused, and killed unjustly, and he murders one of the slave-drivers in his anger. Moses then escapes to Midian for fear of being brought to justice, and he settles down with the local priest's daughter.

3.   When Moses approaches Mount Sinai with his flock of sheep, the Lord lights a nearby bush on fire and speaks from the flame, saying "Moses, you are standing in the presence of the holy God of your ancestors. I have heard the cry of my people in Egypt, and I cannot bear to see them suffer in captivity and oppression anymore. I am sending you to free them and lead them to a good and fertile land. I know you think you are no one special, but I will be with you every step of the way. I will give you all the confidence you need to stand up to the king, and when he doesn't listen to you, I will show him what I'm capable of. By the time I'm done, all the Egyptians will respect you and will send my people away with full pockets."

4.   Moses answers "Please pick someone else. I have a timid, stuttering voice, and this mission scares me to death. What if they laugh at me? What if they won't listen to me?" God miraculously transforms Moses' walking stick into a stick capable of performing miracles and says "With this stick, I will convince the people I am with you. I created your mouth, and I will enable it to speak with skill and confidence. Your outgoing brother Aaron can serve as your spokesman if that will ease your mind a bit." In a new spirit of courage and trust, Moses journeys across the desert back to Egypt, gaining support from Aaron and several of the

Hebrew leaders along the way.

5. Moses and his brother Aaron plead their case to the pharaoh for the first time, asking that the Hebrew people be granted an opportunity to rest for a few days and worship God. The king refuses to take them seriously, responding "I don't know or care about your God, and I will not allow my workers to neglect their responsibilities and go on vacation. Because you have wasted my time with your lazy, stupid questions, your people will now have twice the workload. Get back to work!" The Hebrews' hearts are crushed by the pharaoh's response, which causes Moses to doubt the validity of his mission.

6. When Moses cries out to God that the people are even worse off now, God responds "Just wait. The king will pay for his actions and free the people. I promised your ancestors that their descendants would inherit the land of Canaan, and I intend to rescue them and fulfill that promise. Don't give up, Moses. Go with my authority."

7. After the Lord's pep talk, Moses and Aaron return to the king and throw down Aaron's stick, which turns into a snake more powerful than the ones the Egyptian magicians can produce. When this miracle leaves the king unimpressed, God begins plaguing Egypt with terrible disasters, starting with turning the Nile to blood for seven days, cutting off the people's primary source of drinking water.

8. An outpouring of frogs, gnats, and flies overwhelm the land of Egypt, causing the Egyptians to lose sleep and causing the land to stink. After each disaster, Moses demands that the pharaoh free the Israelites, and he refuses, even when

these acts of God are clearly more powerful than those the palace magicians can reproduce.

9. Plagues continue with a fatal disease that kills all the Egyptian animals while sparing the animals belonging to the Hebrews. The king's stubbornness remains, so God allows disgusting boils to infect the skin of the Egyptian people, followed by a terrible hail throughout the land.

10. God allows a swarm of locusts to kill the crops in Egypt, which causes the king to beg for God's forgiveness and agree to free the slaves. However, as soon as the locusts disappear, the king changes his mind once again, refusing to let the Hebrew people go.

11. Moses announces to the king "Since you refuse to obey our powerful God, he has one more punishment for you. All of Egypt's firstborn sons will die unless you surrender to God and let his people go."

12. God's spirit passes over the land that evening, smiting the Egyptian firstborn sons and sparing those in Hebrew households. Only after this particular plague does the pharaoh finally relent, allowing them to leave the country.

13. On their way out of Egypt, the Hebrew people dedicate their firstborn children and animals to God, thanking the Lord for sparing them from the terrifying plagues and rescuing them from slavery. Moses encourages the people to annually acknowledge God's great power and remember this day of deliverance through the Festival of Unleavened Bread. God produces pillars of cloud and fire to guide and protect the people as they set out across the desert.

14. In one final act of stubborn pride, the Egyptian king leads

600 soldiers into the desert to recapture the Israelites, but he drastically underestimates what God will do to protect his people. God allows Moses to part the waters of the Red Sea, and God literally blocks the king's men from his children with an enormous cloud pillar. God then leads the Egyptian soldiers to follow the Hebrews across the sea, just in time for the waters to rise and drown the enemy. Stunned at God's clear act of protection and deliverance, the Israelite people worship God in great reverence.

15. Miriam and Moses lead the people in singing "God has saved us! He has thrown our slave drivers into the sea! Our powerful God is a mighty Warrior who can take down his enemies with one fiery breath. Lord, there is no one like you. Your miracles are unmatched, and you faithfully keep your promises. As you plant us high on a mountain, the evil nations around us tremble in wonder and fear." Three days into the journey, God answers the people's prayer for fresh water and promises to provide for their needs in exchange for their continued worship and obedience.

16. God provides a daily feast of manna (delicious sweet bread) and quail to nourish his people in the desert. Every seven days, God provides a two-day supply for each family so they can enjoy a weekly day of rest. After a lifetime of slavery, the Israelites resist God's permission to take a break, and some continue to toil away on this sanctioned Sabbath day, showing their lack of trust in God's provision.

17. The Hebrews cry out for more water and complain that the unpleasant desert feels worse than Egypt. God allows water to miraculously flow out of a rock to nourish the whiny

Hebrews. God also **demonstrates** his protection of the Hebrews by allowing them to win an unlikely battle against a group of Amalekites.

18. Moses enjoys a happy reunion with his father-in-law, Jethro. Jethro says "Son, I am delighted to hear about how God has used you to deliver his people. God is good! You are doing a great job leading these people, but Son, why are you trying to do this alone? You will wear yourself out at this rate, so you need to appoint a team of judges to help you settle disputes."

19. The Hebrews set up camp around Mount Sinai, and Moses meets privately with God on the mountain. **Moses** reminds the people to respect God's power and approach the holy mountain with an attitude of awe and purity.

20. God reveals the Ten Commandments to Moses, saying "Always remember I am the God who rescued you; worship me alone with no idols or substitutions. Respect my holy name, and respect yourselves by resting one day each week. **Respect** the people who raised you, and avoid **harming each other with** murder, adultery, theft, dishonesty, and envy." When the people hear God's booming voice from the base of the mountain, they stand in awe and fear.

21. God continues "If someone works for you to repay a debt, treat these slaves fairly and free them from all remaining obligations every seven years. Murderers and kidnappers deserve the death sentence, and those who abuse slaves and pregnant women should be severely punished. Accept responsibility for acts of violence committed by your animals.

22. "Thieves must repay what they stole and accept responsibility for property destruction. I will hold liars accountable by requiring that property disputes be handled in my holy place of worship. Do not practice witchcraft, idolatry, or bestiality. Humbly remember that in Egypt, you were poor slaves, so treat poor people and foreigners with grace and dignity. Allow your actions to reflect a grateful heart rather than an entitled heart.

23. "Keep bribes out of the courtroom, and do not deny justice to poor people. If you see a neighbor in need, do your part to help out. Treat foreign travelers with kindness. Work hard six days a week, and take care of yourselves and your animals by resting on the seventh day. Allow the fields to rest every seven years, and honor me through three annual festivals. If you obey and worship me, I will protect you."

24. Moses, Aaron, and 70 Israelite leaders worship God from the base of Mount Sinai, and Moses reads God's commands to the people, reverently offering an animal sacrifice to honor God's promises. Moses approaches God's dazzling presence on the top of the mountain and writes all the new commands on stone tablets over the next 40 days.

25. God instructs Moses to collect a free-will offering from the people to create a beautiful sacred tent for God's presence, so that he can remain with them once they leave the mountain. He gives specific construction guidelines about the bread offering table, a golden lamp stand, and the covenant box, which will hold the stone tablets.

26. Moses gains a colorful, detailed description of how the

interior of the sacred tent should look upon completion, and God offers Moses step-by-step instructions to break this enormous project into small, manageable chunks.

27. God specifically explains how to build the bronze-covered altar and the enclosure for the tent. He also reveals that the lamp should burn each night as a reminder of God's warm, constant presence among the people.

28. Moses receives instructions from God about colorful robes and accessories that will allow priests to lead with dignity, beauty, and modesty. He also learns that the High Priest will wear an elaborate, beautiful breast piece covered in twelve multi-colored jewels as a reminder of the twelve uniquely precious tribes of Israel.

29. The Lord says "Moses, when you bring your brother Aaron and his sons into my presence to anoint them as my chosen priests, make some biscuits with the best flour you can find. Ask the new priests to bathe and get dressed up in their new sacred garments. Pour oil on their heads and make a generous animal sacrifice to honor me and dedicate their lives to God. Then let the new priests enjoy the meat and bread as a symbol of the blessings and undeserved forgiveness I offer freely to them." Moses also receives instructions about daily morning and evening offerings designed to remind the people of God's ever-present glory.

30. God describes how to build the altar for burning incense and a bronze water basin to sanitize the priests' hands before and after handling food offerings. He also gives a recipe for the sweet-smelling anointing oil, ingredients for the incense, and a description of taxes that will

fund the worship supplies.

31. God talks to Moses about several young men in the community who demonstrate passion and skill in the areas of art, woodworking, metal working, and construction. God encourages Moses to enlist their help and utilize their strengths with the tent-making project. These artists and workers will need to give it their all six days per week, while always remembering to rest and worship God on the Sabbath day.

32. While Moses spends 40 days on Mount Sinai receiving God's instructions, the Hebrew people in the camp lose their patience and turn away from God entirely. They create a gold bull calf as an idol and begin worshipping the statue through a drunken, sexually inappropriate party. Humble Moses attempts to take full responsibility for this act of disrespect, but the Lord spares Moses and punishes only the people directly responsible for this disgusting act of idolatry.

33. God instructs his people to leave Mount Sinai for the Promised Land but instructs Moses to put some distance between the sacred tent and the camp as they move forward. God is concerned that if the people disappoint him like that again with his presence close by, they will not survive his judgment. Moses prays that God will remember his love and dedication to the Hebrew nation, and God looks on Moses with love and favor, allowing Moses to draw even closer to his presence.

34. Since the original stone tablets of the covenant were smashed when Moses discovered his people worshipping the golden calf, Moses rewrites the covenant on a second set

of stone tablets before leaving the mountain. God promises to lead the Israelites to victories that will make their enemies flee in fear. When Moses returns to camp, his face is literally glowing in the aftermath of his meeting with God, which makes the people afraid to go near him unless Moses covers his face.

35. Moses announces to the community that the seventh day of each week should be a holy day of rest, and he asks the wealthy and willing members of the community to donate precious metals, jewels, and nice fabric for the making of the sacred tent. Moses asks for skilled workers to step forward and accept various assignments related to the creation of the sacred items. The people willingly give their time, talents, and treasure to set this project up for success.

36. The people continue giving generously until Moses has to turn them away due to a surplus of help. At this point, the hearts of the Israelites are right with God, and perhaps because of this, they are willing and excited to work together to build the sacred tent according to God's exact instructions.

37. The talented artist Bezalel and his assistant work hard to build the covenant box, the bread offering table, the lamp stand, and the incense alter just as God instructed. They also enjoy mixing various spices and perfumes to make the anointing oil and the incense smell amazing.

38. Hardworking Bezalel constructs the burnt offering alter, the bronze handwashing basin, the tent enclosure, and the metals for the tent, just as the Father commanded.

39. Bezalel's helper Ohiliab uses his garment making ability to sew the priestly clothing according to the Lord's specifications. He pays close attention to every detail as he skillfully crafts these beautiful, durable garments. At this point, the construction process for the tent is complete. Moses happily blesses and congratulates the people for coming together in obedience to God to create something truly beautiful.

40. The Israelites dedicate the sacred tent to God, burning offerings and giving thanks. God's dazzling presence fills the tent and goes with the Hebrews as they continue their journey.

DAY THREE - WORSHIP GUIDE
LEVITICUS

BIG IDEA

It's all about respect for God, each other, and ourselves.

PURPOSE OF THE TRADITIONS

- **Daily offering-** Regular acts of generosity that helped the people habitually connect to God and express humble gratitude for blessings.
- **Fellowship offering-** Communal act of worship to lift up God and provide food for a family meal.
- **Sin offering-** Sacrifice designed to help the people humbly confess mistakes, seek God's forgiveness, and accept his guidance toward positive change.
- **Anointing priests-** Reverent ceremony to dedicate spiritual leaders to God and help them humbly acknowledge their new responsibilities.
- **Purity practices-** Regulations that help the people respect their bodies by maintaining healthy nutrition, safe infection control habits, and a commitment to reserve sex as an intimate act within committed marriage.
- **Community rules-** Laws that recognize all people as God's children, requiring even the most marginalized members of society to be treated with dignity.
- **Annual festivals-** Holidays that celebrate God's amazing

acts of deliverance and provide opportunities for families to pause their work, gratefully reflect of God's provision, and enjoy a relaxing day of food and family.

HOW GOD SHOWS UP

God teaches Moses and Aaron about a style of worship designed to please and honor him. These laws and traditions are meant to refine the hearts of the people, keep them safe, and set their culture apart. God loves the Hebrews so much that he longs for them to have a full life characterized by authentic worship, peaceful community, and strong character.

LEVITICUS

1. God meets with Moses in the sacred tent to reveal his specifications regarding burnt animal sacrifices, ensuring that these offerings of beef, lamb, and poultry will be both aesthetically pleasing to the Father and will remind the people to come to the Lord in a spirit of humility and reverence.

2. Moses learns that God desires grain offerings to be made simply and deliciously with flour, olive oil, and spices. By giving their very best fruits of the harvest to their Provider, the Israelites will be able to honor the Lord as their highest priority.

3. The Lord explains the proper protocol for daily fellowship offerings, which serve to help the people master a spirit of cheerful giving through regular practice and routine.

4.   God describes a humbling and detailed ceremony designed to purify Hebrew individuals of unintentional sins.

5.   If an Israelite gives an incorrect testimony in court, makes a promise he can't keep, or intentionally touches an unclean or unsafe substance, he must repentantly come before God with a burnt sin offering for forgiveness.

6.   God requires that those who lie and steal must pay back those they have cheated and then offer a sin offering in the sacred tent to request God's forgiveness. God also gives instructions regarding daily cleaning and maintenance of the altar, and He specifies which offerings the priests are allowed to eat.

7.   When the priests eat certain foods offered to God by community members, they must respect each other by sharing the food equally. They also must respect God by eating the food in the sacred tent and leaving no food leftover. God also mentions that it would be unsafe and unacceptable for the Hebrews to eat uncooked meat with blood in it.

8.   Moses ordains Aaron and his sons to be priests, anointing them and dedicating them to God through a holy, detailed ceremony outlined by the Lord. Moses instructs his brother and nephews to eat the bread and meat in an attitude of praise, and he instructs the men to commune with God in the tent for an entire week.

9.   After Aaron and his sons complete their week of purification in the tent, Moses invites the entire community to a worship service in which the newly ordained Aaron blesses the people. God appears as an awesome, dazzling light to all the people, causing them to raise their voices in excitement

and bow down in humble adoration.

10. Aaron's sons take it upon themselves to present an unnec-
    essary sacrifice with a disrespectful spirit, failing to honor
    the regulations God had carefully presented to Moses. God
    kills these young men on the spot, and Aaron absorbs the
    news in reverent silence.

11. Certain animals are acceptable for the people to eat, while
    others are unacceptable. Some of these regulations protect
    the Israelites from eating poisonous animals or animals that
    tend to carry diseases, while other food regulations simply
    set the Hebrew culture apart from the crude eating habits
    of other cultures.

12. God describes the process of purification for Israelite
    women following childbirth, quarantining them during
    this time of blood loss, perhaps for the cleanliness of the
    camp and the safety of others.

13. Moses learns how to prevent widespread infection from
    dreaded skin diseases. God reveals how to distinguish
    between non-contagious skin conditions and dangerous
    rashes that could lead to a fatal epidemic throughout the
    camp if not contained.

14. God outlines a purification practice that can physically
    and spiritually restore a Hebrew person after recovering
    from a skin disease. This process includes bathing, washing
    clothes, removing all hair, and presenting sacrifices to God
    so that he might bless the healing process. God also gives
    Moses common sense guidelines about how to rid a home
    of dangerous mildew.

15. The Lord encourages people to bathe and wash their clothes

if they ever come in contact with the unclean body fluids of others. Through these infection control regulations, God shows that he cares about the hygiene and physical safety of his people.

16. Once a year, on the Day of Atonement, the High Priest is allowed to enter into the most holy place within the sacred tent to perform a ritual meant to purify the entire nation of Israel of their sins.

17. God reveals that blood is a sacred substance that contains life and therefore has the power to atone sins when sacrificed on the altar. Since blood holds this special purpose in the heart of God, blood shall not be ingested by the Israelites.

18. God desires his people to be set apart from the wickedness of surrounding cultures, so they should not fall into the unhealthy and unacceptable sexual practices of these cultures. This means Hebrews are not to have intimate relations with animals, family members, or children.

19. The Lord commands the Israelites to respect God by refusing to worship false idols and obediently following God's regulations for worship. God requires that his people should show grace and generosity to poor people and foreign travelers, and he also discusses the importance of treating all people with honesty, fairness, and respect.

20. God promises to turn his back on any of his people who worship Molech, a foreign idol whose followers rape and sacrifice their children. The good Father simply cannot allow such evil to remain under his protection. People who choose to tear apart their families with incest, adultery, and disrespect deserve to be cast out of their family to live in

isolation, far away from those they have hurt.

21. The Israelite priests must be pillars of strength when others are mourning, and they must marry righteous, pure women in order to ensure that their children are raised in righteous households.

22. Priests must respect the offerings brought to God by only coming near the sacrifices and eating them when they are ritually clean. Only high quality, defect-free animals should be offered to God, and they must be given with a heart of humility and obedience.

23. God describes his vision for various annual festivals that will provide opportunities for the people to gather together, worship God, celebrate his blessings, and take a break from work. In addition to the weekly Sabbath, the people are to rest and worship during the Passover, the Harvest Festival, the New Year Festival, the Day of Atonement, and the Festival of Shelters.

24. Aaron must take good care of the lamps by only burning high quality olive oil, so that the lamps will stay in good shape when they are lit each night to remind the people of God's presence. Sabbath bread offerings are holy and may only be eaten by the priests in the holy tent. God reveals an example of the kind of justice that requires "an eye for an eye, a tooth for a tooth."

25. The Lord commands that every seven years will be a year of restoration for the Jewish people. This is a year dedicated to the Lord in which the farmland rests, all debts are forgiven, and all slaves are freed regardless of circumstance. God asks the people to trust that he will provide enough food to feed

the people during this special year of rest. Interestingly, the people never trust God enough to actually put the "year of restoration" command into practice.

26. God instructs the people "Don't make fake gods for yourself. I am the only real God, so honor me and keep my place of worship holy. If you live a good and holy life according to my instructions, I will bless your land with gentle rain, lush crops, and protection from dangerous wild animals. I will wipe out your enemies and will allow you former slaves to enjoy lives of freedom. However, if you choose actions that harm yourselves and each other, I will punish you with increasing intensity until I can get your attention and turn you around. I am your Father who loves you, and I give you these laws and limits for your own well-being."

27. The Lord outlines the process by which slaves should be set free and points out that families that are too poor to free loved ones from slavery may request a lower, more reasonable price from the priest. God points out that a tenth of all animals, crops and possessions are to be dedicated and given to God because it all belongs to Him anyway.

DAY FOUR - LOST IN THE WILDERNESS
NUMBERS

BIG IDEA

The Israelites nearly unravel in the desert, but God still protects them.

CAST OF CHARACTERS

- **Moses-** Fearless leader who continues to work God's miracles but grows frustrated with the people's constant conflict and complaining.
- **Aaron-** Responsible for appointing worthy people to work in the sacred tent.
- **Miriam-** Questions the authority of her humble little brother and gets confronted by God.
- **Caleb-** The first spy to silence the negativity of others and passionately trust in God's protection.
- **Joshua-** Moses' protégé and successor who courageously believes the Israelites can achieve unlikely victories with God's help.
- **Balak-** King of Moab who is intimidated by the mysterious wandering nation and tries to get Balaam to curse them.
- **Balaam-** Courageously refuses the king's request, recognizing the God of Israel as a King much more powerful and glorious than Balak.
- **Israelite Spies-** Twelve men chosen to scope out the

Promised Land and help with battle planning. Ten of them give up the original plan quickly and refuse to believe victory is possible.

- **Frustrated Rebels-** The former slaves quickly lose patience with the desert journey and the lack of menu variety, so they try to rebel against Moses and God himself.

HOW GOD SHOWS UP

God wanted to deliver his people directly to the Promised Land, but unfortunately, the people require a forty-year attitude adjustment. They fear that God can't ensure their victory over the giant Canaanites, and they complain about the heavenly food he provides. God punishes those at the center of the rebellion but continues to try to win the hearts of Israel through miracles, provision, and encouragement. When even Moses becomes frustrated at the stubborn, ungrateful people, the Hebrews finally learn to trust God again. God leads his people to unlikely victories, causing other nations to take notice of the powerful God of Israel.

NUMBERS

1. In the second year after their escape from Egypt, Moses and Aaron take a census and register all men fit for military service. God has allowed the family of Jacob to grow into an astounding army of 603,550 men.

2.   Moses successfully organizes the tribes of Israel into four large divisions that march together through the wilderness and camp with their own clans and families. The multitude protects the Levites who carry different components of the sacred tent between each of the four large divisions.

3.   God commands that Aaron's surviving sons and the rest of the Levite males be set apart for God and dedicated to his service. They are put in charge of maintaining the sacred tent and serve as spiritual leaders of the Israelite community. Moses takes a census of Levites, and the total number of males is 22,000.

4.   Moses assigns specific duties to each clan of the Levite tribe according to God's instructions. He outlines the procedure by which the Levites can safely transport all the sacred items from camp to camp, placing one of Aaron's sons in charge of overseeing this process as they travel.

5.   The Lord commands Moses to enforce infection control regulations, removing unclean or diseased people from the camp until purification is possible. He outlines a ceremony for married people to come before God and learn the truth if they suspect their spouse is being unfaithful.

6.   God requires that the Nazarites demonstrate their vow of holiness and dedication to God by following a specific diet and never cutting their hair. God instructs the priests to offer a blessing of peace, protection, and favor to the Hebrew community.

7.   When the tent set-up process is complete, Moses dedicates all the sacred items to God, and the clan leaders bring practical gifts of wagons and oxen to help the Levites carry

these heavy items from place to place.

8. God gives guidelines for the placement of lamps in the tent, and he describes the purification ritual designed to set the Levite priests apart as God's special children, uniquely qualified to work in the sacred tent. God instructs Moses to delegate duties to Levite men ages 25 to 50. **Priests older than 50** are to retire and serve as mentors to the younger priests.

9. The Israelites celebrate the second Passover Festival, allowing those who are ritually unclean at the time to celebrate a month later. Each time the Hebrews set up the tent in a new place, God's presence hovers over it as a cloud by day and a fire in the sky by night. The people respect God's divine authority over the journey by accepting that whenever the cloud lifts off the tent, this means the Lord is ready for them to break camp and journey to a new place.

10. The Lord guides Moses to use different trumpet signals to communicate with the large community that it is time to break camp, come together as a group, organize the leaders for a staff meeting, or prepare for battle against an approaching enemy. When God lifts the fiery cloud, the massive parade of Israelites continue moving through the wilderness according to his divine instructions. Moses encourages his Midianite brother-in-law to stay with the group and help navigate, since he is more familiar with the wilderness than Moses.

11. Despite God's constant protection and guidance during this lengthy journey, the people complain to God like toddlers on a road trip, whining of their craving for meat instead of manna. The wise Father, in an act of tough love, decides

to teach his children a lesson in contentment. Not only will they have the quail they've been wanting; they will have an all-you-can-eat buffet of it for an entire month, until their ungrateful bellies are sick from the leftovers.

12. When Moses' siblings Miriam and Aaron begin questioning the authority of this sweet, humble leader, God gathers the three siblings together to put Miriam and Aaron in their place. God has called Moses to a special position of leadership and a uniquely intimate relationship with Him. Petty Miriam breaks out in a terrible rash as a result of God's irritation with her.

13. Moses appoints twelve spies (one from each tribe) to secretly explore the surrounding land of Canaan which would eventually be conquered by the Israelites in God's name. Although most of the spies are afraid of the enemy, Caleb silences the negativity, saying "I'm not afraid of the giants and strong warriors in those enemy lands. With God on our side, we are strong enough to win. Let's go!"

14. The people complain to one another in the desert, saying "We've been wandering around this desert for half of forever, and now Moses and Aaron are leading us to die fighting this impossible enemy. Let's pick a new leader and go back to Egypt." Joshua and Caleb boldly and passionately retort "Don't you dare give up now! God is taking us to an excellent, fertile land, and he will shield us as we go into battle. Why are you so afraid?" When the crowd tries to stone these two men for stirring up disagreement, God's dazzling presence comes to their defense. God expresses his anger to Moses about his disappointment with the Hebrews'

ungrateful spirits, and he reveals that of this generation, only the faithful Caleb and Joshua will live to see the land promised by God. The army tries to invade the land of Canaan prematurely without God's help, and they are defeated.

15. The Lord encourages the people to offer food sacrifices that smell pleasing to God, and foreign travelers are to observe the law of the land by respecting God in this way. The people must weekly observe the Sabbath as a holy day of rest. God also proposes that the people start incorporating tassels into the corners of their garments as a visual reminder to practice obedience to God.

16. Several men shout out in rebellion against Moses' leadership, and Moses' first response is to throw himself on the ground in prayer. God gives Moses the courage to defend himself against these verbal attacks, and God causes the ground to literally swallow up the rebels. An even greater rebellion ensues, and God's anger unleashes a deadly epidemic that is only stopped when Aaron offers a sacrifice of purification on behalf of the disobedient protesters.

17. God reminds the people of his almighty power and authority over creation by causing Aaron's staff to sprout overnight into a beautiful almond tree. Moses hopes this miracle will encourage the rebels to return to God and avoid further punishment.

18. God instructs Aaron "As the leader of the priests, you must only hire trusted, qualified people to help manage the sacred tent, while only allowing the ordained priests to handle the sacred objects. You must be good stewards of all the

offerings that come into my place of worship, and you must practice generosity by giving ten percent of your own income as well. Honor the sacred food offerings by eating them with reverence in the holy place, and make sure you manage monetary offerings wisely."

19. God explains a ritual in which person who has become unclean by touching a dead body may participate in a week-long purification process using holy water and the ashes of the red cow.

20. Shortly after Moses' sister Miriam dies, the people choose to complain to Moses and Aaron about the water shortage instead of comforting them in their time of grief. An irritated Moses shouts "Do I have to do everything around here?!" as he makes water gush out of a rock. Since Moses angrily and impatiently mishandles this opportunity to demonstrate God's miraculous power and provision, God reveals that Moses will pass away before the nation crosses over into the Promised Land. The Israelites experience another roadblock when the Edomites refuse to let them pass, and Aaron dies shortly after.

21. The Israelites achieve a much-needed victory over the Canaanites after they reach out to God and renew their dedication to him. Shortly after their triumphant battle, many Israelites still have the nerve to gossip about Moses and complain about the manna. The Lord punishes them in anger, but he forgives the people once they accept responsibility for their words and dedicate themselves to God once again. With renewed trust in the Lord, the Israelites are victorious in their next few battles, and they sing songs of

praise and gratitude to Him.

22. The Moabite and Midianite leaders hear about Israel's recent victories, and they are intimidated by this enormous multitude wandering close to their land. These leaders try to persuade a Canaanite prophet named Balaam to curse the Israelites, and Balaam initially refuses out of respect for God. When Balaam finally gives in and begins journeying to the Moabite king, God places a warrior angel in the road to block Balaam's path and turn Balaam's allegiance toward God.

23. King Balak of Moab tries to force Balaam to curse Israel as they look upon the Hebrew camp from a mountain. Instead of cursing Israel, Balaam says "You brought me a great distance to curse Israel, but how could I curse them when God has blessed them? This curious nation is set apart and richly blessed. As I grow old, I hope to become as peaceful and righteous as them." When King Balak reprimands Balaam, the prophet responds "Hear these words, king. God cannot lie, and he does not change his mind. He keeps his promises, so when I see that he has promised to bless these people, how can I argue with that? God has brought them out of Egypt and leads them as their holy King. No magic spell that I utter could take down this mighty lion of a nation."

24. As the evil king of Moab fumes in anger, God's spirit takes control of Balaam's heart, and he proudly proclaims "God has made me see clearly, and I see beautiful gardens, abundant rainfall, and beautiful tents covering the land of Israel. Their enemies will be crushed under foot. One day,

a bright star of a king will rule in Israel and lead them to an age of power, victory, and security."

25. While camping near the border of Moab, many Israelite men begin having sex with Moabite women and adopting some of their corrupt religious practices. God kills the corrupted men in order to preserve the lives and hearts of the rest of his people, and he commands the people to fight their corrupt neighbors instead of intermingling with them.

26. Moses and his nephew rally the troops and are able to identify 601,730 men fit for military service. Moses uses the information from the census to fairly divide the land among the clans.

27. Some of the unmarried women of Israel boldly request property of their own, and God assures Moses that they have just as much a right to own property as men do. As Moses climbs a mountain and looks down longingly at the Promised Land he will never get to set foot on, God comforts him with the knowledge that his people will be in good hands after Moses passes away. God asks Moses to bless and support the capable and courageous Joshua as the next leader of Israel.

28. Moses reminds the people to please God with daily sacrifices and respect the Sabbath with grain and wine offerings. They must start each month on the right foot with a generous sacrifice and remember to keep an attitude of worship, rest, and joyful celebration during the Passover and Harvest Festivals.

29. Moses reminds the people of God's specifications regarding observance of the New Year Festival, the Day of Atonement,

and the Festival of Shelters. During these holidays, the people should take a break from work and wholeheartedly praise God with generous offerings.

30. Moses reminds the people that when they promise to honor God with their gifts and obedient actions, they must do all in their power to stay true to their word. However, if a person's parent or spouse prevents him or her from fulfilling a promise to God, the broken promise is certainly understandable and forgivable.

31. Moses sends his army into battle against the Midianites, and God allows his people to thoroughly defeat this enemy without losing a single Hebrew soldier. Moses and the High Priest oversee the fair division of the loot won in battle, while remembering to offer a portion to God.

32. The men of the Israelite tribes Gad and Reuben feel at home in the land where they are currently camping, finding that it is an ideal landscape for their livestock. Moses agrees to let them make their permanent home there as long as they agree to do their part in the next mission to cross the river and finish conquering the Promised Land.

33. Moses reflects on the forty-year journey from Egypt to the bank of the Jordan River, making a note of each place that they camped along the way. After remembering how far they've come, Moses prepares the people for where they are about to go. God commands them to take no prisoners and drive out all the wicked people currently living in the Promised Land.

34. God gives a clear and detailed description of the landmarks that will help identify the boundaries of the Promised Land,

and Moses prepares Joshua and several other trustworthy leaders to oversee the division of the land when the time comes.

35. God instructs the people to assign cities and land to Levites throughout the land so that each tribe of Israel will have access to their spiritual leadership. God also provides a blueprint for the distribution of cities set aside as a safe haven for people who commit accidental crimes as well as those awaiting trial.

36. A few men remind Moses of the new policy allowing single women to inherit property, and they argue that this could lead to unequal property distribution if these women eventually marry men outside their tribes. Moses supports God's decision to allow women to inherit property, and clarifies that if these women do eventually marry, they will need to marry someone within their own tribe.

DAY FIVE - EDGE OF A PROMISE
DEUTERONOMY

BIG IDEA

After forty years of wandering and growing, Moses delivers a series of sermons to motivate the Israelites forward into the Promised Land.

SERMON LESSONS

- **Moses has grown-** He started as a reluctant, stuttering leader terrified of public speaking, and now he speaks with a commanding voice and inspired words of seasoned wisdom.
- **God protected and provided-** Every step of the journey, God guided his chosen nation out of oppressive Egypt and through unfriendly lands. He kept their clothes untarnished and their bellies full every day.
- **God deserves our respect-** We must remember how God has rescued and blessed us, and we must remember how awesome and powerful he is. Replacing him with fake gods would be a terrible mistake.
- **Take care of each other-** Whether you are a child, a widow, a leader, or a slave, you deserve to be treated with dignity and respect. Act with kindness and generosity toward each other, and hold each other accountable to the law.
- **Obedience leads to success-** If you trust God and respect his guidance, he will help you conquer great enemies and

lead you into a life of prosperity and peace.

- **Trust Joshua**- Moses' time is almost up, and he passes the torch to Joshua to lead the nation forward. They join their voices in a stirring song of worship and gratitude.

HOW GOD SHOWS UP

God shows up time and time again to carry his children through the desert, even though they are often ungrateful and rebellious. He empowers meek Moses to overcome countless obstacles and rise up as one of the most respected leaders in Jewish history. Through Moses and Aaron, God teaches the people how to set themselves apart as a culture that worships wholeheartedly and lifts up its most vulnerable citizens. He promises to lead them forward into the Promised Land with fresh new leadership and assured victory.

DEUTORONOMY

1. On the shore of the river dividing the Hebrew people from the Promised Land, Moses stands before the great multitude to deliver a sermon of encouragement and inspiration. He says "I've been thinking about my conversation with God at Mount Sinai, when he first sent us forth on this wild adventure through mountain ranges and across rivers. Back then, I was overwhelmed by the massive responsibility of serving as your leader, since God had made you as numerous as the stars. How could I ever keep the peace

among you by myself? God blessed me with incredibly valuable helpers who served as my advisors and your judges as we created this new society together. We came to the edge of this land forty years ago, and with the exception of Caleb, everyone froze up upon seeing the enemy, and they refused to trust God to help us win the fight, even though he had already brought us so far. Then, to make matters worse, some of your fathers took it upon themselves to go into battle without God's guidance, which of course did not work out too well.

2.   "When we approached the country of Edom, the descendants of Esau were intimidated by us, provided us with food, and let us pass through peacefully. We are so blessed that God never failed to provide for our needs and even let us sneak through cities of giants unscathed. And when enemy kings tried to start power struggles with us, we showed them just how powerful our God can be.

3.   "God encouraged us not to be afraid of the armies that tried to attack us. When we faced the evil King Og and his men, we were able to defeat them completely, leaving no enemy soldier alive. When we came to this land near the Jordan River, I assigned different portions of it to the tribes of Reuben, Gad, and Manassah, and as I speak to you, Joshua and our most capable soldiers are preparing to cross the river to conquer the rest of the Promised Land. This is just the beginning! There is no God like our God, and oh how I wish he would allow me to go with you during this next exciting chapter of your journey.

4.   "If you follow God's instructions without trying to rewrite

what he has already written, he will make you successful during this next chapter. Please remember how wonderful and merciful our God is and how many times he has showed up to help you; don't ever replace him with the evil gods of those living around us. One day you will tell your children of the awesome miracles you've seen, and you will remember that we worship the one true God who existed before time began." Moses ends this particular speech to designate three cities in their current land as the cities of refuge.

5.   Moses gathers the Hebrews again to share the following profound speech. "Four decades ago on Mount Sinai, our great Rescuer appeared to me from the fire and revealed the great law to me. He started with the ten most important commandments, which serve as a blueprint for how we might put God first, take care of ourselves, and avoid harming one another. I saw God's awesome presence and lived to tell about it! The tribe leaders heard God's booming voice from the base of the mountain and stood in awe as they promised to obey whatever God spoke to me next. If only that dedication had lasted!

6.   "Listen up! This is the most important thing! Love God with all you've got. Pass what you are about to hear onto your children, and do whatever you need to do to remember these words, even if you have to write them on every wall of your house. God is about to bless you with cities you did not build and fields you did not plant. You've done nothing to earn God's favor, so don't take his blessings for granted or put him to the test. Remember that you were slaves, and he performed many astounding miracles to free

you from bondage.

7. "When our army marches into this new land, God will equip us to drive out seven armies bigger than ours. Take no prisoners. Don't hold back. Know that these people have fallen deeply into wickedness, and if you let any of them continue to live in your land, they will corrupt you. If you stay loyal to God, he will provide you with abundant harvests, healthy livestock, and immunity from fatal illnesses. Have no fear. God is on your side, and he is the only One worthy of fear.

8. "God could have let you go hungry in that desert, but he provided manna instead. Take a look at your clothes and shoes. In all these years, they have not worn out. Have you ever paused to thank God for that? God has made water flow out of dry rocks for you and blessed you with more wealth than you ever could have predicted. Don't forget about him.

9. "Take a look at that lush, fertile land across the river, with giants much stronger than you and cities more impressive than anything you've ever seen. Even though you don't deserve it, God is about to drive out those giants and give you that land. From the day we left Egypt, you have tested God's patience time and time again. Even when I was on the mountain hearing God's holy law for the first time, you wasted no time in making an idol for yourselves and congratulating yourselves with a drunken party. If not for my fasting and prayer on your behalf, he probably would have killed you all.

10. "Since my discovery of your golden idol made me so mad that I broke the stone tablets containing the law, I accepted

God's suggestion to rewrite the tablets and keep them safe in a protective box. It's important for you to know that our loving God created this law for your own good, so that you would live in relationship with him and not destroy each other. Our worthy God is capable of great miracles and reigns over all creation, and yet he has a heart for even the smallest and poorest among us.

11. "You have seen God devastate your oppressors in Egypt and part the Red Sea to allow you to escape. You've seen the ground swallow up those who tried to destroy our community from within. Keep serving God, and you will be amazed at the beauty and rich harvests he will provide in the new land. It is up to you whether you want to cherish these words and be blessed by God or whether you want to turn away from him and fend for yourselves without his protection. It's up to you.

12. "When you cross the river, make sure you destroy all the worship centers for the foreign idols. People burned children and committed such evil acts in those places, and it is not okay to blend in with these cultures and just do whatever you please in worship. God deserves more respect than that. Offer him a portion of the blessings he has given you, and do it joyfully and reverently according to God's instructions.

13. "Foreign magicians and fortune tellers will try to impress you and get you to worship gods that aren't real. Don't fall for this. Even your own family members might turn against God, but you will need to stay strong and remain loyal to the God that rescued you from slavery.

14. "Set yourselves apart from the cultures around you. Don't

cut yourself to mourn the dead like they do. Don't eat unclean animals that could make you sick. Take care of the body that God gave you, and nourish it with food that is good for you. Give ten percent of your wealth to God so that his chosen priests will have their needs met, and feel free to enjoy the rest of your wealth alongside your family.

15. "Every seven years, God wants you to forgive all debts and wipe the slate clean so that he will be able to lift families out of poverty and give them a fresh start. Give freely and unselfishly to people in need; God sees and loves them as much as he loves you. When the seventh year comes, free all slaves, and send them away with full pockets. Treat slaves with dignity, respecting them as members of your family.

16. "When you celebrate the Passover, remember the miracles that allowed you leave Egypt. We had to leave in such a hurry that we didn't have time to let the bread dough rise, which is why we feast on unleavened bread during this holiday. Celebrate the harvest each year by showing joyful gratitude to God and presenting him with a lavish offering. During the Festival of Shelters, enjoy a week of rest as you reflect on how God has blessed you. When you settle into the new land, appoint judges who will keep the peace with fairness and wisdom.

17. "If multiple witnesses catch someone disrespecting God and breaking the law, the community is free to hold that person accountable and even execute him if necessary. When a case is too difficult for the judges to decide, bring it directly to God. If you decide you need a king like the nations around you, choose someone God has prepared

for the task. Choose someone who takes God seriously and who doesn't let himself get distracted by temptations like sex and money.

18. "The Levite priests residing in your land were chosen by God and deserve to be well fed and taken care of through your offerings. Don't follow the disgusting religious practices of foreigners who murder children and perform witchcraft in their churches. Drive them out along with their wicked customs. Keep your eyes peeled for false prophets who may try to mislead you.

19. "Each territory should contain three easily accessible cities of refuge for anyone who has accidentally killed someone. This will prevent grieving families from being tempted to act out in murderous revenge against the person responsible for the accident, and an innocent life will not have to be lost. Judges must require multiple witnesses to convict someone, and the punishment should proportionally fit the crime.

20. "When your enemies outnumber you in battle, don't panic. God delivered you from Egypt, and he'll deliver you again. If an officer's heart is not in the fight, and if he can't stop thinking about his family, send him home so that his distracted focus doesn't spread to the other men. Keep your head in the game, and wipe out the enemy.

21. "When a murder goes unsolved, the priests must offer a sacrifice to recognize the innocent victim and atone whoever is responsible for the murder. If you marry a foreign prisoner of war, allow her to mourn her family and do not treat her like a slave. Be fair to your children when dividing your property among them, and if a child refuses to respect your

household rules, let the community hold him accountable.

22. "If you notice one of your neighbor's animals wandering onto your property, take the animal back to its rightful owner. Respect the animals God created by allowing mother animals to take care of their babies in peace. Don't cut corners when you build your houses, so that your family can safely live there for many years. Remain faithful to your spouses, and don't falsely accuse your wife of having an affair just to divorce her. If a woman is raped and abused, it is not her fault, even though she may feel dirty and broken from it.

23. "God has not forgotten how each foreign nation responded to us when we passed through their lands. God will bless those who showed mercy to us and will curse those who refused to feed us. Keep yourself and your military camps ritually clean during times of battle so that God will bless your mission and stick with you. God wants people to pay their debts honorably and never resort to prostitution to make money. Don't exploit people who owe you money, and when you make a promise to God, don't procrastinate.

24. "Respect the sanctity of marriage, and allow newlyweds to enjoy their first year together without the fear of military deployment. If someone is poor and indebted to you, treat him with dignity. Do not take the clothes off his back or the food out of his child's mouth. Only you are responsible for your actions; if you mess up, it is not your parents' fault.

25. "If your brother dies, don't send his wife and kids away to fend for themselves. Keep them in the family, and make sure they're taken care of. Fight fair, respect the animals

that work hard for you, and don't cheat people out of their hard-earned money.

26. "After God grants you peace and plentiful harvest in the new land, remember the good God that made it happen. He transformed a wandering Aramean and his barren wife into the ancestors of a great nation. He heard our cries of suffering in Egypt and rescued us from slavery. He led us across the desert and conquered giants so that we could have peace and plenty in this new place. Celebrate God's greatness, and freely give him a tenth of the harvest as a result of that gratitude. Obey God, and he will keep his promises to you.

27. "When you cross the river, build an altar to God right away. Write his law on stone, and place it high on a mountain where it can be seen by all. When you cross the river, gather on the mountain and loudly proclaim God's curse on all who disrespect his commands.

28. "If you obey God, he will make you prosper in all you do, and you will gain the respect of all who witness your life. If you turn away from God, he will turn away from you. In the absence of his guidance and protection, you will experience repeated failure, and your enemies will get the upper hand. Your misfortune and suffering may get so bad that you lose your mind and lose the land you've waited so long to inhabit. God has given you much more than you deserve; he has every right to take it all away and send you right back to Egypt."

29. Moses speaks to the people a third time to renew their covenant with God, saying "You have witnessed firsthand

that God is capable of great and wondrous things, but you have not really understood or appreciated these experiences. God devastated Egypt so that we could be set free, and he provided for our needs in the desert. God has already led us to great victories, and he deserves our obedience as we press on. Today we promise to worship him as our only God, knowing that he will continue to fulfill the promises he made to our ancestors long ago. If you turn away from God, this lush country will become a wasteland, and you will be uprooted.

30. "God is giving you a clear choice between a blessing and a curse. If you choose the path of disobedience and become exiled out of this land, it will never be too late to turn back to your merciful God and begin listening to his guidance again. He will lead you back home and make your nation great again. This is not complicated. Just love God and be loyal to him, and you will be blessed."

31. "I am 120 years old, and God will not let me live to see you cross this river. I am passing the torch on to Joshua, and through him, God will lead you to victory. Be brave Joshua, and don't give up." Moses pauses his speech to write down God's law and turn it over to the priests. Then he proclaims "Don't ever forget the words you heard today. Every seven years, I want you to read God's commands aloud to the whole community, so that each generation will be well informed and inspired to live for the Lord." At this point, God informs Moses that his time on earth is coming to an end. God inspires him to write a final song, and Moses offers final words of direction and encouragement to Joshua and the priests.

32. Moses and Joshua recite Moses' new song for all to hear: "Let these words fall like rain upon listening ears. We want to thank our great God for protecting us and revealing his perfect justice to us. We are unworthy to be called his people. He found us wandering in the desert and gathered us under his mighty wing. He filled our bellies and made us rich, and we still turned to gods who weren't real. Those who betray and anger God have earned a lifetime of disaster, but when the bad times cause you to lean on God again, he will look at you with love and mercy. Our living God gives and takes away. He defends his people and flattens his enemies." Then, God directs Moses to go to the top of the mountain to spend his last moments gazing at the Promised Land from a distance.

33. Moses delivers his final words of blessing upon the people of Israel, saying "God's glory dazzles above Mount Sinai with thousands of angels by his side. That same great and powerful God protects his children, and we fall in worship at his feet. We obey him and call him our king. God, keep the tribe of Reuben alive, and help the tribe of Judah rise up in unity and victory. Lord, recognize and strengthen the Levites who serve you faithfully, and dwell among the people of Benjamin who you love so dearly. Bless the people of Joseph with fertile land and rich harvests. As the people of Zebulon and Issachar start international businesses on the shores of our land, I pray that you will bring them peace and prosperity in their ventures. Lord, the people of Gad and Dan gobble up your blessings like hungry lions, and the people of Naphtali enjoy your blessing and favor. God, I see how much you love the people of Asher, and I know

you will grant them peace and security. People of Israel, may God fly across the sky to protect you, trampling your enemies, and nourishing your land. Live in peace."

34. Moses climbs to the top of Mount Pisgah and takes in the view of the entire land, knowing that this is the land God promised to Abraham long ago. Moses dies at the age of 120, and God equips Joshua to lead the people with wisdom. There was no other prophet quite like Moses, and he will never be forgotten.

WEEK ONE REFLECTION

Foundation

DISCUSSION QUESTIONS

- How do you define faith? When do Noah, Abraham, and Joseph each demonstrate great faith through their stories? What other people in Genesis stand out as faithful founders of the Hebrew nation?

- Joseph's brothers sold him into slavery, but the Lord allowed Joseph to rise above great obstacles. How did Joseph demonstrate gratitude, faith, and resilience in the face of his circumstances? Is there an area of your life where you need to learn from Joseph's example?

- Moses resisted God's call initially because of his speech impediment. How can you relate to Moses' reluctance and insecurity? What imperfections hold you back from saying yes to the Father? How might God use your imperfect self to lead or bless others?

- Read the Ten Commandments in Exodus 20:1-17. How does each commandment relate to the overarching concepts of love and respect? How do the other regulations of Exodus and Leviticus relate to love and respect?

- How did God show his love for the Hebrews as they wandered through the desert? How would you rate the people's level of gratitude during this time, and did that level of gratitude change at any point? How would you rate your own level of gratitude for God's blessings in the last week? What are five blessings you can be grateful for today?

- Imagine you are sitting in the crowd listening to Moses' final speeches that are recorded in Deuteronomy. What are the most powerful lessons you draw from these sermons? How would these words motivate you to move forward into the Promised Land?

MUSIC MEDITATIONS

- **Genesis-** Listen to "So Will I" by Hillsong United. Try to pinpoint a few aspects of God's creation that highlight God's beauty, power, and immense creativity.
- **Exodus-** If you'd like to experience the story of Moses on a deeper level, rent *The Prince of Egypt*, and listen to each of its beautiful, insightful songs. "Deliver Us" by Steven Schwartz contains especially powerful lyrics about the enslavement of the Hebrews and their desperate need for rescue.
- **Leviticus-** Listen to "O Come to the Altar" by Elevation Worship, and consider what the modern church might learn from this ancient worship guide. We may not have the same laws and cultural practices today, but we can still approach God's altar with reverent love and gratitude.
- **Numbers-** Listen to "Blessed Be Your Name" by Matt Redman, and reflect on what it might look like to passionately worship God even as you trudge through the uncertain, uncomfortable deserts of your life.
- **Deuteronomy-** Moses emphasizes that throughout the

desert years, God never abandoned them. Listen to "Never Once" by Matt Redman, and consider whether you've ever felt God's constant presence during a difficult season.

APPLICATION IDEAS

- Get up early one day this week, take a walk, and watch in silent amazement as the sun rises. Pray as you walk, and acknowledge that the Lord you are speaking to is also the One who invented all the colors in that sunrise.

- Moses trusted God enough to face his fears and weaknesses, letting God accomplish great miracles through his life. What is a fear or task you have been avoiding? Trust God enough to formulate an action plan and make a small step forward in that area this week.

- Take a cue from Leviticus, and respect your body. You only get one of those, so take care of it. For you, this may mean mindfully choosing healthy foods and reasonable portion sizes at a few mealtimes this week. It could also mean increasing your physical activity, reducing your screen time, or going to bed a bit earlier than usual.

- If you feel yourself wandering in the desert in some area of your life, let yourself pray words of gratitude for the things that are still going well. When you are tempted to complain, recognize this temptation as unhelpful, and ask God to help you adopt an attitude of hope and praise. Notice how your day changes with this simple shift in perspective.

WEEK TWO

History

JOSHUA-ESTHER

DAY ONE - FORGETTING THE DELIVERER
JOSHUA-JUDGES-RUTH

BIG IDEA

God leads the Israelites into the Promised Land at last, and they quickly grow complacent and disobedient.

CAST OF CHARACTERS

- **Joshua-** Courageous leader who guides the Israelite army into dozens of victories and never forgets to give God the credit.

- **Rahab-** Foreign prostitute who recognizes the power of God, works undercover to help the Israelites, and later marries into the family.

- **Barak-** Strong military leader who enthusiastically celebrates Israel's victory and offers plenty of humble gratitude to his soldiers, Deborah, and God.

- **Deborah-** Barak's friend and a highly respected mother figure to the Israelite troops. God lifts up this powerful and influential woman long before women are typically respected as leaders.

- **Gideon-** Meek commander of a tiny army that doesn't stand a chance without God's help.

- **Samson-** Entitled, macho womanizer with uncommon strength and poor judgment. God can use just about anyone to fulfill his greater plans.

- **Ruth-** Hard-working, fearless woman who puts her mother-in-law first.
- **Boaz-** Son of the prostitute Rahab who becomes a successful, respected member of the Hebrew community.

HOW GOD SHOWS UP

God provides Joshua with the courage he needs to face 31 kings and defeat them all. He ushers the Hebrews into the fertile, beautiful land he promised long ago, and they respond with gratitude, obedience, and unity until Joshua's death. When the people grow complacent toward sin, God allows struggle to turn his nation back to him. He lifts up leaders like Barak, Deborah, Gideon, and Samson to rescue the undeserving people from enemy nations. In the midst of sin and chaos, God notices an uncommonly kind woman named Ruth, and he quietly chooses her to be the matriarch of the most important family in history.

JOSHUA

1. As the Hebrew people mourn the death of Moses, God offers Joshua words of assurance as the nation's new leader, asking him to lead the people to the Promised Land with courage, confidence, determination, and obedience. God promises to never leave Joshua's side as he leads the chosen people to victory. Joshua enthusiastically passes on God's encouragement to his troops and orders them to pack their bags.

2. Joshua sends two spies into the city of Jericho, and a pros-
    titute named Rahab takes them in and hides them from the
    king's men. Rahab has noticed the many victories Israel
    has experienced, and she recognizes that those victories
    have come directly from God. In fact, the whole country
    has noticed, and they're scared to death. The spies vow to
    reward Rahab for her loyalty by sparing her household in
    the coming siege.

3. Joshua gets the troops up early the next morning and
    encourages them to trust that God will provide a victory.
    The men on the front lines carry the Covenant Box to
    the bank of the Jordan River, and God parts the waters,
    allowing the army to cross into the Promised Land on dry
    ground.

4. As they cross the river, Joshua instructs a few of his soldiers
    to pick up twelve stones from the river floor and configure
    them on the opposite shore as a permanent reminder of
    God's miraculous power that allowed the waters to part.

5. The Amorite and Canaanite kings fear the Israelites even
    more intensely after hearing of the river parting. Joshua
    leads his men in a mass circumcision to honor their covenant
    with God, and shortly after, a powerful military angel shows
    up to help lead the army.

6. Joshua and the Israelite people demonstrate great faith
    by walking around the city walls of Jericho seven times,
    until God causes the walls to come down. As the Israelites
    overtake the city, they spare the household of the loyal
    prostitute Rahab as promised.

7. God commands the people to take nothing from the ruins

of Jericho, but a greedy Israelite named Achan disobeys
this order. When the Hebrew army is forced to retreat in
its next battle, Joshua recognizes right away that God's
miraculous protection is gone, and he identifies Achan as
the culprit. Achan is stoned for stealing, lying, and jeop-
ardizing their mission.

8. The Lord allows his people to defeat the people of Ai in
    battle after the Hebrew army pretends to retreat and then
    surprises the enemy with a hidden battalion. In a spirit of
    gratitude, Joshua builds an altar to God and reads the Law
    to his soldiers.

9. When the people of Gibeon hear about the Hebrew army's
    miraculous victories, they recognize that they don't stand
    a chance against God's chosen people. The Gibeon-
    ites convince Joshua they are from a distant land so he
    will make a peace treaty with them. Joshua mercifully lets
    these people live as servants of the Israelites, even after
    learning the truth about where they really live.

10. The evil king of Jerusalem and several of his allies learn
    that Gibeon has now teamed up with Israel, and they swarm
    Gibeon with their armies right away. Joshua brings his best
    troops to defend the city, and God sends giant hailstones
    upon the enemy army. Joshua leads his men into a series
    of important victories, and in the midst of the action, he
    encourages his officers to proceed with confidence, knowing
    God is on their side.

11. Several enemy kings learn of Israel's recent victories, and
    they decide to band together to form an enormous army
    that should logically be able to defeat Joshua's men. God

drives out Joshua's fear and equips his army to wipe out this massive army as well as an entire race of giants. The Hebrews realize they have won the war, and they are finally able to rest.

12. In the invasion of the Promised Land, God allows Moses and Joshua to defeat 33 kings, and 31 of these are overtaken during the time of Joshua. Pretty impressive!

13. In Joshua's old age, God informs him of the land still to be taken, noting that the current occupants will retreat as Israel advances. Joshua divides the territory east of the Jordan among the tribes of Reuben, Gad, and East Manasseh, according to the instructions Moses had left long ago.

14. The leaders of Israel begin to fairly divide the freshly conquered land west of the Jordan among the nine and a half remaining tribes. Joshua gives the city of Hebron to the family of Caleb, a man who demonstrated courage and obedience to God when everyone else refused to trust in his divine protection.

15. As the people enjoy this new era of peace, Joshua and the other leaders assign territory to the tribe of Judah. Meanwhile, the brave warrior Caleb easily drives out the occupants of Hebron. When Caleb's daughter boldly asks him for a piece of land as a wedding present, Caleb generously blesses her beyond her request.

16. The leaders assign a certain portion of land to the tribe of Ephraim, and instead of driving out the Canaanites as God had requested, the Hebrews in this area allow the enemy people to live with them as servants.

17. The tribe of West Manasseh learns which portion of land

will belong to them. When the people of Ephraim and West Manasseh complain that their territory is too small, Joshua says that if they drove the enemy people out as God had instructed, the land would not feel so crowded.

18. After the community of Israel sets up the sacred tent in Shiloh, Joshua maps out the rest of the territories which would be divided among the remaining seven tribes. He starts with the tribe of Benjamin.

19. Joshua assigns the remaining land to the tribes of Simeon, Zebulun, Issachar, Asher, Naphtali, and Dan. Last but not least, Joshua finally assigns a city to his own family.

20. With the help of his fellow leaders, Joshua decides where the cities of refuge will be located in each territory. These cities are meant to serve as safe havens for people who commit accidental crimes as well as those awaiting trial.

21. Joshua and the other leaders assign 48 cities to the Levites. These cities are scattered throughout Israel so that these priests can provide spiritual leadership for the entire nation. God ushers in an era of peace throughout the land, just as he promised. Not one enemy could stand against the army God protected.

22. Joshua thanks the soldiers of Reuben, Gad, and East Manasseh for a job well done, and he sends them back across the Jordan River to be with their families. In an attitude of celebration and gratitude, these soldiers build an impressive altar on the western river bank before they cross. The western tribes initially view this as an act of disrespect for the territory boundaries, but those who built the altar clarify that the altar is simply meant to honor God.

23. Joshua gives a farewell address to the Israelite people, saying "Friends, together we have seen God fight for us again and again. He has already driven out many nations, and the rest will flee as you advance. God has generously kept his promises to you, so honor him by following his law and faithfully standing by him. Beware of the corrupt foreigners that may try to steer you away from God, and for goodness sake, don't marry them! My life is almost over, so before I die, I want you to understand how great our God is. Worship him alone, and don't take his protection for granted."

24. Joshua reminds the Israelite leaders of their remarkable history, and he challenges them to choose whether their households will serve foreign idols or the one true God. As for Joshua, he's with God. Joshua and the head priest Eleazer die of old age.

JUDGES

1. With the confidence that the Lord is on their side, Judah leads the way in a battle to take control of the mighty city of Jerusalem. Caleb and his future son-in-law work together to conquer another bit of land, and Caleb generously gives a portion of that land to his daughter and son-in-law as a wedding present. God leads the Hebrew army into many victories, with only a few enemy towns being able to defend themselves. The Hebrews disobey God's command to drive the enemy out entirely, and they allow some Canaanites to

continue to live among them as servants. In the territory of Dan, this disobedience backfires, and an enemy nation forces the people of Dan into the hill country.

2.   An angel shows up to remind the people that God delivered them out of Egypt and deserves their complete loyalty. The Hebrews must tear down the evil altars of the enemy; otherwise God will not drive them out as he previously promised. After Joshua dies, the next generation forgets all about the Lord who had brought them so far. The Father is understandably angry when his children betray him to worship false gods, and without God's miraculous protection, Israel's enemies are able to raid and overtake their cities.

3.   God allows certain enemies to stay in Israel to test the people and motivate them to fight for their faith. Unfortunately, the Israelites begin intermarrying with these enemies instead of fighting them. It's only when the Moabites start to take control of Israel that God's people cry out to him in desperation. The Lord mercifully sends a military leader named Ehud to assassinate the king of Moab and help Israel regain independence.

4.   After nearly a century of peace under godly leadership, the Hebrews sin again, and God allows them be conquered by a violent Canaanite king named Jabin. Israel eventually cries out for help, and a man named Barak leads them to victory with the encouragement and friendship of a prophet named Deborah.

5.   Deborah and Barak do a victory dance and sing the following celebratory song: "Our soldiers stepped up, fighting with determination. Take notice, all you evil kings of the world!

The nation of Israel is back! Our powerful God shook the mountains and scared away unfriendly travelers from our roads. I want to brag about our brave army to everyone I see. Men all over the country left their jobs and families behind to risk their lives on the battlefield. Praise God for our dynamite team! Deborah, thanks for being like a mom to us. Lead on, girl! May God curse anyone else who tries to take us on, and may he let our allies shine like the sun." Israel lives in peace for 40 years under the excellent leadership of Deborah and Barak.

6. The next generation of entitled Hebrews forgets about God again, and the Lord allows the Midianites to rule over the people for seven years in an effort to humble them. When the people cry out for help, God reminds them that the people continually turn away from him, even after he rescued the people from Egypt and led them to complete victory when conquering the Promised Land. How disappointing! The Lord then calls a faithful but seemingly unimportant man named Gideon to rise up and lead Israel into victory. Sometimes, God works powerfully through those ignored by the world.

7. The meek and self-conscious Gideon must battle the enormous Midianite army with only 300 men, and this tiny Hebrew battalion is miraculously victorious. God protects these 300 warriors to prove to the self-righteous Israelites that they can accomplish anything if they keep God in the driver's seat and acknowledge his blessings with gratitude.

8. The people of Israel do not show proper honor to God or Gideon's army after the battle of the 300, whining that they

weren't kept in the loop. In fact, two Hebrew towns will not even feed the victorious battalion until they defeat the two remaining Midianite kings. The Israelites still engage in idol worship despite God's miracles, yet he mercifully allows peace in the land for 40 years. Gideon dies after fathering 71 children.

9. Gideon's greedy son, Abimelech, convinces the men of Shechem to support him as king, and he kills 69 of his brothers to avoid sharing power. Abimelech's youngest brother, Jotham, escapes this wrath and proclaims publicly that the men of Shechem made a terrible mistake. God lets the power-hungry Abimelech rule Israel for only three years before allowing an outbreak of chaos and violence to result in his death.

10. After Abimelech's death, men named Tola and Jair lead Israel for 23 years and 22 years respectively. Once again, Israel stops worshipping the Lord, and God angrily tells the people to ask their fake gods for help, and see how that works out for them. Unsurprisingly, the idols can't stop Philistia and Ammon from conquering Israel.

11. A seemingly insignificant soldier named Jephthah is is rejected by his embarrassed family because he is born out of wedlock to a prostitute. When he is called upon to help in a war against Ammon, Jephthah boldly prays that if God allows him victory, he will sacrifice the first person to visit his home afterward. God helps this warrior defeat the Ammonites, and tragically, the first person he sees afterward happens to be his beloved daughter. This remarkable young woman bravely sacrifices her own unfinished life so that

her dad can keep his promise to God.

12. The men of Ephraim have their feelings hurt due to Jephthah going into battle without their help, so he reminds these whiners that when he asked for their help in the past, they didn't show up. Jephthah leads a slaughter of 42,000 Ephraimites in a power struggle that the Ephraimites pointlessly start. Jephthah and several leaders that follow him rule Israel for about seven years apiece.

13. Israel turns away from God yet again, and the Philistines take over for 40 years. An angel appears to an infertile couple with no status to predict that they will have a miracle child named Samson who will become a great warrior and rescue the Hebrews from the Philistines. The couple celebrates this vision with joy and amazement. When Samson is born, his grateful parents dedicate him to God based on the angel's instructions.

14. Showing that God can truly use any imperfect person to serve his higher purposes, he uses Samson's hot temper and his poor taste in women to ultimately set up the fall of the Philistines. God gives Samson strength great enough to tear apart a lion with his bare hands, so when he's angry, he can do some serious damage to his enemies. Samson marries an untrustworthy woman based on her looks rather than her character, and she betrays him by telling a group of locals about her husband's great power. Samson kills these 30 Philistine men in a blind rage. Samson discovers that his wife has been given away to his former best man, and he acts out in revenge toward the Philistines. He ultimately kills a thousand of them with the jawbone of a donkey, and

he rules Israel for 20 years.

15. Aside from his terrifying temper, Samson's biggest weakness is his stupidity and recklessness when it comes to his love life. He endangers himself by sleeping with a prostitute in enemy territory, and then he falls in love with an untrustworthy woman named Delilah. Delilah accepts a bribe from the Philistine kings, and she nags him until he reveals his secret weakness to her. He reveals that his miraculous God-given strength will disappear with a haircut, since his long hair symbolizes his dedication to God. Delilah wastes no time in cutting off her lover's long hair while he sleeps, which allows the Philistines to capture him, torture him, and make him blind. Despite his many flaws, God allows Samson to die as a hero, taking all the Philistine kings down with him in a building collapse.

16. During a time of religious chaos in Israel, a man named Micah steals everything in his mom's saving's account, and when he confesses his crime to her, she forgives him, and they make an idol with the silver. A Levite traveler from Bethlehem wanders into Micah's town and agrees to live with Micah as his spiritual advisor.

17. At this point, the Israelites have not yet assigned land to the tribe of Dan, so explorers from Dan pass through Micah's area looking to conquer it. They kidnap the Levite priest, steal Micah's silver idol, and attack the peaceful city of Laish. The people of Dan set up Micah's idol in their place of worship and begin worshipping this dead object instead of the living God. The people of Dan name Moses' grandson as their pagan priest.

18. During the time when Israel is actively rejecting God, a concubine leaves her Levite lover to return to her father's house after a quarrel. The man makes peace with his concubine and the two of them have so much fun catching up at her father's house that they lose track of time and don't leave for five days. In the middle of the journey home, they have trouble finding a place to stay but are eventually taken in by a sweet, hospitable old man. In the middle of the night, a gang of corrupt perverts from the tribe of Benjamin rape and kill the concubine as well as the sweet old man's daughter. The grieving Levite man makes sure each of the Israelite tribes know about this tragedy, demanding that something must be done to hold the criminals accountable.

19. Eleven of the Israelite tribes declare war on the tribe of Benjamin because they refuse to punish or reveal the identities of the ones who had brutally killed the young woman. God agrees that the Israelites need to punish this tribe for their corrupt decision, and the tribe of Benjamin is nearly wiped out in battle.

20. The Israelites as a whole take pity on the remaining Benjaminites and agree that they should not allow an entire tribe to be destroyed because of the sins of one generation. They instruct the remaining men of this tribe to kidnap women from the town of Shiloh to be their wives, so the family of Benjamin would not die out completely. The Israelites continue floating through life without a stable government and without any consistent connection to God during this dark time.

RUTH

1. During the violent and corrupt time of *Judges*, a kind
    Hebrew woman named Naomi loses her husband and two
    sons while living in Moab. Naomi shows compassion for
    her two daughters-in-law by saying "Don't worry about
    me, girls. You don't have to waste your youth looking after
    a broken down old woman like me. I want you to go back
    to your hometowns, find handsome husbands, and raise a
    family with them. If you stay with me as I go back to Israel,
    I will only hold you back." One of the girls takes her moth-
    er-in-law's advice and hugs Naomi goodbye. However, the
    uncommonly selfless Ruth looks her grieving mother-in-law
    in the face and says "Not a chance! You are my family, and
    I will not leave you alone. If you're going back to Israel
    to be with your people and worship your God, I will do
    the same because I love you." So, hand in hand, Ruth and
    Naomi journey to Bethlehem.

2. With Naomi's blessing, Ruth takes it upon herself to pick
    corn with the locals, to show the field owners what a hard
    worker she is. Naomi's wealthy and influential relative Boaz
    takes notice of the lovely and scrappy young woman and
    hires her right away to work in his field. Ruth humbly thanks
    Boaz for the job, and Boaz responds "Well, I heard how
    you left your country and your whole family to take care
    of your mother-in-law. I think that's pretty awesome, so I
    think you deserve all the rewards and blessings God has in
    store for you." Boaz then invites Ruth to eat lunch with him
    and encourages the other workers to let Ruth gather extra

corn to feed and bless her household. Naomi is excited to learn that the kind Boaz is Ruth's new boss and encourages her to keep working there.

3. With Naomi's advice and encouragement, Ruth dolls herself up and crawls into Boaz's bed with him, boldly proposing marriage to her kind friend and employer. While Boaz is flattered and perhaps a little bit tempted to take advantage of the situation, he acts like a perfect gentleman toward Ruth and even suggests that he might be able to match Ruth with someone who could be an even better potential husband for her. Ruth returns to Naomi's house the next morning and patiently waits for Boaz to make the next move.

4. Boaz's matchmaking attempt falls through, so Boaz himself agrees to marry Ruth. The town leaders offer a kind and generous blessing upon their new family. Ruth and Boaz become the great-grandparents of David, the godliest king in Israel's history.

DAY TWO - RISE OF A SHEPHERD KING
1 SAMUEL-2 SAMUEL

BIG IDEA

God humbles an arrogant giant and lifts up an overlooked shepherd.

CAST OF CHARACTERS

- **Hannah-** Gratefully celebrates when God answers her prayer for a child.
- **Samuel-** Innocent leader who listens to God and finds the first chosen kings.
- **Saul-** Strong warrior who looks like a king but grows paranoid of losing power. He doesn't have the obedience or mental strength to keep the job.
- **Jonathan-** Prince who protects his friend David from his bloodthirsty father.
- **David-** Musical shepherd who is stronger than anyone realizes. He leads Israel to great victories and becomes the first truly worthy king of Israel.
- **Goliath-** Prideful giant who terrorizes Israel's army and mocks their God.
- **Abigail-** Clever woman who soothes conflict and earns David's respect.
- **Nathan-** Unafraid to confront the king with the difficult truth.

- **Bathsheba-** Solomon's mother who endures the unfair loss of her husband and newborn son because of David's sense of entitlement to be with her.
- **Absalom-** Murders his sister's abuser in anger, betrays his father, and greedily steals David's throne.
- **Joab-** Successful military commander willing to kill to stay at the top of King David's list of royal advisors.

HOW GOD SHOWS UP

God looks past the physical strength of potential kings to find someone with a strong and determined heart. He trusts David to put the welfare of the people ahead of his own selfish desires. When David grows a bit prideful and entitled, God forgives him but firmly reminds him to get his heart back on track. When Goliath, Saul, Nabal, and Absalom try to overpower David, God sends unlikely heroes to protect David every step of the way. After the dark and disobedient time of *Judges*, God allows the first kings to usher Israel into a new age of victory over enemies.

1 SAMUEL

1. A godly woman named Hannah falls deeply into depression because she has not been able to have children. Hannah's husband doesn't know how to help her, and his other wife humiliates and torments Hannah over her infertility. Hannah boldly and desperately prays for a son and does not care when other worshipers think she's making a fool

of herself. God answers her prayers by giving her a son named Samuel, who she agrees to dedicate to the Lord.

2. In response to the joy of baby Samuel's birth, Hannah shouts "God has made my heart so happy! There is no other God who blesses and protects like our God. He humbles the proud and lifts up weak people like me. Hungry people are fed, and barren women bear many children with His help." Keeping her promise, she leaves Samuel at the house of God to serve the priest Eli. God blesses her with more children and allows Samuel to grow into a godly young man. Meanwhile, a prophet reveals to Eli that his sons will die due to their corrupt practices.

3. God speaks aloud to young Samuel during the night, and since messages from God are so rare during this time, Samuel assumes initially that he is hearing the voice of Eli. God reveals his plan to wipe out Eli's wicked family, and Samuel obediently tells his guardian and mentor the difficult truth. Samuel continues to grow into a widely respected leader who draws many insights and prophecies from his close relationship and daily communication with God.

4. The Philistines brutally defeat the Hebrew army in two battles. During the second battle, 30,000 Israelite soldiers are killed, God's sacred Covenant Box is captured, and Eli's corrupt sons meet with an early death, as predicted. The startling news surrounding this battle leads Eli and his pregnant daughter-in-law to die in a state of shock and depression.

5. The Philistines set up the Covenant Box among their idols, and God punishes these thieves with a plague of tumors.

This enemy nation begins to panic and cry out to their false gods for help.

6. After seven months of God wreaking havoc upon the Philistines, this enemy realizes that God won't let up until his sacred Covenant Box is returned to his chosen people. With respect and fear for the Almighty Lord, the Philistines decide to return the Covenant Box across the border into Israel, along with a few golden statues to serve as apology gifts to the Hebrew people.

7. The Covenant Box stays in the Hebrew town of Kiriath Jearim for twenty years, and during that time, the people cry out to God and seek the wise spiritual council of Samuel. Samuel responds "Well, if you're really serious about turning back to God, he must be the only God that you worship. All the disgusting foreign idols and religious customs must go." Once the people destroy the idols and seek God's forgiveness, God allows Israel to experience a time of peace, with Samuel leading the people as head judge.

8. In Samuel's old age, the people of Israel insist that they want this prophet to appoint a king so they can "be like all the other nations". Samuel explains that a monarchy would result in less freedom for the Israelites, but the people remain stubborn, demanding a king. God advises Samuel to give the people what they want and let them reap the consequences.

9. Samuel meets a handsome, strong, charismatic man named Saul, and God immediately assures Samuel that this young man will be a great warrior who will save Israel from the

Philistines.

10. Samuel anoints Saul as the first king of Israel and asks God to bless him in all he does. God proves his power to Saul by taking control of his body and making the new king dance enthusiastically. Most of the Israelites accept Saul's new leadership, but a few skeptics choose to remain unsatisfied

11. When the evil king of Ammon surrounds a small town in Israel, Saul snaps into action to protect his people, and uses his anger and passion to motivate 330,000 Hebrew soldiers to come together against the Ammonite army. After a solid victory, even the skeptics and doubters in Israel become convinced that Saul is in fact a strong and capable leader.

12. In his old age, Samuel addresses the people, saying "Now that I am an old man, it is time for me to step down and hand the reigns to this king I found for you. I have led you since I was a boy, and if I have hurt any of you, I promise to make it right." The people respond "Of course not, Samuel. You have treated all of us with dignity, and you've been a great and innocent leader." Samuel continues, "God chose Moses to lead our ancestors out of Egypt, and he performed great miracles to lead them to freedom. The people forgot the Lord again and again, and when God let their enemies overtake them, the people cried out for mercy, and God granted them that mercy. God sent great leaders like Gideon, Barak, and myself, and now, he has given you this king that you asked for. Even though God intended to serve as your King himself, he'll honor your request for a human king and bring good from it like he always does. As long as you, Saul, and future kings obey

God, you can trust that he'll protect you."

13. Saul's soldiers find themselves in a desperate situation when warring with the Philistines, and instead of trusting God's timing and waiting for Samuel's guidance as instructed, Saul hastily takes matters into his own hands. Samuel informs the king that God will anoint a more obedient and patient man to take Saul's place.

14. Trusting that God will protect and help them, Saul's son, Jonathan and his friend sneak into the Philistine camp and attack. The two men kill over twenty enemy soldiers and cause great calamity in the Philistine camp. Without taking time to consult God, Saul irrationally commands his army to enter into the chaos after commanding the army to fast until complete victory is won. Despite Saul endangering his hungry, unprepared soldiers with his rash, unwise decisions, God still swoops in and saves the day. Jonathan convinces his father that it is ridiculous to not allow the soldiers to refuel their bodies, and the remaining Philistines retreat. During Saul's reign as king, he frequently finds conflict with other nations, and God must save them again and again in various wars.

15. God commands Saul to wipe out the evil people of Amalek without sparing anyone or anything. He disobeys God by preserving the lives of the enemy king and some of the best Amalekite livestock. Saul further sins by lying to Samuel about this. God informs Samuel that he is sorry he ever made Saul king, and Samuel carries out God's order to execute the corrupt Amalekite king.

16. Samuel searches for a potential leader to replace Saul, and

God leads him to a humble shepherd boy. A man named Jesse presents his seven older and stronger sons to Samuel, but overlooks his youngest son David, leaving him in the field to watch the sheep during Samuel's visit. However, Samuel recognizes David's kind heart and courageous spirit right away, anointing him as the next king of Israel in front of David's shocked father and brothers. Soon after this, King Saul calls upon David to soothe his troubled, anxious mind by playing the harp.

17. A nine-foot-tall Philistine soldier named Goliath dares the Israelite soldiers to choose their strongest comrade to fight him, and Saul's army fearfully shrinks away from this challenge for 40 days. When David delivers food to the army camp, he remarks "Who does this Goliath think he is to come against the army of the living God? We have no reason to fear him. Let me fight him!" After hearing the doubts of Saul and the laughs of the other soldiers, David says, "God has enabled me to kill lions and bears protecting my father's sheep. I'm certain that he'll save me today, too." David confidently approaches the giant with nothing but a simple slingshot and kills him with one quick stone to the forehead. This causes Philistines to flee in fear and causes the king to learn the name of this curiously brave young shepherd.

18. Saul hires David as an officer in his army, and Jonathan befriends and deeply admires this rising star. The king becomes jealous of David's popularity and numerous military victories, so he endangers David by sending him on a dangerous and unnecessary mission. The plan backfires, and with God on his side, David succeeds and earns

the right to marry Saul's oldest daughter, Michal.

19. The king makes it known to Jonathan that he is plotting to kill David, and Saul's son passionately defends his friend, saying "Why would you kill David? He has been loyal to you every step of the way and has won battles none of your other officers were brave enough to even attempt. He is perfectly innocent, and your jealousy of him is incredibly unfair." Saul refuses to listen to his good-hearted son and later tries to stab David suddenly during his harp practice. David's wife, Michal, sneaks her husband out of her father's house, and David escapes to Samuel's house for protection. When the king sends several groups of men to arrest David, God causes them to lose control of their bodies in fits of dancing. The same strange phenomenon happens when Saul attempts to arrest David himself.

20. David flees from Samuel's house to reunite with Jonathan, and the king's son has trouble believing that his father truly wants to kill David. Jonathan insists on setting a trap for Saul to confirm that the suspicions are true. Jonathan realizes through one of Saul's angry outbursts that David is right about the king's murderous intentions, and the two best friends share a tearful goodbye.

21. David shrewdly acquires food and the sword of Goliath from a local priest named Ahimelech, saying that's he needs the sword to carry out orders from King Saul. With sword in hand, he flees to the city of Gath. David pretends to have a mental illness in order to not be perceived as a threat by the local king.

22. David flees from Gath to a series of caves to protect himself

from Saul, and along the way, he reunites with his family and acquires 400 followers who are also dissatisfied with Saul's leadership. Meanwhile, when Saul discovers that the priest Ahimelech provided David with food and Goliath's sword, the king accuses all his priests of conspiring against him, and he kills 85 of them in a paranoid rage. But he doesn't stop there. King Saul orders a senseless massacre on the priests' entire town, destroying their property and killing their wives and children.

23. The courageous and big-hearted David plans to save the town of Keilah from the Philistine thieves who are stealing the town's corn. Saul marches his armies toward Keilah, seeing this as his chance to overcome David, and upon learning this, David cries out to God and heeds God's advice to flee into the hill country. Jonathan joins David on the journey and says "Don't worry, my dear friend. My dad knows full well that God has chosen you as the next king, and I will proudly serve as your right hand man." A few locals reveal David's secret location to Saul, and just as the king is closing in on him, a messenger pulls Saul back to his royal duties with the news that Philistine troops are invading Israel. Saul must abandon his murderous search for now.

24. After handling the conflict with the Philistines, Saul tracks down David's location again, and in an act of wisdom and mercy, David sneaks up on Saul and cuts off a piece of his robe. David comes out of hiding and bows down in respect saying "Your Majesty, I know people have gotten into your head, saying I'm trying to harm you. But look at this piece of cloth in my hand! Does it look familiar? I could have killed you just now, but I didn't. Please stop hunting me.

May God see me as innocent and continue protecting me as he has so far." Saul responds with gratitude that David spared his life and promises to stop pursuing him. David remains in hiding just in case Saul's heart hardens once again.

25. Samuel dies after a lifetime of service and dedication to God. Meanwhile, David asks for the hospitality of a wealthy man named Nabal, and he rudely turns David away. Nabal's wife, Abigail, makes up for her husband's insult saying "Sir, ignore my idiot husband. Please accept this generous supply of groceries to nourish your men, and may God keep you safe on your journey. With his help, I know you will become king one day." David thanks Abigail for her good sense and walks away from a potential conflict with Nabal. God causes Nabal to have a stroke, and David takes beautiful Abigail as his wife.

26. When Saul goes after David yet again, David boldly sneaks into Saul's tent and steals his spear and water jug from his bedside. Once he is a safe distance away, David wakes up the whole camp, saying "Hey guard! You're not doing a great job protecting your king. Why don't you check and see if his spear and water jug are still in his tent? Saul, what have I ever done to harm you? Why do you insist on hunting me down like an animal? God put your life in my hands again, and I showed mercy to you. May God see this and have mercy on me." Upon hearing David's words, Saul stops his pursuit and returns home.

27. David and his 600-man army settle down in the town of Ziklag and gain the trust of Achish, one of the Philistine

kings. While David secretly raids and conquers many of the surrounding enemy towns, right under Achish's nose, this local king assumes that David is no longer loyal to Israel.

28. Achish gathers his troops against Israel, trusting David as his personal bodyguard. In desperation and fear, Saul consults a psychic medium to ask the ghost of Samuel for advice. Saul says "Samuel, my friend, I'm in big trouble! The Philistines are gathering their armies, and God is silent when I pray. What should I do?" The spirit of Samuel responds "You have disobeyed God, and your heart is far from him, so God is taking the kingdom from you and giving it to his servant David. Tomorrow, you and your sons will die." In terror and grief, Saul falls to the floor and refuses to eat for the rest of the day.

29. When the remaining Philistine kings see David and his small army of Hebrews tagging along behind Achish, they confront their fellow king saying "Is this the same David that has overcome tens of thousands of our people in the past? If he goes into battle with us, he and his men will turn on us." Achish refuses to believe this, saying "David, you have been loyal to me for a long time, and I fully trust you to remain by my side. But if my fellow kings refuse to let you fight, I will send you home in peace before the battle begins."

30. David and his men return to Ziklag shortly after a group of Amalekites raid their camp and parts of Judah. After seeking God's advice, this band of Hebrews follows the raiders, attacks them by surprise, and saves all the wives, children, and valuable possessions that had been taken.

31. The Philistines achieve a solid victory over the Israelite army, and Saul and his sons die in battle. The enemy army brutalizes the corpses of the fallen king and his three sons, eventually nailing their bodies to a city wall. A few Hebrew allies in Gilead learn of this disgusting and shameful tragedy, and they bravely return the king's and princes' remains across the border for a proper burial and funeral.

2 SAMUEL

1. David learns of Saul and Jonathan's deaths, and he mourns bitterly for them, singing "Our brave soldiers and leaders have fallen, their weapons abandoned on the ground. May our enemies never learn the extent of our grief because it would only bring smiles to their wicked faces. Jonathan, you and your dad lived and died together as strong, swift warriors. Your dad provided generously for the women of this nation, and you were like a brother to me. I love you more than I can say."

2. With God's permission and the people's blessing, David assumes the throne in Judah. He thanks the men of Gilead for rescuing the remains of Saul and his sons and giving them a dignified burial. Meanwhile, Ishbosheth, one of Saul's surviving sons, is named king over the rest of Israel. Judah and Israel go to war with each other after a petty armed contest between several dozen men.

3. King David's forces become stronger than those loyal to Saul's family, and God blesses David with six sons.

Meanwhile, King Ishbosheth falsely accuses his most loyal commander, Abner, of sexual misconduct. This accused man turns his loyalty to David because of his anger toward Ishbosheth, but the Judean official, Joab, kills Abner to avenge his brother's death. David mourns this senseless murder with great passion and requires Joab to sit beside him at Abner's funeral.

4.   Two of Ishbosheth's leading officers assassinate him in his sleep, and they proudly go to David with this news. The peaceable king shouts that it is never good news to learn that an innocent man has been killed in his sleep, and he puts the two men to death for the murder. During this time of danger toward Saul's surviving relatives, Jonathan's five-year-old son Mephibosheth is taken into hiding by his nanny, who accidentally cripples him in a rush to escape the area.

5.   Because of King Ishbosheth's death, the leaders within each tribe of Israel pledge their loyalty to David and anoint him king over the entire nation. Seeking God's council every step of the way, David leads this reunited kingdom into a series of solid military victories, driving the Philistines out of the land at last.

6.   King David leads the people in a musical victory parade, carrying the Covenant Box from Baalah to Jerusalem. The journey is cut short when a man comes too close to the Covenant Box and dies. David reverently allows the Covenant Box to stay in a nearby house out of fear of the Lord. After God richly blesses the family housing the Covenant Box, David courageously decides to transport

it all the way to Jerusalem. He honors God with generous sacrifices and passionate dancing throughout the journey, ignoring the embarrassed complaints of his wife Michal.

7.   During a time of peace, David humbly notices that God has allowed him to live in a great cedar house, and God's place of worship is just a tent. A prophet named Nathan reveals God's message to David, saying "Dear boy, you are not the one who will build a temple for me, but I am honored by your love and consideration for me. I was with you as a young shepherd boy, and I am proud to see the leader you have become. I promise to keep you safe and turn your family into a dynasty of great kings." David responds in prayer "My God and King, I am not worthy of your lavish blessings and promises. There is no one like you and no nation as blessed as the one you chose. Thank you so much for all you have done and all that you've promised to do!"

8.   During David's time as king, God leads him to overwhelming victories over the corrupt nations of Philistia, Moab, Edom, Ammon, Amalek, and Syria. He rules Israel with a spirit of justice and fairness.

9.   David discovers that Jonathan's son Mephibosheth is still alive and disabled. Mephibosheth is initially fearful of the new king, but David says "Don't be afraid. Your father was a dear friend of mine, and I will honor him by blessing you. I want to give you all the land that used to belong to your grandfather Saul, and you will always be welcome at my table."

10. The king of Ammon dies, and David sends a sympathy gift to the new king, gently requesting continued peace between

the two nations. The Ammonites humiliate the Hebrew messengers, and David swiftly defeats the Ammonites and their Syrian allies because of this.

11. David commits adultery with a beautiful woman named Bathsheba, and she becomes pregnant. David tries to take her husband, Uriah, out of combat to send him home so that he might sleep with his wife and believe the expected child is his. When Uriah refuses to go home and leave his comrades behind, David arranges for him to be killed in battle, so he can legally take Bathsheba as his wife without truly accepting responsibility for his sin. God becomes very displeased with David for this cowardly act.

12. The royal spiritual advisor Nathan boldly approaches King David, saying "If you discovered that a rich man in your kingdom made himself wealthier by stealing and cooking the only precious lamb in a poor man's flock, you would see that as disgusting and dishonorable. Well, that dishonorable man is you right now. Uriah was a good man who loved and honored his wife, and you stole her and added her to your houseful of wives. You harbored an attitude of greed and discontentment, which caused you to feel entitled to be with Bathsheba, and now, the child she is carrying and future generations of your descendants will pay for your sin." When David comforts Bathsheba after the death of their newborn son, she becomes pregnant with Solomon. Meanwhile, David's commander Joab defeats the capital city of Ammon.

13. David's daughter Tamar is raped by her half-brother Amnon, and she is completely broken by the trauma, living

the rest of her life in depression and isolation. David is furious to learn of this crime, and Tamar's brother, Absalom kills Amnon in vengeful anger two years later. David grieves over his son, and Absalom flees.

14. Joab sends an actress into the king's presence to play the role of a poor widow whose son had killed his brother and then fled into exile. David empathizes with the widow's desire to reunite with her surviving son despite his crime, so that she won't lose both of her boys. David realizes that Joab had used this story to mirror David's situation and convince him that Absalom should be allowed to return from exile. The king allows Absalom to return to the city, and after two years, David is finally ready to forgive him face-to-face.

15. Although Absalom is welcomed back into the palace, he greedily begins a campaign for more power and influence, loudly recruiting followers at the city gate. Absalom creates a stronghold for himself in Hebron and mobilizes his men to overthrow King David. David learns of Absalom's plans and mournfully flees Jerusalem with his most loyal officials and soldiers. David convinces his friend Hushai to stay behind and work for Absalom as a double agent.

16. David learns that Jonathan's disabled son has betrayed him in a campaign for selfish power. Shortly after this, one of Saul's relatives begins throwing stones at David, cruelly and falsely calling him the murderer of Saul's family. Meanwhile, David's friend and spy, Hushai, pledges his loyalty to the newly minted King Absalom.

17. Fortunately, Hushai is still loyal to the true king, and he

misleads Absalom with advice that delays a sneak-attack on David and his men. Hushai warns David of the pending attack, so he can safely escape into the wilderness.

18. David arranges an attack upon his son's men to take back his rightful crown, but he insists that Absalom himself be spared in battle. After all, corrupt or not, the king still loves his fallen child and wants to forgive him. David's loyal commander Joab is so angry with Absalom that he kills him anyway, and the king bitterly mourns the loss of another son.

19. Joab warns David "I know you are grieving the loss of your son Absalom, but with all due respect, sir, he was a traitor, and there are a lot of good people who just risked their lives for you. Please honor those who fought for you by pulling yourself together, reassuring your men, and returning to your rightful place on the throne." David accepts his commander's advice and returns to Jerusalem, showing mercy and kindness to the people who previously betrayed him; right away, he regains the people's trust.

20. A loud and worthless protestor named Sheba convinces most of the Israelite tribes to rebel against David's restored leadership, but the people of Judah remain faithful to their king. Joab cannot accept that David's relative Amasa is gaining power and influence within the king's inner circle, so Joab kills Amasa so that he might take credit for the coming victory. Joab's men track down Sheba at the city of Abel, and they allow the locals to execute Sheba independently instead of raiding the peaceful city.

21. David consults the Gibeons about righting the wrongs done

to their people by Saul, and they demand that seven of Saul's descendants be publicly executed since Saul had tried to wipe them out. David honors several promises by sparing Jonathan's son and obediently handing over seven other men from Saul's family. God then leads Judah's army into victory over the Philistine giants.

22. When God leads David to victory over Saul and many other enemies, the humble king sings "God is my strong fortress and shield, and when I am surrounded by death and danger, he keeps me safe. God shakes the earth and breathes fire like a mighty dragon to scatter his enemies and scoop me up from the wreckage. I am so thankful that God notices my innocent, obedient heart and rewards my loyalty with his protection and fool-proof guidance. Our strong and loving God deserves all the credit for our success!"

23. As his last words to the people, David sings "Your Protector wants you to know that if you choose kings who rule with justice and obedience to God, your nation will continue to sparkle and shine like the sun. God has blessed and equipped my family for the task, so I will be so happy if you honor God's intention to lift them up." The author delivers a list to honor David's most valiant and most famous soldiers who fought alongside him.

24. Late in his reign, David takes a census of the Israelites, arrogantly numbering and taking ownership of the people while ignoring the fact that the great multitude and all their victories actually belong to God. God humbles David by allowing him to choose a punishment for the people, but God stops the fatal epidemic early because of David's pleas for mercy.

DAY THREE - SPIRALING INTO EXILE
1 KINGS-2 KINGS

BIG IDEA

God has great plans to lift up his chosen people, but prideful kings destroy that plan.

CAST OF CHARACTERS

- **Solomon-** Much of his reign is characterized by unmatched wisdom and prosperity, but fame unfortunately makes his heart proud and his kingdom divided.
- **Elijah-** Prophet and miracle worker who boldly confronts evil Ahab and takes down a multitude of Baal worshippers.
- **Elisha-** Elijah's protégé who brings short bursts of victory to a hurting nation.
- **Hezekiah-** Trusts God to protect Judah from Syrian bullies, and reverses his father's damage to lead a new generation to God.
- **Josiah-** The last pure-hearted king of Judah who works hard for reforms that are thrown away a generation later.
- **Nebuchadnezzar-** Powerful emperor of Babylonia who conquers Judah.
- **Good kings of Judah-** Effective leaders who trust God and fight idolatry. These men include Asa, Jehoshaphat, Joash, Uzziah, and Jotham.
- **Unworthy kings of Judah-** Descendants of David who

let immaturity, pride, and selfishness lead the nation away from God and into disaster. These men include Rehoboam, Abijah, Amaziah, Ahaz, Manasseh, Amon, and Zedekiah.

- **Unworthy kings of Israel-** When the kingdom splits, Israel falls far from God and is ruled by a series of power-hungry assassins. These men include Jeroboam, Baasha, Omri, Ahab, Ahaziah, Joram, Jehu, Jehoahaz, Jeroboam II, and Hoshea.

HOW GOD SHOWS UP

Even in the darkest periods of the Hebrew monarchy's history, God reveals his power through prophets like Elijah who try to turn hearts away from worthless idols. God lifts up good-hearted kings who bring peace and light to their generations, and he allows their reigns to be much longer than that of evil kings and worthless assassins. God gives Israel and Judah many opportunities to change but eventually cannot bear to watch them destroy themselves any longer.

1 KINGS

1. When elderly King David is on his death bed, his overly ambitious eldest son, Adonijah, conducts a ceremony to assume the throne and neglects to invite David's inner circle to the feast. When Solomon's mom and the prophet Nathan come to David with the news, David quickly

clarifies "Adonijah acted without my consent. I have already promised the throne to my son Solomon, and we need to announce my decision to the people right away to prevent any further confusion." David's announcement is pronounced throughout the land and interrupts Adonijah's self-celebration. His guests disperse quickly out of fear of being seen as disloyal to the true king. Solomon mercifully tells his brother that he will be allowed to live as long as he remains respectful of their father's decision.

2.   David calls Solomon to his bedside and says "My dear son, when I die, I want you to lead with confidence and determination. If you obey God and listen closely for his direction, you will prosper, and he will continue to lift up our family. Follow our Lord faithfully with your whole heart. Commander Joab killed two of my dear friends and advisors out of jealousy; I am trusting you to bring him to justice. You must also punish the man who kicked me when I was down, throwing stones at me and shouting lies that I had murdered my best friend Jonathan." King David passes away, and Solomon fulfills his father's last requests. Adonijah shows signs of rising up against Solomon, so the new king must have his brother killed.

3.   When God appears to good-hearted Solomon in a dream, the young king prays "Lord, my father followed you with all his heart, and I am humbled and honored to take his place. I know that I am young and inexperienced, so please give me the wisdom to do this job right. I want to fairly and peacefully rule the great, precious multitude you have chosen." God answers "It makes me smile to hear your mature, unselfish request. Because of your uncommonly

beautiful heart, I will bless you more than you asked. You will be wiser and wealthier than anyone in the world, and you will live a long life." Solomon wakes up with an attitude of worship and cleverly handles disputes in a way that brings truth to the surface and protects the innocent.

4. Solomon appoints a team of trustworthy officials, including Nathan's son as his royal advisor. He also chooses twelve district governors to collect a fair tax from each territory. Due to Solomon's unmatched level of insight, he is able to maintain peace and diplomacy with neighboring countries. Kings from all around send him generous gifts and seek his advice.

5. Solomon approaches King Hiram of Tyre and says "I understand that my father was a friend of yours, and I'd love to continue a mutually beneficial relationship between our two great nations. Dad always wanted to build a proper temple of worship for our God, but he was always too busy solving military conflicts to act on that dream. Since God has blessed me with a time of peace, I'm hoping you can send some of your best men to help us with the construction project." Hiram welcomes the economy boost that comes with Solomon's generous pay for the men of Tyre. The kings shake hands, and construction begins.

6. Israel's young king orchestrates the building of God's Temple, and the construction project lasts a total of seven years. He leads the project with a spirit of patience and obedience to the Lord. The finished project is ornate and beautiful.

7. After the temple is built, Solomon takes thirteen years

to build a palace for himself, and he locates a brilliant craftsman to design and create bronze columns and other furnishings to finish the Temple.

8. Solomon has the Covenant Box transported to the new house of God, and God's dazzling presence overwhelms the whole place. Solomon announces "Our God put the sun in the sky, and he has chosen to live in this beautiful Temple we have made together. My father wanted to build this place, and I'm so grateful that God has allowed me to lead this project on his behalf. God of heaven and earth, you keep your promises and love those whose hearts are close to you. It blows my mind that you are bigger than the galaxy, but you can fit your overwhelming presence into this place. Watch over this sacred house of worship, and let this be a place where liars are held accountable. When our land is in trouble, hear our cries for help. Welcome good–hearted foreigners here, and give your obedient soldiers victory when they pray. We all mess up sometimes, and when we humbly turn back to you, forgive us. Give us peace! Stay with us, and make us better people through your guidance. Let everyone see our remarkable nation and know that you are with us." Solomon offers generous sacrifices to God and leads the people in a week-long joyous celebration.

9. After the construction projects and celebrations are complete, God says "Solomon, I've been listening to your prayers. I will be happy to protect and inhabit the Temple you built for me. If you continue to serve me with the integrity and obedience your father showed me, I will continue to bless your family. However, if future generations forget about me, I will leave the Temple and exile the Hebrews

from this land." The wise and considerate Solomon compensates King Hiram generously for providing high-quality cedar, pine, and gold for the Temple construction. He also allows the surviving Canaanites to do all the manual construction-related labor, while the Israelites act as managers of the project.

10. The queen of Sheba hears of Solomon's success and tests him with difficult questions. As she witnesses Solomon's wisdom and takes a tour of his ornate palace, she breathlessly says "Wow! Solomon, my friends have told me remarkable things about you, but I always thought they were exaggerating. Now I realize I didn't even hear the half of it! All I can do is praise your God for showing his love so generously to your household and your nation." This queen and many other impressed visitors offer generous gifts to Solomon, and he uses the wealth to improve the equipment of his military and furnish the palace with many luxurious things.

11. At the height of his wealth and prosperity, Solomon forgets that God is his true provider, and he falls deeply into temptation and pride. The king sleeps with literally a thousand foreign women and picks up their corrupt and idolatrous religious customs. God angrily allows some of Solomon's enemies to come against him, and the Lord informs a man named Jeroboam that he will be the next king. Solomon dies after 40 years of leadership.

12. Solomon's son Rehoboam takes over as king and seeks the advice of his young and inexperienced friends. His immaturity leads to the Hebrew kingdom splitting into Israel (the

northern tribes) and Judah (Judah and Benjamin). David's grandson stays in control of Judah, and Jeroboam becomes king of Israel. Unfortunately, Jeroboam allows his fear of being overthrown to turn his heart away from God.

13. A prophet from Judah boldly predicts that a king from David's family named Josiah will rise up and destroy the pagan altars built by Jeroboam. When Jeroboam hears this, he acts out in anger and ignores the prophet's encouragement to turn back to God. Jeroboam sins further by ordaining extremely unqualified people to be priests.

14. When Jeroboam's son becomes fatally ill, the king sends his wife to a blind prophet, who reveals God's message that "I hand-picked your husband to lead my people, hoping he would remain loyal and obedient to me like David. But he has angered me and rejected me, so your family will not be in charge much longer." Jeroboam's son dies as soon as his wife returns home, and after 22 years as king of Israel, Jeroboam dies as well. Meanwhile, Rehoboam leads Judah into pagan worship, fully disrespecting his family's legacy.

15. In Judah, young King Abijah, follows in his father's sinful footsteps. Fortunately, his son, Asa, pleases God by banishing prostitutes from the pagan worship centers and tearing down many of the idols and pagan altars his father had built. In Israel, Jeroboam's son is assassinated and overthrown after only two years in power, which fulfills the prophecy against Jeroboam's family.

16. In Israel, the assassin Baasha sins against God like Jeroboam before him, fighting against the noble King Asa of Judah. God promises to end the reign of Baasha's family, as he

did with Jeroboam's family. Baasha's son has a short and violent reign over Israel that ends with an assassination. The assassin is overtaken and killed after only a week on the throne. In the midst of chaos and national division, military commander Omri rises up as king, and his son Ahab takes evil to a new level by marrying a corrupt foreign princess named Jezebel and building worship centers for the cults of Baal and Asherah.

17. A prophet named Elijah warns Ahab that God will punish Israel with a three-year drought due to this king's sin. During the drought, God provides Elijah with water from a hidden brook, and God leads his prophet to the house of a starving widow. She kindly takes him in, and through their trust in God, God allows her last morsel of food to nourish both of them for many days. When the widow's son dies, Elijah cries out to God, and the boy comes back to life.

18. In the third year of the drought, Elijah heads toward King Ahab's palace and runs into a brave man of god named Obadiah along the way. Operating as a trusted member of Ahab's cabinet, Obadiah had secretly saved the lives of a hundred men of God after Jezebel began killing the Lord's prophets. Obadiah nervously presents Elijah to the king, worried the king will realize he is a follower of God. Elijah boldly says "Ahab, you are nothing but a trouble-maker, and your dad was too. You've abandoned the one true God for all these fake idols, so I have a challenge for you. We'll prepare identical sacrifices for each of our gods, Baal and Yahweh, and we'll get to find out which one is real." The next day, 450 Baal prophets dance furiously around their altar all day, and nothing happens. Elijah

mocks them, saying "Pray louder! Maybe Baal is asleep or on a bathroom break. Maybe he's on vacation or just not paying attention to you." After a day of Baal doing nothing, Elijah dumps water on the altar and says "Okay God! Show them that you're real." God immediately sends fire down that destroys not only the sacrifice but the altar as well. The people worship God in awe, and arrest the prophets of Baal, which ends the drought.

19. Queen Jezebel threatens Elijah after learning of the execution of Baal's prophets. Elijah fearfully flees to Mount Sinai, praying "God, I've always been loyal to you, and the rest of Israel has abandoned you and killed your prophets. I'm the only one left, and they're about to kill me too!" God eases Elijah's anxiety with a whispered promise to anoint a farmer named Elisha as the next prophet of Israel. Elisha follows Elijah without hesitation.

20. The Syrian king seeks to steal gold and silver from Ahab's kingdom and declares war on Israel when Ahab refuses to meet his enemy's demands. Despite Ahab's history of wickedness, God allows Israel to achieve victory over Syria in the first battle. When Syria attacks again the following spring, God shows Syria his power again, but Ahab disobeys God by preserving the life of the evil Syrian king. A prophet predicts that Ahab will be punished for his disobedience.

21. Ahab wants to turn a man's vineyard into the royal vegetable garden, and the owner says "My family has lived here and worked this land for years. I have nowhere else to go, and I won't sell it to you." Ahab refuses to eat dinner that night and whines to his wife about not getting to take this

guy's home to make his yard bigger. Jezebel arranges the murder of the vineyard owner just so her husband can take over the vineyard, and Elijah predicts that this evil king and queen will die humiliating deaths because of their complete dedication to sin. Ahab humbly repents after Elijah tells him this, and God has mercy on him.

22. In Judah, Asa's son Jehoshaphat is faithful to God but does not completely wipe out pagan worship in the nation. When Jehoshaphat and Ahab join forces to battle Syria, Judah's good king suggests they consult the Lord before taking action. Many of Ahab's hired prophets only say favorable things to the king, but God's true prophet Micaiah is bold enough to tell Ahab the difficult truth that Ahab will not survive the coming battle. Ahab turns to Jehoshaphat and says "See? I told you that guy never predicts anything good for me." He stubbornly proceeds into the battle that kills kim. Ahab's son Ahaziah becomes the King of Israel and follows the sinful example of his parents.

2 KINGS

1. The sinful King Ahaziah of Israel falls off his balcony during his second year in power and consults a pagan god about his injuries. Elijah boldly declares that the king will not recover due to his refusal to consult the one true God. When the king angrily sends large groups of soldiers to kill Elijah, God wipes out each group with heavenly fire. Since Ahaziah has no sons, his brother Joram succeeds him as

king of Israel.

2. Instead of dying a natural death, the obedient prophet
    Elijah is swept up to heaven on a chariot of fire. His loyal
    protégé Elisha stays by his side until the very end and pas-
    sionately mourns when he is separated from his mighty
    teacher. Elisha has big shoes to fill, but his first two public
    miracles show that God has truly granted Elisha great
    authority.

3. When Joram takes over as king of Israel, he is sinful but
    not as corrupt as his parents Ahab and Jezebel. The nation
    of Moab rebels against Joram, and King Jehoshaphat of
    Judah agrees to help him fight. The kings consult Elisha,
    who predicts a victory for the Hebrews. When the Israelites
    attack the next morning, they destroy the enemy so fully that
    the Moabite king sacrifices his own son in his desperation
    to flee the land.

4. God works through Elisha, allowing him to perform miracles
    that enrich the lives of those who love God. He produces
    excess olive oil to help a poor widow pay her husband's
    debts. He also correctly predicts that a hospitable, rich
    woman would have a son after years of infertility. Years
    later, the son dies, and Elisha brings him back to life. During
    a time of famine, Elisha removes poison from a pot of stew
    and multiplies a small portion of food to fill the bellies of
    a hundred men.

5. A Syrian commander named Naaman travels to Israel in
    search of Elisha, hoping the prophet can cure him of a
    fatal skin disease. Elisha's servants instruct him to bathe
    in the Jordan River, and at first, Naaman huffs "He can't

even show up in person to tell me this? I don't even like the Jordan River; our rivers back home are much cleaner." After being humbled a bit by the messengers, Naaman follows their instructions and declares "I'm healed! Now I know that Israel's God is the only real God." Elisha's greedy servant Gahazi tries to collect Naaman's gifts that Elisha had refused to accept, but Gahazi gets caught and contracts Naaman's former skin disease.

6. When one of his travelling companions drops a borrowed axe in the river, Elisha makes the heavy axe float to help him recover it. During a war between Syria and Israel, Elisha helps Israel's army avoid a potential ambush site and later blinds an entire division of enemy men to lead them directly to King Joram's throne room. The enemy army is so terrified that they return home peacefully and stop raiding Israel for a long time. Years later, a Syrian raid of Samaria causes a food shortage in Israel so desperate that a woman eats her own child. King Joram angrily blames God for this tragedy.

7. Elisha encourages the angry and skeptical king that the famine will end the following day. This prophecy comes true when the Syrian army mistakenly fears they are being attacked, and they flee from their camp, leaving abundant supplies of food, clothing, and equipment for the Israelites.

8. Elisha warns the woman whose son he had resurrected of the terrible seven-year famine before its onset, and she intelligently flees to Philistia during that time. When a Syrian official named Hazael visits Elisha on his sick king's behalf, the prophet bursts into tears because he sees the terrible

things Hazael will do to Israel as the next Syrian king. That night, the power-hungry Hazael smothers his king and takes over Syria. In Judah, Jehoshaphat's son marries into evil Ahab's family and dies in a war against Edom. Judah's next king, Ahaziah, follows the wicked example of his grandfather Ahab and only reigns for a year.

9. Elisha anoints a man named Jehu to be the next king of Israel, and it is his duty to kill Queen Jezebel and the rest of Ahab's corrupt family. Jehu obediently kills King Joram of Israel, Queen Jezebel of Israel, and King Ahaziah of Judah.

10. Jehu kills the remaining relatives of Ahab as well as the relatives of Ahaziah who travel to Israel to mourn Jezebel. He then wipes out the worship of Baal in the land, and God promises that four generations of Jehu's family will reign because of his obedience. Tragically, Jehu still falls into idol worship and away from God's commands. After his 28-year reign, Jehu dies, and Hazael of Syria begins to conquer much of Israel.

11. Ahaziah's mother takes over Judah after her son's execution, and she orders all remaining members of the royal family to be killed due to her greed and fear of being overthrown. Ahaziah's infant son, Joash, escapes his grandmother's wrath under the protection of his aunt. At the age of seven, Joash becomes king after his grandmother is assassinated, and his primary advisor, priest Jehoiada, destroys the Baal worship centers and renews Judah's covenant with God.

12. King Joash loves the Lord and starts to make reforms with the counsel of Jehoiada. Joash restores and renovates the Temple but does not destroy all the pagan worship centers

in the land. He wisely offers King Hazael of Syria a large monetary gift to prevent him from attacking Jerusalem.

13. In Israel, Jehu's son Jehoahaz takes over and leads the nation back into sin. When he prays for relief from the Syrians, God mercifully rescues his people, even though Jehoahaz and his son, Jehoash, refuse to break the pattern of idol worship and widespread corruption in Israel. Elisha dies, and the power of God in him is so strong that another dead body is brought back to life in the presence of Elisha's remains. Syria once again comes against Israel, but God never allows this enemy to completely destroy his covenant people.

14. In Judah, Joash's son, Amaziah, follows his father's example of faithfulness to God, but he allows pagan worship to continue in the land. After a great victory against the Edomites, Amaziah becomes filled with pride and declares war upon King Jehoash of Israel. Israel defeats Judah, and Amaziah is later assassinated and replaced by his teenage son, Uzziah. In Israel, the wicked Jeroboam II takes over, and God allows him to be successful in battle out of pity for his rebellious, unhappy children.

15. King Uzziah in Judah loves God like his father and grandfather but still refuses to destroy the pagan places of worship. During Uzziah's 52-year reign in Judah, Israel's government falls further into chaos with a series of wicked kings, three of which are assassinated within twelve short years. Uzziah's son, Jotham, pleases God by taking care of God's temple but continues to tolerate pagan worship in Judah.

16. In Judah, Jotham's son Ahaz goes against the godly example

of his family. He even defaces the Temple and offers his son as a burnt offering to idols. God allows Jerusalem to be attacked by Syria and Israel, but Ahaz aligns with the emperor of Assyria to avoid capture.

17. A sinful assassin named Hoshea takes over as king of Israel. In the ninth year of his reign, Emperor Shalmanesar of Assyria forces the Israelites into exile. God allows his people to be removed from the Promised Land after generations of Hebrews ignoring the Lord's warnings, destroying themselves and each other in sin. The Assyrians who take over the land of Israel learn to worship God but continue worshiping their idols as well.

18. In Judah, King Hezekiah completely reverses the damage done by his father Ahaz, destroying the pagan places of worship and helping a new generation of Judeans learn to worship God. When Assyria attacks Jerusalem, Hezekiah sends a large sum of money to Assyria in an effort to make peace with them. Unfortunately, the Assyrian attacks continue, and an enemy official shouts "Does Hezekiah really think his words can help him in the face of Assyria's strength? He and your precious God can't save you Hebrews now. You may as well surrender and come live in Assyria, where we have plenty of food. Your God couldn't save Samaria, and he can't save you either!" Hezekiah's officials remain quiet and dignified in the face of these terrible insults, but they are clearly hurt and troubled by the Assyrian official's words.

19. King Hezekiah consults with the wise prophet Isaiah and says "The Assyrians are disgracing us, kicking us while

we're already down. I feel like a laboring woman in terrible pain who is too weak to finish the delivery. That Assyrian official insulted the God I love, and I just hope the Lord comes to our defense. Our armies are too tired to finish this war without him." Isaiah encourages Hezekiah to ignore the naysayers and trust in God's promise of protection. In response to Hezekiah's faithfulness, an angel of God kills an entire camp of Assyrian soldiers numbering 185,000.

20. Hezekiah becomes seriously ill, and God compassionately answers his prayers for healing. Later, messengers from distant Babylonia send the king a gift in honor of his recent recovery. Trusting these foreign messengers, Hezekiah gives them a complete tour of the palace. Later, Isaiah informs him that one day the Babylonians will reign in that same palace.

21. Hezekiah's son, Manasseh, takes over as ruler of Judah at the age of twelve. This immature king destroys his father's progress, rebuilding the pagan places of worship and killing many innocent people in Judah, including his own son. God is fed up with the disappointing and disgusting decisions of Judah's kings. Even good kings like David, Solomon, and Hezekiah are unable to have a lasting impact because their children and grandchildren destroy their reforms, forget about God, and destroy innocent lives. God decides it's finally time to exile the Judeans as he did the Israelites. Manasseh's son, Amon, follows the sinful practices of his father and is assassinated by his officials two years into his reign.

22. Amon's son Josiah becomes king at the age of eight and

follows all God's commands throughout his reign. He discovers the book of the Law and is saddened because of how far the people have fallen into sin. The king seeks the advice of an old woman prophet who reveals God's message saying "My people have rejected me time and time again, turning their loyalty to foreign gods and corrupt behaviors. My anger toward the people is not going away, but Josiah, I have seen your humble, repentant heart. It would break your heart to see how I will punish Jerusalem, so I will wait until after your life is over, so you can die in peace."

23. Josiah initiates many moral and religious reforms in Judah. He informs the people about the Law, destroys the pagan places of worship, and executes all the pagan priests. This righteous king restores the annual celebration of the Passover, and he banishes the fortune tellers and other wicked people from the land. When Josiah's sinful son takes over, the king of Egypt captures him during his third month as king.

24. The Egyptian king appoints another son of Josiah as King of Judah, and the land is heavily attacked by King Nebuchadnezzar of Babylonia and other enemies. Josiah's grandson is quickly captured by the Babylonians in his third month as king, and Nebuchadnezzar replaces him with his uncle Zedekiah.

25. Zedekiah rebels against Nebuchadnezzar, and the Babylonians attack Jerusalem with enough force to destroy the city and the Temple. Many of the best and brightest Judeans are exiled to Babylonia, and Nebuchadnezzar appoints one of his officials to govern the people who remain in Judah.

DAY FOUR - HONORABLE MENTIONS
1 CHRONICLES-2 CHRONICLES

BIG IDEA

As the Hebrew kingdoms unravel, a few righteous individuals stand out from the pack to honor God and selflessly lead others during their generations.

BRIGHT SPOTS IN THE DARKNESS

- **Jabez-** Trusts God to protect him, and manages his blessings responsibly.

- **King David-** Consults God before each battle to ensure success and earn the nation's trust. He worships with passionate boldness and longs to build God a grand Temple to replace the worn-out tent.

- **King Solomon-** Humbly prays for wisdom to lead God's people effectively and live up to his father's example. He oversees the Temple construction project and creates peaceful alliances with neighboring nations.

- **King Rehoboam-** Humbled by Egyptian looters and allowed to lead 41 years.

- **King Asa-** Wipes out pagan worship and strengthens Judah's military.

- **King Jehoshaphat-** Teaches a new generation of Judeans about God's Law.

- **Jehoiada-** Rescues infant King Joash from his murderous grandmother, and advises Joash toward widespread reforms.

- **King Jotham-** Remains obedient to God and earns his protection.
- **King Hezekiah-** Offers heartfelt prayers that inspire a lost nation to repent.
- **King Josiah-** So saddened by the people's sins that God agrees not to let Babylonia conquer Judah in his lifetime.

HOW GOD SHOWS UP

Although Judah eventually falls into a time of exile, God reaches out again and again to try to turn the nation around. God blesses and extends the reign of leaders who obey him and treat the people with dignity. He leads good-hearted kings to times of victory and peace that the people could not have achieved on their own. When his chosen leaders recognize their mistakes, God forgives them without question.

1 CHRONICLES

1. Ten generations link Adam to Noah, and ten generations link Noah's son Shem to Abraham. The nations that stem from Noah's son Ham include many of Israel's future enemies such as Canaan and Egypt. The descendants of Ishmael and Esau are listed, along with a record of the original inhabitants of Edom, the land of Esau's family.

2. The family tree from Judah to King David starts with deception and scandal. Judah is tricked by his daughter-in-law,

Tamar, into sleeping with him so that she will not have to die childless. Seven generations link Tamar's son to Boaz, Ruth's successful and good-hearted husband. Three more generations link Boaz to Jesse's youngest son David. Other notable descendants of Judah are also mentioned.

3. King David has twenty sons through his seven wives, and he has even more children through his concubines. King Solomon rises above David's many other children to become the ancestor of seventeen generations of Judah kings. The family then falls away from power after the Jewish exile to Babylonia. Twelve generations of lesser known, post-exile descendants of David are listed.

4. Another family tree stemming from Judah leads to a respected man named Jabez. Jabez prays fervently "God, bless me richly, and give me more responsibility. Be by my side, and protect me from evil things that would bring pain on me and my family." God hears his simple and profound prayer and richly blesses his life. The descendants of Jacob's son Simeon are recorded as well as the descendants of several other noteworthy Israelites.

5. The Hebrew tribes who settle east of the Jordan are Reuben, Gad, and East Manasseh. Reuben is Jacob's oldest son but loses his firstborn privileges after sleeping with his father's concubine. The eastern tribes include thousands of well-trained soldiers who God protects in times of war. However, these tribes are eventually so unfaithful to God that they are deported from the land by the Assyrian Emperor.

6. Jacob's son Levi is the great-grandfather of Moses and Aaron. Aaron's descendants include twenty-two generations

of high priests until the time of exile. Other descendants of Levi include temple musicians and other religious professionals who serve as spiritual leaders for all other tribes of Israel.

7. The six other sons of Jacob are Issachar, Benjamin, Dan, Naphtali, Asher, and Joseph; their most notable descendants are listed here. Since Jacob offers a special blessing on Joseph's sons, Manasseh and Ephraim, these two men become patriarchs of two separate tribes of Israel.

8. King Saul and his family stem from the tribe of Benjamin. Many of the Benjaminites settle in Gibeon and Jerusalem.

9. After a time of punishment and exile in Babylon, a thousand Hebrew families humbly return to Jerusalem. This includes people from the tribes of Judah, Levi, Benjamin, Ephraim, and Manasseh. This new generation appoints priests, Levite leaders, and Temple guards to restore and protect God's house. King Saul's ancestors and descendants are also listed.

10. Saul and three of his sons die while trying to retreat from a Philistine battle. They die this way because of Saul's jealousy of David and his abandonment of God.

11. Upon Saul's death, the people approach David and say "You feel like family to us, and we pledge our loyalty to you. Even when Saul was king, you led our armies to great victories, and we are happy to lift you up as our next king." King David begins his reign by conquering and rebuilding Jerusalem and achieving many other victories alongside hundreds of loyal and valiant soldiers.

12. Toward the end of Saul's reign, David's army grows from a few skilled Benjaminites to around 340,000 men

representing each tribe of Israel. The soldiers fight to defend David as their future king and celebrate with great joy when David assumes the throne.

13. David's troops support him in the transport of the Covenant Box from Kirith Jearim to Jerusalem. God makes it clear that this object is sacred, powerful, and not to be touched by human hands. Unfortunately, a man named Uzzah accidentally grabs the box and is struck dead. After Uzzah dies, David is afraid to continue with the journey, and he leaves the Covenant Box with a man named Obed Edom.

14. God allows David to have many sons, a prosperous kingdom, and victory over the Philistines in battle. David faithfully consults God before each battle and faithfully follows the Lord's guidance every step of the way. The surrounding nations grow in respect for David and come to fear the mighty God that protects him.

15. David finally musters up the courage to move the Covenant Box from the house of Obed Edom to a sacred tent in Jerusalem. The Levite leaders transport it carefully, and the king joyfully leads the procession in music, worship, and celebration. David is so passionate during the parade that his wife Michal is embarrassed by him.

16. David and several Levites lead a celebratory worship service and feast when the Covenant Box is finally placed in Jerusalem. The people sing "Let the whole world hear of our great God! He has chosen us, blessed us, and done great miracles on our behalf; he deserves all our thanks. We were a small family of wanderers, and God led us through enemy lands unscathed. No one could keep us down, and God kept all

his promises to us. Let us sing the good news that the God who made heaven now fills this Temple with his power and joy. Let the whole earth shake and roar in worship, shouting that the love of our good God lasts forever."

17. David feels guilty for living in a strong house while the Covenant Box is stored in a tent. God's prophet, Nathan, assures him that the Lord is happy with David's work and that David's son will be the one to build the Temple. David joyfully thanks God for allowing him to grow from a lowly shepherd to a beloved king, and he trusts that God will continue to lead his family into greatness.

18. David leads thousands of Hebrew soldiers in victory over Philistine, Moabite, and Syrian armies. Surrounding nations submit to this good, powerful king and pay taxes to him. David's victories cause other kings to send him gifts and declarations of peace in order to align with him. King David treats his people fairly and allows justice to reign.

19. David reaches out compassionately to the mourning Ammonite king, and the leaders of Ammon reject David's sympathy and humiliate his messengers. David retaliates against the Ammonites as well as their Syrian allies, and God leads Israel to victory.

20. Israel's armies capture the city of Rabbah in Ammon, and David puts the jewel from their most prized idol into his own crown. The Hebrews also enjoy victory over the giants of Gath, and David's nephew kills one of their most nasty warriors.

21. Satan tempts David to self-importantly number the Hebrews to take ownership of his successes and turn his attention

away from God. God allows David to choose one of three extreme punishments upon Israel for this sin, but the Lord mercifully cuts the punishment short when he sees his chosen king's repentant heart.

22. David tells Solomon "We're not wandering around the desert anymore. It's time for God's presence to have a permanent home in this land instead of being relegated to a tent. I will prepare the building materials for this project during my final days as king, but it will be up to you to lead the construction process. God will give you peace on all sides of our land as you do this. Proceed with confidence and serve God wholeheartedly with an attitude of trust."

23. During the time of desert wandering, the Levite clans were tasked with transporting the sacred tent and the sacred objects from place to place. Since the wandering is now over, David reassigns duties to the Levite clans, including supervising the building of the Temple, keeping records, settling disputes, guarding the construction zone, tending the grounds, and leading worship through music.

24. David organizes the Levites into 24 separate family groups and allows each group to draw lots to determine their new job assignments. King David and the head priests oversee this process to ensure fairness and honesty.

25. King David instructs the temple musicians to lead worship with a spirit of joyful thanks. The king emphasizes that worship leaders can lead the people in praise whether they are beginner musicians or virtuosos. All members of the team should do their best to learn from the experts among them, but having a worshipful attitude is most important

to fulfill this role.

26. The men chosen as temple guards are from highly respected Levite families and show great skill and promise in terms of maintaining safety. Other Levites are chosen to manage the treasury, keep accurate records, and fulfill other administrative duties.

27. Each month, the Israelites rotate military commanders, perhaps to prevent burnout or temptation to abuse power for those assigned to fulfill this role. King David's administrators, royal property managers, and royal advisors are also noted here.

28. David gathers his sons, his cabinet members, and the clan leaders to say "Gentlemen, I have done what I can to prepare materials for the new Temple that will honor God and house his sacred Covenant Box. During my reign, I was too busy leading our nation's military to see this project through, but God has chosen my son Solomon to reign in peace and build his Temple. My son, I challenge you to serve our great God with an undivided heart and mind. God has chosen you, so go and fulfill his plans with a determined spirit. With God on your side, no one can stop you, and you will have many capable Levites, architects, and artists to help you.

29. "Solomon, since you are young and inexperienced, I have made every effort to gather high quality building materials for the Temple. I care so deeply about this mission that I have funded many of these materials from my own retirement fund. Would any of the rest of you be willing to give to this worthy project as well?" Following David's generous

example, the leaders of Israel happily donate hundreds of tons of precious metals to set Solomon up for success. David responds "Your generosity makes me so happy! Thank you God of our ancestors for letting your power, splendor, and majesty reign supreme over heaven and earth. You are the source of all our earthly riches, and any strength we have comes directly from you. We cannot offer you anything that you did not give to us first. Keep our devotion and integrity strong as we strive to honor you through the building of this beautiful Temple. Please bless my son and these capable leaders as they turn this dream into a reality."

2 CHRONICLES

1. As David's son, Solomon, takes control of the kingdom of Israel, he gathers the government officials to worship at the sacred tent made during the time of Moses. God asks Solomon "How would you like me to bless you?" Solomon responds "God, you loved and fulfilled great promises to my father, so please do the same for me as I take his place. Give me the wisdom to lead this great multitude that you have chosen and blessed." God answers "It is great that you recognize that your level of wisdom is more important than your monetary wealth or physical strength. I will grant your unselfish request and also reward you with unprecedented amounts of earthly riches and fame."

2. The new king prepares to build the Temple by assigning 150,000 of the Hebrew men to provide physical labor for

the construction process. Solomon tells King Hiram of Tyre "I am building a Temple to honor the God of Israel, and I know my father had positive business dealings with you in the past. Could I buy some of your high quality timber to help us build the Temple? I also see that the metal workers and artists in your land are especially skilled, so I would love to recruit some of your talented men to work alongside my guys. I will pay them generously for their help." The King of Tyre praises God for giving David such a wise, capable son to take his place, and Hiram and Solomon shake hands to begin their partnership.

3. King Solomon oversees the building of the Temple in the place where God appeared to David. The workers skillfully build this beautiful, golden house of God, complete with decorative statues, colorful wall hangings, and sturdy, durable columns to support the structure.

4. The king supervises the design and construction of all the Temple equipment including the altar, washing tank, lamp stands, courtyard gates, carts, and basins. These objects and other furnishings are constructed carefully from bronze and gold.

5. Upon completion of the Temple, Solomon arranges for the sacred Covenant Box to be transported to its new home. The Covenant Box contains the stone tablets inscribed by Moses to honor God's promise to protect and deliver his children to freedom. The priests and musicians lead the Hebrews in a celebratory worship song, and the service has to end early due to God's bright and overwhelming presence in the place.

6. During the celebratory gathering, Solomon prays "God, thank you for coming from your home in the clouds to fill this Temple with your light. Thank you for keeping your promises to my father and allowing me to fulfill his dream of building a beautiful home for you. There is no other god like you, so continue to love us as we humbly serve and obey you. Protect this Temple and open your heart to hear the fervent prayers for forgiveness and deliverance that will come from this place."

7. The people are amazed as God's holy fire ignites the animal sacrifices on the altar and illuminates the entire structure. The king leads the multitude in a seven-day celebration that leave all participants feeling happy and grateful for God's many blessings. The Lord later comes to Solomon and says "I have listened to your prayers, and I will happily protect the Temple and allow Israel to prosper. All I ask in return is that you and the people continue to worship me and live honorable, respectful lives according to my commands."

8. After building the temple, Solomon oversees the construction of a new royal palace, renovates several cities, and strengthens military storage areas throughout the land. Solomon offers reverence and gratitude to God with the success of each building project, and he enjoys a positive, rewarding alliance with King Hiram.

9. The queen of Sheba visits King Solomon to witness his famous wealth and wisdom for herself. She tests him with difficult riddles and takes a tour of the breathtaking Temple and palace. In amazement, she says "You, sir, are even wiser than people say, and this place is more beautiful than I ever

could have imagined. The people who work for you are incredibly lucky because your great God has clearly smiled upon you and his beloved nation." Throughout Solomon's forty-year reign, many people travel great distances to seek Solomon's counsel, and they make the wise king extremely wealthy with their generous gifts.

10. Solomon's son, Rehoboam, takes over as king, and he ignores the wise counsel of his more seasoned advisors, harshly announcing that he plans to rule the people with an attitude of brute force and control. The northern tribes rebel against his foolishness and choose a man named Jeroboam to rule over their territories. Aside from the tribes of Judah and Benjamin, the Israelite people never again fully trust the dynasty of David.

11. A prophet convinces Rehoboam not to re-conquer the northern tribes, assuring the young king that God has chosen to divide Israel and reduce Rehoboam's territory. Rehoboam fortifies Jerusalem, and Levites from all over Israel migrate to Judah when Jeroboam unexpectedly rebels against God in Israel.

12. Rehoboam leads the people of Judah to abandon God, and God allows Egypt loot the palace in Jerusalem. When the people humbly admit their wrongdoing, God eases up on Rehoboam and allows his rule over Judah to last 41 years.

13. When war breaks out between evil Jeroboam and Rehoboam's son, Abijah, the young king of Judah stares down the army of Israel, declaring "Hear this, Jeroboam! God made a binding promise with my great-grandfather, David, and even though your army is twice the size of ours, you

and your golden idols are no match for the powerful God that the people of Judah still serve faithfully." Although the massive army of Israel surrounds them, the army of Judah lets out a roaring battle cry and achieves an overwhelming victory.

14. The next king of Judah, Asa, pleases God by destroying pagan worship centers in the land and always doing the right thing as a leader. He strengthens the walls of Judean cities and recruits a huge army to defend the nation. Asa's army defeats Ethiopian attackers in one swift battle.

15. A man named Azariah goes before King Asa and proclaims "For a long time, our country lived in chaos and oppression, far from God's law, but now, God is blessing and strengthening us with good kings. God is clearly with you, sir, and if you continue to seek out the Lord, he'll continue to reveal himself to you." Heartened by these encouraging words, Asa repairs the altar in the Temple courtyard and rids Judah of as many idols as possible, including the obscene fertility goddess worshipped by his grandmother.

16. During the 36th year of Asa's reign, evil King Baasha of Israel attempts to invade a portion of Judah. Asa foolishly aligns with the King of Syria instead of leaning on God for help. When a prophet confronts Asa about his foolish act of distrust in God, Asa bitterly punishes the prophet and spends his final three years as king treating his people cruelly.

17. King Jehoshaphat of Judah follows the good example of his father's early life, leading the people in worship and obedience to God. This dedicated king sends priests

throughout the land to teach God's law to a new generation of Judeans. God blesses this obedience by making the kingdom of Judah more wealthy and secure. Other nations are afraid to go to war with Jehoshaphat and seek to align with him.

18. As God increases Jehoshaphat's wealth and fame, this wise king has a momentary lapse in judgment when he allows his son to marry into the family of evil King Ahab of Israel. When these two kings come together to attack the city of Ramoth, the good prophet Micaiah predicts bitter defeat for Israel. Ahab turns to Jehoshaphat and huffs "I knew talking to this guy would be a mistake. He never predicts anything good for me." Ahab stubbornly proceeds with his plan of attack and dies in on the battlefield as predicted.

19. A prophet named Jehu reprimands Jehoshaphat, saying "You have a great heart, and you have done a great job of following God's will in most respects. However, it makes no sense that you allowed yourself to work together with Ahab, a wicked man who hates God." Jehoshaphat takes this feedback to heart and continues to reform Judah by removing bribes from the courtroom, thereby restoring honesty and honor to the justice system.

20. When Jehoshaphat learns that the Edomites are invading Judah, he immediately prays "God, this is scary, but I know you will guide us. You are powerful over all nations and drove many wicked people out of this land long ago. I know you can rescue us again. We are powerless without your help!" God offers words of comfort and encouragement to the king through one of the Levites, and the soldiers

of Judah go into the battle without fear or hesitation. A band of musicians marches ahead of the army to lead the battalion in worship as they approach the enemy, and this throws the enemy armies into a state of confused panic.

21. Jehoshaphat dies as a godly and highly respected king, but his son Jehoram follows the wicked example of his father-in-law, Ahab. This corrupt ruler kills his six brothers simply because he doesn't want anyone to threaten his leadership, and he rebuilds the pagan worship centers that his father and grandfather worked hard to remove from the land. Jehoram is hated throughout Judah, and after he ignores Elijah's warnings, God allows him to die of a painful intestinal disease.

22. After being the only royal son to survive an Arab raid, young King Ahaziah of Judah follows the wicked advice of his mother (daughter of Ahab) and other relatives on the corrupt **branch** of his family. He is assassinated one year into his reign by a man named Jehu. In a thirst for power, Ahaziah's mother kills the remaining members of the royal family except her infant grandson, Joash, who escapes under the protection of a priest named Jehoiada.

23. Jehoiada raises Joash secretly in the kingdom of Judah, and with the support of the people, he overthrows the evil queen and places the crown on seven-year-old Joash's head. The priest becomes the child king's greatest advisor and leads Joash to destroy the temple of Baal and return the Levites to leading music and worship as they did during the time of David.

24. Joash places a collection box on the front steps of the

Temple to fund an extensive renovation of the sacred house of worship, and the people give large sums of money to help out. Unfortunately, after Jehoiada dies, the Judeans manipulate the young king into reversing many of his own reforms, and Jehoiada's son, Zechariah, is publicly stoned in his attempts to get the king to return to God.

25. Joash's son begins his reign by reluctantly following God but falls into idol worship at the first opportunity, thanking false gods for Judah's victory over Edom. God allows the army of Israel to attack Judah and take the arrogant young king as a hostage.

26. Joash's grandson, Uzziah, begins his kingship at age sixteen and rules successfully for 52 years. Uzziah's wise advisor Zechariah leads him to numerous military successes and widespread fame, but he arrogantly fails to give God the credit. Toward the end of his life, God allows this arrogant king to contract a dreaded skin disease, which means he can no longer enter God's Temple and cannot be buried in the royal tombs.

27. Uzziah's son, Jotham, remains obedient to God through-out his reign, which leads God to protect him against the Ammonite army. Despite Jotham's leadership, the people of Judah remain lost in a lifestyle of sin.

28. King Ahaz begins his reign over Judah by building Baal worship sites and sacrificing his own children to fake gods. Israel captures 200,000 Judean women in children, and the prophet Oded tells the army of Israel "You seem awfully proud of yourselves, but the God of your ancestors is the one who allowed you to defeat Judah. The people there

have angered him, but now he is even angrier with you for slaughtering them so viciously and taking their wives and children as slaves. These people are children of Jacob, just like you. Let them go immediately!" The Israelites obediently let the prisoners go, but when other enemies take more prisoners from Judah, King Ahaz makes things even worse for his nation by turning his allegiance to Syrian gods.

29. Good King Hezekiah wastes no time purifying the Temple and leading the people in worshipping and returning to God. He offers a heartfelt sacrifice to God to apologize for the many sins of his father Ahaz and to recommit the nation of Judah to God. His passionate prayer and joyful singing inspires the people to join in worship and turn their hearts back to God as well.

30. Hezekiah reinstates the annual celebration of the Passover Festival, celebrating it two months in a row to re-educate the people about this tradition. He sends a message throughout Israel and Judah, saying "Children of Jacob, you have survived the attack of many enemies in this Promised Land, and now the God of your ancestors wants you to return to him. To my brothers and sisters in Israel, many of you were exiled because you refused to remember the God that brought us here, and I would hate for the same fate to fall upon Judah. Our Lord is kind and merciful, and if we come back to him with humble, obedient hearts, he won't be angry with us anymore." Some Israelites laugh at Hezekiah's messengers, but others see the truth in the king's message and decide to move to Jerusalem. The people of Judah come together in joyful worship, and God forgives them.

31. Hezekiah leads many religious reforms in Judah out of a spirit of complete devotion to God. He successfully destroys the pagan worship centers and re-establishes a sense order among the Levites. When this great king encourages the people to give ten percent of their wealth to the church, they respond so enthusiastically that the Levites must prepare huge storerooms in the Temple to house the huge surplus of gifts.

32. When the emperor of Assyria invades Judah and begins to approach Jerusalem, Hezekiah wisely cuts off the water supply to the enemy armies and assembles his armies, saying "Don't be afraid, friends! These Assyrian bullies are operating under human power, but we have the God of heaven on our side!" Assyrian messengers go before Hezekiah and say "You are giving your people false hope, stupidly declaring that your precious little God will save you from us. We have ravaged other nations, and their gods didn't save them. What makes you think you're so special that your fate will be different?" Upon receiving this vile, disrespectful message, Hezekiah and the prophet Isaiah cry out to God, and an angel wipes out the Assyrian army and allows the Assyrian emperor to shamefully die at the hands of his own sons. Other nations respect and act peacefully toward Hezekiah from that day on.

33. Hezekiah's twelve-year old son reverses much of his father's progress, defiling the Temple with altars for star worship and sacrificing his own sons on those altars. Young King Manasseh and the people refuse to hear God's command to return to him, so the Assyrian army captures Manasseh and takes him to Babylon in chains. This frightening experience

humbles the young king into turning Judah back to God and removing the idols from the Temple. Manasseh's son later rules for only two years and is assassinated because of his wickedness.

34. Hezekiah's great-grandson, Josiah, becomes one of the most righteous and pure kings since David. Josiah attacks the practice of pagan worship in Judah, and upon discovering the book of the Law hidden away in the Temple, he passionately mourns how far God's people have fallen. God assures Josiah "You are right that the people of Judah have fallen far from me, and I must punish them for that. However, I have seen your deep grief and humble heart, so I will not punish the nation during your lifetime."

35. Josiah reinstates the tradition of Passover, leading the celebration with a sense of joy and reverence for God that hadn't been experienced in the land since the time of David. Josiah tragically dies in battle against King Neco of Egypt, and the prophet Jeremiah writes a lament to honor this beloved king of Judah.

36. The four final kings of Judah each reign for a short time as Egypt and Babylonia gradually weaken the nation. The first king is captured by the king of Egypt in the third month of his reign. The second and third kings are carried away to Babylonia, and King Nebuchadnezzar of Babylonia appoints Judah's final king shortly before destroying Jerusalem completely and sending many Judeans into exile. After seventy years, the Persian emperor honors God by allowing the Judeans to return to their homeland and build a new temple.

DAY FIVE - THE COMEBACK
EZRA-NEHEMIAH-ESTHER

BIG IDEA

A new generation of humble Hebrews return from exile, ready to respect their powerful God, and willing to work together to rebuild the ruins.

CAST OF CHARACTERS

- **Emperor Cyrus-** Compassionately allows the Hebrews to journey home, giving back the riches Nebuchadnezzar stole.
- **Emperor Xerxes-** Fears the Jews may be a threat and orders them to stop rebuilding. He later marries Esther and adjusts his attitude toward the Hebrews.
- **Emperor Darius-** Approves of the Temple rebuilding project and asks his officials to stop interfering with their work.
- **Ezra-** Enthusiastic spiritual leader who convinces the people to stop making the same mistakes that led to exile.
- **Nehemiah-** Royal wine steward who moves to Jerusalem with a longing to help the nation rebuild. He effectively leads the workers to overcome oppressors and stay motivated.
- **Sanballat-** Leader of the Arabian bullies who attempts to discourage and derail the Jewish workers.
- **Queen Vashti-** Embarrasses her husband by refusing to satisfy his every whim.

- **Queen Esther-** Courageously reveals her Jewish heritage to her husband in an effort to save her people.
- **Mordecai-** Boldly refuses to bow to Haman, and convinces Esther to overcome her fear for the greater good.
- **Haman-** Arrogant prime minister who gets his feelings hurt whenever someone doesn't treat him like a god.

HOW GOD SHOWS UP

Through the humbling time of exile, God teaches his children to adjust their priorities and their attitudes. When their hearts are sufficiently transformed through trial, God softens the hearts of the Persian emperors. He supplies the Hebrews with courageous leaders and protects them from further oppression. Their buildings may be broken, but God smiles with an understanding that his children are stronger than ever before.

EZRA

1. Emperor Cyrus issues a message throughout Persia, saying "The God of heaven has allowed me to come to great power. He wants me to send his people back home to Judah, so they can rebuild his Temple in Jerusalem. If you live near one of these Jewish exiles, please help him get back home, provide him with food for the journey, and fill his pockets with money to help fund the rebuilding of their Temple." Cyrus mercifully returns the golden Temple items that King Nebuchadnezzar had stolen from Judah seventy

years earlier.

2. Over 42,000 Israelites from dozens of clans return to the town of their ancestors. Descendants of Levite priests, musicians, and temple workmen settle near Jerusalem, and they begin accepting freewill offerings to help rebuild the Temple in its old location.

3. After seven months of settling back into the Promised Land, the Jews tentatively begin burning sacrifices to God again, despite the presence of powerful neighbors in the land that disagree with the Jewish laws and customs. As Temple reconstruction begins, these humbled and spiritually restored people sing ever more boldly, "Our God is good, and his love lasts forever!" The sounds of joyful singing and worshipful sobs ring out throughout the land.

4. The Arabian people who had been living in Jerusalem during the time of exile try to discourage the Jews from rebuilding the Temple. When that doesn't work, they threaten the Jews, bribe Persian officials to sabotage them, and even write a letter to the new emperor Xerxes. They write "Honorable king, we thought you should know what's happening in your kingdom. The Jews have traveled from your other territories and are taking over Jerusalem, rebuilding it into the same rebellious city that was hard for kings of the past to control." Upon receiving the letter, Xerxes instructs the Jews to stop building while he investigates their loyalty to the Persian government.

5. Several years later, the Jews boldly continue building the Temple despite the fact that the new emperor has not yet given his stamp of approval. Almost immediately, Persian

officials write a letter to Emperor Darius, saying "Your Majesty, the Jews are building a Temple to honor their God here in Jerusalem, and they are making fast progress. When we asked them if this construction project was sanctioned by you, they said 'We are acting under God's authority. Our ancestors turned away from God and were exiled to Babylonia, but Cyrus allowed us to return seventy years later and rebuild this place to honor our Lord. If you don't believe us, look it up."

6. Emperor Darius rediscovers Cyrus' order to return the Jews from exile and support the Temple reconstruction, and he sends a reply letter to his governors in Jerusalem: "Do not interfere with the construction of the Temple anymore. In fact, from now on, I am ordering you to help supply them with whatever they need out of my royal funds." With Darius' support, the Jews are able to complete the Temple and joyfully dedicate it to God, offering an enormous sacrifice to atone the many sins that led the Hebrews into exile. The people assign various duties to the Levite priests and celebrate the first Passover since their homecoming.

7. Ezra is a descendant of the high priest Aaron, and like many Levite priests before him, Ezra has a particular passion for learning about God's laws and scriptures and teaching them to the people. The new emperor sends Ezra to Jerusalem, giving him a generous salary and the authority to appoint judges to teach God's law and enforce it throughout the land. In response to the emperor's letter of support, Ezra says "Thank you God! Somehow I have won the emperor's favor, and God has made him sympathetic and supportive of the Hebrew people. Thank you God for giving me the

courage and passion I need to be an effective leader for my people."

8.   As Ezra travels from Babylonia to Jerusalem, over 1500 men representing fifteen Hebrew clans journey with him. Prior to the journey, Ezra gathers Levites to join their group and identifies several non-Levite leaders, teachers, and workers in their group who are excited to help in the Temple. The capable leader instructs his group to humble themselves and fast to show their trust in God's protection and guidance. With many gold and silver gifts for the Temple in tow, the group arrives in Jerusalem unharmed, and they present offerings of gratitude before God.

9.   Ezra learns that even after the dark time of exile, the Jewish people are making some of the same mistakes they made before. They are marrying people outside the Jewish culture and picking up their corrupt religious customs. Ezra grieves over this terrible mistake, and prays "Lord, I'm ashamed to even look at you right now. From the time of our ancestors until today, your chosen people have let you down again and again, even after you saved us from slavery and exile. You allowed us to start a new era of peace and freedom here in Jerusalem, and we are already messing up that opportunity. God, I know we deserve to be destroyed completely for this, but please have mercy on us and let us survive."

10. As Ezra weeps and prays for the people, many others gather around him and promise to re-dedicate themselves to God and his law. Ezra speaks to the entire community and inspires at least a hundred men in Jerusalem to divorce their corrupt spouses and ask for God's forgiveness as they move forward.

NEHEMIAH

1. My name is Nehemiah, and my story started when my brother returned home to Babylonia from Jerusalem to report how our fellow Jews were doing since returning from exile. It was not good news. The city walls were still broken, and our people's rebuilding efforts were being mocked and sabotaged by the locals. I was devastated by this and prayed "God, you have always kept your promises, and I know you hear my prayer. I confess that my people have sinned, and when you warned us that the exile would happen, we ignored you. But now they have returned home, and they are doing their best to make things right. Please give me an opportunity to help."

2. Back then, I was the emperor's wine steward, and one day, he asked me why I looked so sad and broken. I said "I can't stop thinking about my people living in ruins. If it's okay with you, sir, could I go to Judah to help them rebuild Jerusalem? Would you send building supplies and give me the authority to lead the way? I know I can do it with your support." My boss and his wife kindly granted my request, and when I first arrived in Jerusalem, I spent three days quietly assessing the damage. When I finally announced that the time had come to rebuild the walls and start living with dignity again, the people jumped up and began working right away. When a local Arabian bully mocked our efforts, I responded "God will help us achieve this goal, and we will serve him every step of the way. This land does not belong to you, and your opinion is not welcome here."

3. As we got to work, I split our men up into forty groups (including a dozen groups of Levites and priests) and gave each of them a section of the city walls and gates to rebuild. I divided the men according to their clans, and along with respected leaders within each group, I oversaw the whole process.

4. When we began to rebuild the wall, a group of local Samaritan troops said "Do these Jews really think that their God will help them rebuild this rubble? What they are attempting is futile. Wild animals could easily knock down this sad excuse for a wall." Upon hearing these unkind words, I prayed that God would judge their insulting behavior and humble them, but we didn't let their words stop us from working. Our workers were more motivated than ever, and soon the work was half-done. The bullies upped their game and actually planned a violent attack upon our workers, but I armed our men and said "Don't be afraid, brothers. Remember that we serve a great and powerful God who will enable you to defend your families and homes." Seeing our determination to guard every inch of our construction area, our enemies abandoned their plan of attack. I'm pretty sure I didn't sleep or change clothes until our work was complete.

5. Once construction was complete, I began to hear complaints from Hebrews who were having trouble feeding their families; some had to borrow money or even sell their daughters into slavery to avoid losing their homes. I arranged a community meeting and angrily announced "This is a disgrace! You are exploiting and oppressing those who suffer in our community. Out of obedience for our

good Father, show mercy to these poor people. Cancel their debts and give them a chance to live with dignity. If you can't do that, maybe God should take your homes, and then you will see how it feels." I did my best to lead by example in my passion to help the poor. During my twelve years as governor, I gave away most of my salary and regularly fed 150 needy people from my own table. I worked hard, and I kept my eyes open to the burdens of others.

6. When the Arabian bullies heard we were done building and tried to meet up with me, I told them very plainly on four separate occasions that I was too busy to give them the time of day. Finally, the head bully Sanballat wrote "I heard a rumor that now that your new fancy city walls are built, you Jews are planning to attack us, and you are going to declare yourself king. Just wait until the emperor hears about this." I responded "None of that is true. I will not run and hide from you idiots. God is making me strong, and he sees every sin you commit." They continued to send their lying, threatening letters, but I didn't let it stop us.

7. Now that the city was functional again, and the Levites and musicians were getting into a stable routine, I appointed my brother and another capable leader to serve as the new governors of Jerusalem. I instructed them to assign guards to protect our newly constructed city, and I finally took a look at the city records. I learned that over 42,000 Israelites from nearly ninety clans had returned from exile, and many of them worked together to restore the Temple and reestablish a stable society in our old home.

8. Seven months after settling back into the towns of Judah,

the respected priest Ezra read the Law at a great community gathering **where many were moved** to tears. We told the people "Today is a holy day to worship, so don't be sad. Return home with joy in your hearts. Feast with your families, and allow God to strengthen you from within." Following this command, the people happily dove into the Law. **They** celebrated the Festival of Shelters by building temporary shelters to **remember their** time of wandering in the desert. Since we were fresh from exile **with a renewed appreciation for the blessing of shelter, we expressed reverence and gratitude** that hadn't been included in this festival since the time of Joshua.

9. Later that month, we gathered again to fast and solemnly ask forgiveness for the many sins our ancestors had committed. Our Levite leaders led us to stand and offer our imperfect human praise to God, and we prayed "God, you gave life to every creature that lives; you gave light to every star. You saw the faithful heart of our ancestor Abraham and promised this land to his family. When our ancestors were oppressed by Egyptian slave drivers, you parted the sea and performed great miracles that still astound us a thousand years later. You nourished them with manna in the desert and gave Moses our sacred law on the mountain. You delivered them to this great land, but in their pride and stubbornness, they refused to yield to your commands and worship you as you deserved. They insulted you and abandoned you again and again, but you didn't give up on them. You let them grow in number and conquer great nations, even as they continued to rebel against you. In times of war and times of peace, they ignored your prophets and

your commands. We deserved all the suffering that came upon us during the time of exile, but now that we're back home, take away our suffering. Bless us, and return us to the glory you intended us to have."

10. Those of us providing political and spiritual leadership to the people signed a written agreement that stated "As leaders we are set apart for God's purposes, and we promise that along with our families, we will do our best to obey the laws God gave us. We will marry people who support our faith, rest from work on the Sabbath, and protect poor people by canceling debts every seven years. We will give generously to the Temple and take care of those who serve there so that our spiritual community will grow stronger in this land."

11. We conducted a lottery to determine which families would be allowed to live in Jerusalem, so that this desirable, renewed city would not become too overcrowded. Many of those chosen were from the tribes of Judah, Benjamin, and Levi.

12. Another wave of priests and Levites returned from exile. Some Levite clans were in charge of leading inspiring worship services, and some formed a choir. Others were in charge of guarding the Temple and the storage rooms for the food offerings. When we dedicated the new city wall to God, several of the priests formed a lively marching band of trumpets, harps, and cymbals to lead a celebratory parade around the city. Even our children joined in the fun by singing thanks to God at the top of their lungs, and the music could be heard for miles around.

13. At one point, I journeyed to visit the king of Babylon to report our community's great progress to him, but I returned to discover that one of priests was lending Temple storage space to one of his buddies, and many of the Temple musicians and priests were forced to quit because the community refused to pay them a living wage. I immediately corrected these disgraceful mistakes and appointed more trustworthy Temple leaders to oversee these responsibilities in the future. I reprimanded local merchants for treating the holy Sabbath like any other work day and reminded the men with corrupt spouses that even wise King Solomon was led astray by wicked-hearted wives. I know God has seen and noticed my hard work and dedication to this community.

ESTHER

1. Once upon a time, in the kingdom of Persia, King Xerxes and Queen Vashti throw a week-long festival to honor their people. The party includes beautiful decorations, an all-you-can-eat feast, and specialty drinks served in gold cups to make even the poorest guests feel special. On the last day of the party, the queen refuses to show her face to a group of the king's friends. Some of the king's advisors say "Your wife refused to respectfully honor your request, and if word gets out, all the women of the kingdom will follow suit and start standing up to their husbands. Put that Vashti lady in her place and find a new queen who will respect you as the leader of your household."

2. Xerxes searches for a beautiful, young virgin to replace the queen, and he falls in love with a shapely young woman named Esther. He is so smitten with her that he throws a feast in her honor and proclaims a holiday throughout the whole land. Esther's adoptive father Mordecai advises her to hide her Jewish heritage from the king for her protection. Mordecai and Esther later save the king's life by preventing an assassination attempt.

3. When Prime Minister Haman requires that his subjects bow down to him, the bold Mordecai refuses to bow to anyone but the one true God. With his pride bruised and his anger stirred, Haman approaches the king and says "These Jewish people scattered around our land refuse to observe our customs and show us leaders the respect we deserve. They are lawbreakers and troublemakers. If we put them to death, your kingdom would be better off." Easily deceived by Haman's proposition, King Xerxes announces a date that the Persians would be allowed to slaughter the Jews in the land. As the capital city falls into a state of panic and confusion, the oblivious king celebrates the proclamation over drinks with Haman.

4. Mordecai and the other Jews are beside themselves with grief upon learning of the coming day of genocide. When Mordecai desperately asks Queen Esther to change her husband's mind, she nervously makes excuses, saying, "I'm a woman. I can't just come into his presence without being summoned. If Xerxes sees me as disrespectful, my life could be in danger." Mordecai responds, "You may be a queen now and think you are above the law, but you are a Jew just like the rest of us, honey. If you remain silent, your family

and friends will die, but maybe God made you queen so you can prevent that." Heartened, Esther says "Tell everyone to pray for me. I will break the law to approach the king unsummoned, and if I must die for my people, so be it."

5. After three days of fasting, Esther boldly goes before her husband, and to her surprise, the smitten king says "Come in, Esther, and tell me what's on your mind. I will give you whatever you ask for, even if it's half my kingdom." She replies "I want to make dinner for you and Haman tomorrow, and then I'll tell you what I want." Haman leaves the dinner full and happy, but his mood is ruined when Mordecai ignores him on his walk home. When Haman tells his wife and friends of this disappointing encounter, they respond "If you kill this Mordecai fellow, you won't have to cope with his disrespectful attitude anymore, and that will make you happy."

6. While reading over royal records in bed that night, the king is reminded of the assassination attempt Mordecai had prevented. He meets with Haman to say "There is an honorable man in the kingdom who has done me a great service, and I want to reward him. What do you think I should do?" Prideful Haman assumes he is the one the king plans to honor, so he says "give this man a royal robe and a crown to wear. Send one of your highest officials to the city square to proclaim his greatness." The king says "What a great idea! Get those robes and a horse for Mordecai right away, and you can announce my favor on him in the city square." Needless to say, Haman hurries home in embarrassment and frets that Mordecai is starting to become more powerful than him.

7. When Esther meets with Xerxes and Haman for another dinner, she says "Your majesty, I have one humble request for you. My people are about to be exterminated, and I want them to live." The king responds "Oh no! Who would do such a thing to the family of the woman I love?" Esther nods toward Haman and says "There he is." The king cannot control his anger and storms out into the garden to take a walk. In his absence, Haman throws himself on the couch next to Esther to beg for mercy, and when the king returns to see the prime minister sitting next to his wife, he shouts "Haven't you done enough?! Now you're going to rape my wife too, right in my own house? Guards, hang this man on the gallows he built for Mordecai! Get him out of my sight!"

8. After Haman's execution, Xerxes gives the prime minister's property to Queen Esther, and emboldened by her husband's regard for her, she reveals that his hero Mordecai is actually her adoptive father and deserves a place at the king's table. When the king honors this request, she then begs her husband to revoke Haman's proclamation against the Jews. The king thoughtfully responds, "Unfortunately, that proclamation bears my royal seal and cannot be reversed. However, I can issue a new proclamation encouraging the Jews to organize themselves in self-defense against any attacks that come against them."

9. On the day the genocide was originally scheduled to be carried out, the Jews throughout the Persian capital stand strong against their enemies, including evil Haman's ten sons. Realizing she still has the respect of her husband, Esther says "I know I have already asked a lot of you on

behalf of my people. Could I be so bold as to ask for a few extra days for my people to rise up against the people in Persia who hate them?" The king honors his wife's request, and the Jews are able to rid Persia of 75,000 of their enemies that week. Mordecai initiates the Festival of Purim to allow Jewish families to annually remember and honor this victory.

10. Xerxes promotes Mordecai to be second in command in the entire empire of Persia. The king works for the good of all the Jewish and Persian people throughout his reign, thanks to his wife having the courage to open his eyes.

WEEK TWO REFLECTION
History

DISCUSSION QUESTIONS

- First, let's just acknowledge that Week Two covers a lot of historical ground and tells a complex story of a nation that spans centuries. It's a lot to digest, even if you've been in the church for years. Who are a few Biblical people you knew nothing about before reading this week's readings? What did you learn about these folks?

- When you came across familiar stories or people within the Week Two readings (i.e. David and Goliath), did you gain a new or different perspective about these stories and how they fit into the larger story? If so, what did you learn?

- Which people stood out as particularly courageous in the readings this week? How might their extraordinary courage be linked to extraordinary faith?

- Of the many eras covered in the historical books, which time period struck you as the most corrupt? What do you suppose led to that corruption? How did the Lord respond during that time?

- What makes David stand out as one of the greatest kings in Jewish history? Why do you think God chose him to replace Saul?

- Of all the kings that followed David and Solomon, who did

you most admire and why? Which kings most disappointed you and why?

- Why do you think God allowed the Hebrews to experience a time of exile? Did anything seem different about their hearts or actions when they returned from Babylonia?

MUSIC MEDITATIONS

- **Joshua-** Listen to "Courageous" by Casting Crowns, and consider the bravery it would take to trust God in the midst of battle.

- **Judges-** Listen to "Slow Fade" by Casting Crowns. Consider whether you can relate to any temptations the people fell into during this era.

- **Ruth-** Reflect on where you notice unconditional love in this story, and listen to "I'll Stand By You" by The Pretenders.

- **1 Samuel-** Listen to "Voice of Truth" by Casting Crowns, and consider the courage David showed against Goliath. Pray for the courage to boldly face the giants in your life.

- **2 Samuel-** Reflect on David's passionate, worshipful dancing while moving the Covenant Box, and listen to "Undignified" by Matt Redman to determine what it would take for you to do likewise.

- **1 Kings-** Listen to "Build Your Kingdom Here" by Rend Collective, and consider the prosperous kingdom Solomon was able to build by trusting in God's guidance in the early years of his reign.

- **2 Kings-** Notice how the corruption and political turmoil seen throughout this text mirrors the chaos and division that exist today. Listen to "Where is the Love" by The Black Eyed Peas, and pray about how you might promote unity and heal divisions in your own corner of the globe.

- **1 Chronicles-** Listen to "Legacy" by Nichole Nordeman to reflect on your favorite leader during this time and what you might learn from that person's example.

- **2 Chronicles-** Listen to "Get Back Up" by TobyMac, and reflect on the ups and downs you notice throughout this book.

- **Ezra-** If you haven't seen *The Greatest Showman*, please know that I'm a big musical nerd and will highly encourage you to check it out. As I listen to the lyrics of "From Now On" by Justin Paul and Benj Pasek, I'm reminded of the many humbling lessons the Hebrews learned before they were able to return home.

- **Nehemiah-** Listen to "The Comeback" by Danny Gokey. Reflect on the positive attitude and energy the Hebrews must have had in order to overcome obstacles and rebuild their nation.

- **Esther-** Listen to "Born For This" by Mandisa, and consider the courage Esther must have had to boldly confront her husband and defend her people.

APPLICATION IDEAS

- When the Covenant Box was moved, David worshipped so hard that his wife was ashamed of him. What can you do to "go all out" in worship this week? Commit to worshipping with your whole heart focused on God regardless of how it looks to others.

- Esther used her position as queen to cleverly and courageously save her people. Think about the power or connections you have through your career or otherwise. How can you use that influence to better the lives of people in your midst who may be overlooked or marginalized?

WEEK THREE
Wisdom

JOB-SONG OF SONGS

DAY ONE - PERSPECTIVE FROM PAIN
JOB

BIG IDEA

God is bigger than the worst trials and traumas a person can face.

LESSONS FROM JOB'S STRUGGLE

- **God loves Job-** Although Job assumes at times that God is out to get him, God sees Job's strong heart and believes he can endure this time of hardship.

- **Satan exists-** God never wants his children to hurt, but he allows all humans and angels to make their own choices. The fallen angel Satan chooses to spread pain and destruction throughout our world, and he often convinces misguided people to spread senseless destruction as well. God doesn't condone this destruction, but he enables us to survive it if we lean on him.

- **Job didn't deserve it-** He really was a loving, responsible man of good deeds, but that didn't make him immune to pain. When trauma struck his life, he deserved comfort and validation instead of unfair judgment.

- **Job's friends were the worst-** They consistently mock and condemn Job for expressing his real emotions. They assume Job and his family must have angered God to earn this series of disasters. These "friends" only care about winning the debate and refuse to offer Job even a modicum of comfort.

- **God is bigger than the pain-** Just when Job feels completely lost and broken, God emerges from the storm and reminds him that he is stronger than any monster and larger than the universe. God condemns the friends who refused to comfort him and blesses Job even more richly than before.

HOW GOD SHOWS UP

God feels silent to Job at first, but he later understands that he simply could not see through his pain to recognize God's bigger picture. God was reaching out all along, but Job was too distracted by untrustworthy friends and too smothered by depression to notice. When the men stop arguing and fall silent, Job is finally able to hear God's voice and learn to trust him again. God reminds his defeated child that he created the whole world and is more than capable to relieve Job's pain. God lifts up this broken man and restores his blessings even greater than before.

JOB

1. Once upon a time, a man named Job enjoys a blessed life in close relationship with God. Job is the richest man in his region and is highly respected by his servants. This proud dad awakens early regularly to pray for the continued success and purity of his ten adult children who gather regularly for family dinners. One day, the proud Father God gathers his angels to say "Look at my faithful child, Job! He is a good man who worships me with his whole heart. I love him so much!" Satan argues

"He only obeys you because you have given him a perfect, charmed life. If all his blessings went away, he'd curse you to your face!" God responds "You are wrong about him, and to prove it, I will let you test him and take some of his blessings away. Just don't hurt him." Satan eagerly allows thieves to steal his livestock and allows lightning to destroy his sheep. The same day, a wind storm destroys his house and kills all his children. Job crumples in grief and cries "God sent me into the world with nothing, and that's how I'll leave it. My heart is broken, but I still know that God is good."

2. God proudly says "Satan, did you notice how Job continues to be loyal to me, even though you punished him for no reason?" Satan replies "Yeah, but he is still able-bodied and healthy. If I take away his health, he will surely turn away from you." The Lord responds "You're wrong about him, but go do whatever damage you're about to do. Just don't kill him." Satan happily causes Job to break out in painful, itchy sores over his whole body, and Job's wife says "How can you continue to honor God when he has made you miserable like this? Why don't you just give up, curse God, and die?" Job responds "That's crazy! God has blessed me so much, so why would I curse him just because I'm experiencing a chapter of trouble?" When Job's three friends come to town, they barely recognize him and grieve in stunned silence with him for seven days.

3. Job finally breaks the silence, crying out in misery, "God, I wish I had never been born. Can you go back to that day and just blot it from history? If I had died as a baby, I'd be at peace now, blissfully sleeping like all those who have

gone before me. God, why do you let people go on living when they're in this much pain?"

4. Job's friend, Eliphaz, responds "I'm sorry, Job. I can't stay quiet any longer. I've seen you lift up many people who were struggling, and now that it's your turn to struggle, you can't even handle it. If you were actually close to God, you wouldn't be so worried. God lifts up the righteous and destroys the wicked. Truly, none of us have a right to be blessed by God. We are just stupid, imperfect lumps of clay. If God wanted to crush us like bugs, he could.

5. "Look around, Job. No angel is coming to your rescue. Don't foolishly dwell on worry or resentment. You brought this mess upon yourself. If I were you, I would stand humbly before God and present my case to him. He lifts up the needy and makes justice reign everywhere. He will correct your mistakes and rescue you from harm no matter what. You know I'm right; just accept it."

6. Job says "If you really understood the heavy burden I'm carrying, my words of sadness wouldn't surprise you. I feel like God has pierced me with painful arrows, and my body is filling with poison. I don't understand why God won't just answer my prayer and put me out of my misery. I know God is holy. I've followed him my whole life, but that doesn't make me immune to the pain and hopelessness that has overwhelmed me. I need loyal friends at a time like this, but you are starving me of that nourishing comfort. If you're so smart, go ahead and tell me what I need to do differently. You are spouting nonsense, and I wish you would stop cruelly calling me a liar, kicking me

while I'm down.

7. "The truth that you refuse to acknowledge is that life is just hard sometimes. Believe me when I say I have nothing to live for. My body is broken and disgusting. God, my life is like a passing wind with no meaning, and soon my pathetic life will be forgotten. What's the point?! I'm so mad I can't keep quiet! As for you people, why can't you just leave me alone? Do you think I'm some monster who will escape this house and ravage the city? Just go away! God, why are people so important to you? Why do you watch us so closely? Can't you just forgive me and stop using me for target practice?"

8. Without hesitation or sympathy, Job's friend, Bildad responds "Are you done? Can I talk now? Your children must have died for a reason; they were probably not as pure as you thought they were. God's justice is perfect, and he is never wrong. If you're so great, why hasn't God miraculously restored your household? Let's remember what our wise ancestors have taught us; when people choose to live apart from the nourishing spring of God, they wither quickly like weeds in the sun. God lifts up those who worship him and punishes all his enemies without fail."

9. Job argues "I've heard all that before, and guess what? God is a whole lot more powerful than people; it's not fair to oversimplify how he operates. How could insignificant me possibly bring a case to God as you suggest? God could shake the earth without warning and could stop the sun from rising if he wanted to. Even though I'm innocent, how could I possibly make him listen to me? He's God. My

pitiful little life couldn't possibly matter to him. I don't see the point in trying to pretend like everything's okay. It's not okay, and I'm not afraid to tell the truth about how I feel.

10. "God, what have I done to deserve this? You formed me with your own hands, and now you're destroying me. Why? You gave me life, love, and blessings, and now all of it is gone. I didn't know you were planning to punish me like this. What's the point of that? Why did you even let me be born in the first place?"

11. Zophar mocks his friend's grief-stricken words, saying "Oh Job, do you really think none of us will be able to debate your dramatic nonsense? You say you've done nothing to deserve this, but I'd love to see what God has to say about that. I'm sure he's actually punishing you less than you deserve. God's greatness stretches beyond the universe, and his knowledge encompasses things we could never understand. Just turn back to him, and I'm sure he'll give your bright, shiny life right back to you."

12. Job shakes his head and sarcastically remarks "Oh wise Zophar, voice of the people. How did any of us ever get by without your genius perspective? Look! You may laugh at me and think that I'm inferior to you because you have no problems in your life, but take a look at yourselves, kicking me while I'm down. You have a lot to learn. Even the birds have more reverence for God than you; even animals are better listeners. God is wiser, stronger, and more powerful than anybody; he can humble the most powerful king and the most righteous priest. I wish he would humble you.

13. "I'm not stupid; I fully understand all the pretentious things

you're saying, but there's no point even debating with you. My beef is with God, not you. He doesn't need your half-truths and false humility to defend him. Do you really think you can fool him into thinking you're decent people? Your words are unbelievably empty. God, are you gonna kill me or what? Why won't you answer me? I just want to know why my life has completely fallen apart.

14. "We are all born weak and helpless, and then we disappear as quickly as we came. Look at me, God! I'm aware that I'm an imperfect, unclean human with a pitifully short life, but why won't you leave me be? I want to just hide away until this time of pain is over. When that happens, I know you'll forgive me, and I will make you proud of me. I know there will be a time when this mountain is moved away from me, but until then, I'll sit here in grief and pain."

15. Eliphaz smirks and chortles "I see your mouth moving, buddy, but I don't hear anything worth listening to. Do you think you're some special snowflake that God granted with wisdom only you can access? We have learned from people older and smarter than you, boy. Why are you so angry with God? Why can't you just accept his comfort and be grateful for whatever he gives you. We don't deserve any of his blessings to begin with. There's really no hope for wicked people like you who torment others and throw tantrums in God's presence. You'll wither away just like all the godless people before you."

16. Job mourns "Why do you insist on torturing me rather than comforting me? Why must you always have the last word? If you were in my shoes, I could do the same to you.

God, talking about my pain doesn't help, and being silent feels even worse. I don't know what to do. I'm worn out, and everyone I love is gone. I was living in peace, and now I'm being attacked from every side. All I can do is pour out my tears to God and beg him to reveal why all this is happening. I wish someone in heaven or on earth would bother to defend me.

17. "It's getting harder to breathe. Everyone mocks me as I die, and no one will try to understand me. God, you know it's true. First my precious children were taken from me, and now those who should comfort me are blaming me for their deaths. This is unbearable. I cannot see the light at the end of this hellhole of a tunnel."

18. Bildad mocks poor Job, saying "Oh shut up already, and listen! You call us stupid, but your anger is doing no good. God will not move mountains to soothe your tantrums. He will put a stop to wicked people like you just like he always does; he'll let you trip over the consequences of your own misguided beliefs. Many wicked people were rich like you were once, and now they are homeless and forgotten with disgusting diseases covering their bodies. God is doing this to you so that others will repent as you refuse to do. You obviously don't care about God."

19. Job tells his friends "Why do you keep abusing me and shaming me like this? How do you benefit by tearing me down? You think you're better than me, but why wouldn't I cry out to God about my pain? Why shouldn't I ask for answers and justice? He has taken everything from me and left me to die. My wife is disgusted my me, my former

servants pretend they don't know me, and children in the street laugh at me. You are supposed to be my friends! Why can't you just take pity on me? I hope someone will notice my story and write it down. I hope someone will care."

20. Zophar replies "Job, I feel hurt and insulted by your words. It's a fact that for as long as humans have been alive, evil people have not prospered for long. They try to rise up, but God blows them down like a pile of dust. They disappear, and the things they stole are returned to the poor. Those who oppress others and enjoy the taste of evil will be crushed in the end. Justice will always prevail!"

21. Job sighs "I wish you would just listen. That's all I ask of you, please. This may shock you, but my impatience is justified, and my quarrel is not with you; it's with God. The truth is that the world isn't as black and white as you make it out to be. There are plenty of evil-hearted people who live to see their grandchildren frolic and play like little lambs. They live in peace and die with plenty of money in the bank for their families. They don't care about God and choose to believe that they got where they are due to their own strength and intelligence. I can't accept their arrogant way of thinking, and I wish God would hold them accountable. You say that God tears down all the wicked in this world, but that's just not true. Some wicked people fly under the radar and die happy. Why do you continue to come at me with these nonsensical lies?!"

22. Eliphaz asks Job "Even the wisest man with a resume full of good deeds is not impressive to our God. God judges you because you deserve it. You have taken the clothes off

your brother's body, and you've refused to feed those who are tired and hungry. You took advantage of widows and orphans, and now you are reaping the consequences of those dark deeds. You cannot hide your sins from God; he sees everything. Job, you continue to reject God and think you are above his law. Good people like me can only laugh as you get what's coming to you. Stop treating God like an enemy, already. Return to him with a humble heart, and he'll bring you joy and success."

23. Job declares "I can't hold back the truth; I'm in pain, and I'm mad about it. I keep crying out to God, hoping to hear from him. I know that he hears me and sees my innocence. I know God sees every step I take; I only wish he would put an end to his silence and allow me to find him. I have to trust that our unchanging God has a plan for me, and all I can do is stand in fearful respect as I await whatever's coming next.

24. "I wish God would judge all the good and evil people once and for all. People lie. People steal. They take advantage of poor, defenseless orphans, and they get away with it. Homeless people work tirelessly in fields of rich people and have nothing to show for it. Children are enslaved and overworked, and God has not answered their prayers yet. Sinners sneak around in the dark killing, stealing, and cheating on their wives. They're afraid for the truth to come out." Zophar argues "The wicked are already being cursed and swept away. Their land is shriveling and their bodies are decaying. They may prosper for a while, but God will avenge every act of unkindness."

25. Bildad says "God is all-powerful, and his heavenly light shines everywhere. Compared to his awesome presence, human beings are nothing."

26. Job sarcastically says "What a fine help you are, sharing your pretty words with a fool like me." Bildad continues "God causes ghosts to tremble; he fills the clouds with rain, and hung the Earth in its exact spot in space. He holds up the sky and could wipe out the most terrifying sea monster with a single breath. But that's not even the half of it; God is greater than we can imagine."

27. Job responds "You guys, I'm aware that God is unimaginably powerful, but I swear I am innocent. I don't deserve this pain, and God knows it. I hope he will punish you people for making my pain worse." Zophar proudly retorts "God always punishes the wicked, violent people of this world. He allows their children to die and gives their riches to honest people. Disaster will strike them and take away everything they love."

28. There are mines deep in the dark earth where miners sift through copious amounts of dirt in the darkness to find tiny specks of gold and silver. Miners have to chip away at the hardest rocks to discover precious stones underneath. Wisdom is more beautiful and precious than any of the precious rubies and crystal the miners search so hard to find. Its beautiful colors are buried under the surface, hard to see amidst all our struggles. God alone can see under the hard rocks and past all the dirt; only he can see things clearly. The only way we can understand anything at all is by humbly acknowledging that God is smarter than us.

29. A deeply broken Job starts a final statement of his case, saying "I guess what I'm really trying to say is I miss my old life. God protected my home and my family. I was surrounded by my children and my wealth. People looked up to me and respected me. I was a champion to people in need, and people really valued my help and advice. I never thought that life of happiness and comfort would end.

30. "But now look at me. How the mighty have fallen! The people who make fun of me are lazy, pitiful nobodies I wouldn't have even hired in my field a few months ago. Now even they think they're better than me; I'm a joke to them, and they spit in my face. I am about to die without any dignity whatsoever and without any way to relieve the aching in my bones. God won't answer my cries for help, even though I used to answer the cries of others. I'm so unbearably lonely and afraid; there is no trace of sunshine or music in my life anymore.

31. "I have never even thought of being unfaithful to my wife, and I have never turned my back to a hungry orphan. I did my best to be fair as a boss, and I have never allowed my wealth to make me prideful. I have never worshipped anyone but God, and I have never tried to hide my flaws from others. I don't care what others think; it only matters what God thinks. God has seen my actions and my heart. He knows I'm innocent, and if I'm wrong about that, I will gladly accept whatever punishment is coming to me."

32. The three friends realize Job is convinced he is innocent, and they realize nothing they say can convince him otherwise. However, a young bystander named Elihu is overcome

with anger at all four men and can no longer stay silent. He says "I know I'm a lot younger than you, and I was afraid to speak up until now. But it's not age that makes men wise; only God can do that. I listened patiently to your attempt to speak wisdom into this situation, and each of you failed miserably. Job, these friends of yours have nothing more to say to you, but I can't wait to say what's on my mind. With God's help, I will speak plainly and honestly without flattering any of you.

33. "Job, I hope you will really hear me and know that my words are sincere. God made both of us from lumps of clay, and I don't think I'm better than you. I heard you say that you're perfectly innocent, and God is finding some excuse to attack you, but with all due respect, I think you've lost sight of who God is. Maybe God has been trying to speak to you this whole time, but you haven't stopped arguing with your friends long enough to listen. God loves to save us from pain, but sometimes he allows us to experience physical pain or disease to teach us a bigger lesson. Once we learn what we need to learn from a time of struggle, I believe God is fully capable of sending angels to make us strong and healthy again. I believe God can save you and bring you joy again. Job, if you disagree with me, I'd love to hear what you have to say. Just please hear me out first.

34. "You keep saying you're perfect and that God is holding out on you, but don't you think that's kind of an arrogant thing to say? Who are you to condemn God? None of us are smarter or better than him. He is perfectly just and has complete power over our lives. We have no right to question what he does or doesn't do to help us. Job, you'd

probably be better off if you stop mocking God and try to learn from him instead.

35. "When you ask God why he cares so much about sin and ask how our actions hurt him, you're assuming that God is acting out of revenge or spite. No! God lives above the clouds and is completely unharmed by any of our actions. He created the Law for our own good, so that we wouldn't destroy ourselves and each other. You say you can't see God, but just be patient and wait for him to show up. He has heard every word you've said.

36. "Please be patient and listen a little longer. I believe this wisdom was given to me by the God that made me. You think God hates you, but he doesn't hate anyone. He understands the big picture when we don't. Sometimes he uses a time of suffering to humble us and reveal our sins to us, and when that happens, it's for our own good. It helps us turn back to him and receive his blessings once more. Godless people stay angry and refuse to ask God for help. Be better than that, Job. Remember the great God who blessed you so richly before? He's still the same God, and he's there to teach you and love you through this. He is greater than we can imagine. He orchestrates the lightning storms and fills the deep oceans with rain.

37. "Look at the beautiful and terrifying lightning storm that is starting around us. God's voice is roaring from the thunder, making my heart pound and my knees shake. He sends the snow and rain that makes us stop working and makes animals hide in their dens. Stop and think about it, Job. How does God do all these amazing, mysterious things?

God is too bright and beautiful for us to even look at; our earthly wisdom pales in comparison."

38. Finally, out of the great storm, God speaks up, saying "Okay Job. Stand up straight, and answer this! Were you there with me when I made the world and heard the angels shout for joy on that very first day? Did you wrangle the powerful sea to keep it from overtaking the earth? Job, have you ever helped the sun rise or visited the creatures at the very bottom of the ocean? Do you control the weather, guide the stars to change with the seasons, or provide food for the animals of the earth? Did you do all that, Son, or was that me?

39. "Have you ever witnessed the beauty of a baby deer being born? Can you teach the mama deer how to keep that baby safe? Who gave the wild animals their freedom? Do you have the power to tame them? Did you design the ostrich to outrun every horse in the world? Did you make the majestic horse brave and strong? Did you teach the hawk to fly or the eagle to hunt?

40. "My child, you challenged the Creator of the universe. Now, what do you have to say for yourself?" Job stares at the ground and replies "I'm a fool, Lord. I've already said too much." God continues "Stand up straight, Son, and answer this. You have called me unjust and have called yourself blameless, but let's set the record straight. Can your voice thunder like mine? Can you humble the proud and crush the wicked where they stand? If you can do those things, go ahead and show me what you're made of. I'll be the first to congratulate you. Look at the mighty Behemoth

with legs like tree trunks. He eats only grass but contains strength in his muscles only his Creator can defeat. That's just one example of the humbling power that exists in this world I've made.

41. "Can you catch or tame the mighty sea monster Leviathan? No man can even touch this guy and live to tell about it! He breathes fire and causes even the bravest men to fall down in fear. His armor is impenetrable, and I made that armor. Think about it! If I made that powerful, indestructible monster, how much more powerful am I?"

42. Job meekly replies "I feel terrible for questioning your power or your wisdom. I ignorantly spoke about things I know nothing about. I thought I knew something about life, but now I have seen you with my own eyes. I'm so ashamed of myself and want to turn back to you. Please forgive me!" God then turns to Job's three friends who had spent so much time insulting Job and tearing him down, saying "I'm angry with you three as well. You could have helped Job or revealed the truth about me, but you disgraced your-selves and only spouted ignorance and lies. You owe your friend a huge apology, and if he decides to forgive you, I'll consider forgiving you as well." The three men obey God right away, and once Job forgives his friends, things begin to turn around. Job's relatives and friends come from all around to offer him sympathy and gifts to rebuild his wealth. God blesses Job and his wife with ten more children, and he lives long enough to see his great-grandchildren. As God knew all along, Job was able to withstand the worst tests of life and come out even stronger and wiser than before.

DAY TWO - LOVE SONGS
PSALMS 1-75

BIG IDEA

A multitude of songs praise our awesome Father for creating us, delivering us from danger, and showing us how to live our best possible life.

SONG THEMES

- **Obedience leads to joy-** Treat others with kindness, honesty, humility, and authenticity, so that you might lead a fruitful life. Sin corrupts our hearts and leads to wealth that doesn't last.

- **God rescues and protects-** Have no fear because our strong Father can defeat any enemy. When we're surrounded, he shows us the way out and gives us what we need to press on.

- **Life is hard-** The world gets us down, and God embraces us as we cry. He offers us hope and peace in the midst of the storm.

- **The Creator loves us-** He made every big and beautiful thing that exists, and still he knows and loves each of us more than we can imagine and better than we deserve.

- **Good will win-** Evil overwhelms the world, but God will have the last word.

- **Grace frees us-** We trap ourselves in worry and guilt, but

God's unconditional forgiveness releases us from all shame.

- **God is beautiful-** No light shines brighter than the glory of God. He deserves all our gratitude and worship.
- **He teaches us to lead-** God can guide us to lead others well and do great things in this world.

HOW GOD SHOWS UP

These songs tenderly and emotionally reveal great truths about our great God. No matter what trials we face, he longs to protect us and show us how to cope. When things are going well, he compels us to recognize our many blessings. Regardless of our circumstances, God reveals his breathtaking beauty throughout his created world, and he offers us love and grace far beyond anything we could ever imagine or deserve.

PSALMS PART 1

1. Despite what misguided folks try to tell you, true joy comes in living God's way. This will help you blossom like a tree by the river, with good fruit that will outlast temporary temptations.

2. Enemy nations try to rise up against the chosen king, but God laughs at their feeble attempts to take charge. They cannot win. The Lord protects our king like his own son, so those rival kings should be afraid.

3. David sings "God, I'm surrounded. These enemies think you can't help me, but prove them wrong. You shielded

me through the night. Please make me brave this morning.

4. "Answer my nighttime prayers, and don't let these people insult me anymore. Let those sinners tremble and lie awake tonight, thinking about what they've done. Show me kindness like you always do, and remember that I am yours. Thank you for giving me unspeakable joy and allowing me to sleep soundly, assured of your peace and safety.

5. "Hear my desperate cries, good King. I know you're listening all the time. You only love good things and don't put up with violence, conceit, or lies. You love it when your beloved children bow before you. Blaze a path for me, and show me how to defeat the liars who plot against me.

6. "Don't be mad at me, Father. I'm desperate and worn out. Have pity on me! I cry myself to sleep every night and cannot see through the tears. I know that you see my tears and will come to my rescue.

7. "Deliver me from the ones who want to tear me to shreds. Judge their wicked motives, and bless my innocent heart. If I have harmed or betrayed anyone, feel free to give me what I deserve.

8. "Great Lord, no enemy can come against you, and children sing your praises. You hung the stars, and still you care about small people like me. You entrusted us with your glorious creation that fills the world with beauty and life.

9. "I can't stop shouting with joy about how awesome you are. Your enemies fall down dead at the very sight of you. You judge the world fairly and without fault. You are our perfect King, our Shelter from the storm. When we cry out in pain, we can trust you to help. You don't tolerate those

who hurt your children."

10. Arrogant, greedy people try to turn my failure into their success. They don't care about God. They only care about themselves, and it feels like God's just letting it happen. These snakes wait in darkness for their opportunity to strike their innocent victims, and they think God doesn't see. Our King will punish them as they deserve in the end.

11. David writes "Father, I trust you to keep me safe, even as you send me into the line of fire. I feel helpless against the arrows that come my way, but I know you are on the throne. You are in control, and you will watch over those who live in your shadow.

12. "Help me, God! All I see are boastful liars who will say anything to get what they want. Look past their nonsense to offer safety to the poor and hurting. Your promise to protect us is more precious than silver.

13. "How long will this agony last, Father? How long will you hide your face? Look at me with love, and make me strong in the face of danger.

14. "Fools don't believe in you, Lord. They only know how to do the wrong thing. They fill the earth, and you struggle to pinpoint anyone who does what's right. When you show the world your power, those who oppress your faithful few will be terrified.

15. "Lord, who is worthy to come into your house? People with good hearts who are honest, authentic, kind, and generous. They love those you love and keep their promises.

16. "Great Protector, I trust you. You are the source of all good

things, and those who abandon you for fake gods are asking for trouble. You give me everything I need and guide me toward unshakable ground. Thank for filling me with joy and showing me a path that leads to my best possible life.

17. "God, I cry out for help and justice from the most honest part of my spirit. You know me better than anyone, and you see that my heart longs to be like your heart. I never want to stray from your path. Reveal your love to me, and protect me under your wings. Defeat my enemies and fill me with your joy.

18. "My Fortress and Defender, you shield me from the dangers all around me. You make the mountains tremble, and your voice thunders from heaven against those who destroy what you love. You pluck me out of the deep ocean and reward my innocent heart. You create light in me, and I can trust you to blaze a safe path. I have never fallen into enemy hands, and you beat the odds to make me king. I was a shepherd boy, and now foreign kings bow to me. I praise you, God, because you deserve all the credit for my victories.

19. "When I look at the sky every morning and night, I stand speechless and know there is a God. The sun greets each day with its beautiful colors, warms the earth, and travels to the other end of the sky each day to paint its beauty again. God's commands make me strong, wise, and safe from sin. This trustworthy, sweet way of life makes me acceptable to God."

20. "May the God of our ancestors deliver you from trouble. May he answer your prayers and make you prosper. Some trust in weapons and chariots of war, but we trust in the

power of the King that makes us rise up.

21. "Thank you, powerful God, for putting a crown on my head and giving me a prosperous, victorious life I couldn't have dreamed up. I trust you to keep my throne and our country secure because I feel your blazing love. Your love warms me and burns up my enemies."

22. "I cry out to God, but I feel all alone. I lie restless at night waiting for the holy King to show up for me. My ancestors trusted him, and I've got to trust him too. I feel like a worthless worm of a person; everyone hates me. Lord, you've been my Protector all my life; don't give up on me now! I'm surrounded by hungry lions, and I'm helpless to stop them. Save me! I want to tell everyone how great you are. You feed the forgotten and humble the proud. Let the whole world and future generations know of your glory.

23. "I am a helpless sheep, and you are the Shepherd that feeds me and strengthens my body. You keep my path safe when the night falls, and I don't have to be afraid. You walk with me wherever I go. You honor me like a guest at your dinner table and make my cup overflow with blessings.

24. "Everything that has life belongs to God. He built the earth with his own hands and designed the ocean floor. Only innocent followers should come into God's house and be blessed. God, fling open the gates of our hearts and come in.

25. "If I trust in you, I can't be crushed. Teach me your ways. Reveal the truth to me. Look at me with love and kindness, and forgive my many mistakes. I am weak, but you calm all my worries. Preserve me in your goodness.

26. "Look at my innocent heart, God. It's a heart that trusts

you and avoids evil hypocrites. Test my motives, and make them like yours. I sing my gratitude to you. Have mercy on me when you judge the world.

27. "With God lighting my path, I have no reason to fear any darkness. When I'm surrounded, I trust my Savior. I want to see our beautiful Lord, accept his shelter, and obey his advice forever. God, don't abandon me in anger. Stay with me, and take care of me.

28. "Help, God! I hope you hear my cry and don't lump me in with all these folks who ignore your greatness. Hurt those who hurt the world. Thank you, great Defender, for giving me a happy life.

29. "Let the mightiest angels bow and sing before our glorious, praiseworthy God. His voice thunders across the sea. It shakes the earth and strips the leaves off trees. The King of the deep ocean strengthens his people with blessings and peace.

30. David sings "Thank you for saving me from those bullies, God. I called for help, and you saved my life. You healed me, and now I dedicate my restored life to you. Thank you for being a good God who brings joy to us and never stays mad for long. You've squashed my depression, and I celebrate with a happy dance."

31. David writes "Shelter me, God, and lead me past all the traps in my way. Through your love, I am safe and free. When I'm exhausted from crying, you have mercy on me. When everyone treats me like garbage, I trust you to shelter me from their insults. Thank you for silencing the arrogant liars and keeping my hope alive.

32. "I am happy, forgiven, and free. When I was holding tightly to sin, I was torn up inside, punishing myself with tears of worry. Once I stopped hiding my flaws from you, you forgave every last mistake. You saved me from my flood of troubles, and I can't stop singing about it. You make me wiser and show me where to go from here."

33. Let all who follow God sing with happy thanks to him. He always does what's right, and his love fills the whole world. He spoke the moon and stars into being. Let the whole earth yield to his plans, and let us be glad he is on our side. When famine or war overwhelms our land, he's always watching.

34. After a priest helps him more safely run from King Saul, David writes "Thank you, God for listening to my fears and freeing me from them. You guard me in this time of helplessness and oppression. I am happy in your arms that give me everything I need. I want to teach young people to honor you so that they can lead a long, happy, peaceful life. You watch over your followers, and you draw near when we've lost all hope."

35. David writes "Fight the ones who fight me, God. Shield me, and rescue me! Let them fall into the very traps they set for me, and I will happily shout that there's no one like my Protector. I thought these guys were my friends. When they were sick, I prayed for them, but they don't care for me at all. They mock me when I stumble and accuse me of crimes I know nothing about. How long until the truth comes out? Declare me innocent, and cover those liars in shame.

36. "When sin infects the heart of a man, he thinks he can

get away with anything, and he lies all the time. But your love stretches higher than the mountains and the sky. You protect your children like a mama bird, filling our bellies and sheltering us under your wings. Continue to love us and protect us from arrogant bullies.

37. "Don't be jealous of sinners who are succeeding, and don't feel sorry for them when they wither away. Trust in God's way of life, and you will stay safe and content. Surrender your plans, stop fretting, and wait patiently for the answers that will surely come. Murderers kill and steal to get ahead, but their wealth won't last. God will take it away and give it to generous givers. If you stumble along God's path, he'll pick you back up. I'm an old man now, so believe me when I say God won't abandon his good-hearted children. Be fair and wise. Do the right thing, and God will keep you safe.

38. "Lord, spare me from your anger. My foolish mistakes have left my body broken, and my heart is heavy with unbearable, crushing pain. Sin has taken the light from my eyes and the strength from my bones. I trust you to save me from these sins that have caused me to lie awake in worry. Don't leave me, God! Save me from myself!

39. "I tried to keep quiet so I wouldn't say the wrong thing, but my anxiety overwhelmed me still. The more I escaped into my thoughts, the more worried I became. It got so bad that I wanted to die. Life is as short as a puff of wind, and sometimes it's hard to see the point. God, help me find hope. Save me from myself and those who mock me. Hear my cries, and let me enjoy what is left of my short, meaningless life.

40. "When I was drowning in the quicksand of anxiety, you pulled me out and put me high on a rock. You saved my life. I'm glad I waited for you instead of turning to fake gods; you are unlike any other. I love to listen for your guidance and tell everyone how you saved me. Your love and mercy are unstoppable.

41. "If your heart loves to help the poor, God will make you happy, safe, and healthy. God, forgive me and heal my body of this sickness that keeps me in bed. My enemies send flowers and pretend to care about my recovery. Make me well so that I can pay them back. Thank you for your help, God. I love you now and forever!"

42. The Korah clan is a group of respected leaders within the Temple choir. Following the tragedy of exile, these musicians write "Lord, I need you like a thirsty deer needs water. I starve without the life you give. As we sit in exile, my heart misses the days when we gathered to shout joyfully to you. Chaos and sorrow flood my soul because I can't find you anywhere. You are my only hope. Show me your love, and teach me how to sing again.

43. "God, defend my innocent heart against cruel liars. Why do you let them hurt me like this? Bring me back into your light so that I can see clearly and find happiness again. Why am I so sad? I hope one day I will make joyful music like I did before.

44. "Our ancestors told us about the great miracles of the past. They told us how you drove your enemies out and helped us prosper. They did not need to trust their swords and bows because you had their back. Today, you no longer protect us

in battle; we are slaughtered like sheep and scattered across foreign lands. People laugh at us, and we cover our faces in shame. Some of us still love you, and you've abandoned us. Wake up and help the people you used to love!

45. "On today, the king's wedding day, I see a handsome, majestic groom whose life God has smiled upon. Nations fall at your feet, good king, and you never fail to do right by us. We are happy to bless you and your beautiful bride with sweet music. Dear queen, you are radiant today, and everyone tries to win your favor. We hope your marriage is filled with respect, loyalty, and devotion to each other. Let the whole world admire our great king and queen!

46. "No need to fear when storms come our way; the mighty God of Jacob shelters us from all of it. Joy fills his house and security fills his kingdom. Wars stop with one word from him; he can do anything.

47. "Everybody clap your hands! Dance and sing with all you've got! Our great King chose our nation and gives us victory again and again. Let the trumpets blast from God's throne room! He is more powerful than any army that could ever come against us.

48. "Praise God from his beautiful mountain! It is a place of joy and safety. When faraway kings tried to attack this mountain, we watched as they fled in fear. Your Temple is filled with your unending love for us and our admiration for you. With your justice comes a joy that covers our cities. Lead future generations to look at your mountain and know you'll be our guiding force forever.

49. "Whether you're rich, poor, big, or small, these wise words

are for you. Listen close. When enemies surround me, I don't need to be afraid. All the wealth in the world won't save me, but God can save me. When I die, my riches won't return me to life."

50. A man named Asaph writes "God shines from his radiant city, and his light reaches the whole world. Judgment Day will not be quiet or tame; God's voice will ring out like a furious storm. God doesn't need our gifts; the whole world belongs to him, and he has all the food he needs. But offerings are important because it reminds us to be grateful to God. Obey the law with a spirit of honesty so that you don't fall into company with thieves."

51. After Nathan confronts David about his adultery with Bathsheba, the humbled king writes "Let your mercy and love wash me clean of my faults. I am not a perfect man, and when I slept with another man's wife, I betrayed you. Make my heart sincere, honest, and wise, as pure as untouched snow. My fresh, clean heart will be filled with joy, and I will return to you with a humble and grateful spirit."

52. When an enemy reveals David's location to King Saul, David writes "Why do you brag about betraying me? Your lies cut me like razors, and you love to see me hurt. God will ruin you before you know it. People will see that you trust in your wealth over God, and you'll pay the price while I bask in God's good presence."

53. David writes "Corrupt fools refuse to believe that God exists. God looks at the world and only sees hearts that are far from him. Soon enough God will reveal himself to these thieves and unbelievers, and their bones will be scattered

while God's people prosper."

54. "Save me, and set me free, faithful Protector! Cruel, arrogant enemies are coming to get me, and you are my only defense.

55. "I hope you hear me, Father. Worry and fear batters me like a raging storm. I wish I could fly away and finally find rest from this mess. There are riots in the city and destruction everywhere. But I know I can call on you day or night, and you listen. I lay my troubles at your feet, and I trust in your shelter."

56. After being captured by the Philistines, David writes "Merciful God, these opponents are everywhere, and they never let up. When they sneak in the shadows and try to kill me, my trust in you calms my fear. You collect my tears and keep me safe in the warm light of your presence. No man can stop me with you on my side."

57. After escaping from Saul, David writes "Until the hurricane stops, I will snuggle under your merciful wings. Saul is like a lion that hungers for my flesh, but I feel your love as you provide for my needs every day. Your goodness stretches across the whole earth, and each morning I wake up to sing and dance about it!"

58. David writes "Rulers of the world don't know how to be fair or just to their people; they are only good at telling lies and committing crimes. These slimy snakes are full of poison, and I will happily watch as God blows them away like dust."

59. As Saul's men actively pursue David, he writes "Rescue me from these murderers, Lord! I haven't done anything to

deserve their sharp insults and snarling threats. Show the world how you feel about their prideful lies; scatter them, and show them no mercy. I will sing every morning about the shelter of my loving Father."

60. Just before a victory over 12,000 enemies, David instructs and inspires his men by saying "Lord, our land has been wounded and rejected by you. We are staggering around like drunks without you to guide us. Turn back to us and lead us today. Remind this enemy that you are a victorious God who defends and loves your people."

61. David cries out "I am depressed and homesick, Lord. Shelter me under your wings today and forever. Let me live a long, full life, and I will offer you songs of thanks every day.

62. "As I wait and hope for God's refuge, I know he is the only one I can depend on. These enemies happily tear me down, even though I'm too weak to fight back, but I trust God to help. No amount of wealth and deception can give these people the upper hand over the Lord; all our lives are like a puff of smoke to him."

63. From the harsh desert, David writes "My soul is like this dry wasteland in desperate need of your nourishing water. Your love satisfies my thirst like nothing else, and I can't stop clinging to your presence. Thank you so much for your abundant help! I'm obsessed with you!"

64. David sings "I'm scared, God! Bad people are hiding in the shadows trying to hunt me down; they spread lies to turn the nation against me. Strike them with your arrows, and make them as scared as I am.

65. "Lord, you forgive your chosen people and allow us into your sanctuary; let us be content and determined to keep our promises to you. The whole world stands in awe of the impossible things you've done, and we see how you tenderly nourish our land with sunshine and rain. Our fertile, blessed land shouts for joy!"

66. Let everyone praise our powerful God! He parted the sea to save our ancestors, and he has allowed us to survive countless tests. The whole world can see how glorious our God is. You strengthen us during times of trial, but you never allow the tests to break us. We offer you our best sacrifices and songs. Thank you for opening your ears to us.

67. God, bless us with your kindness and mercy. Let the world joyfully celebrate your justice and guidance.

68. David writes "God makes our enemies melt like wax and disappear like smoke. We joyfully worship as our God offers the homeless a place to stay and nourishes their parched land with rain. God carries our burdens and marches with our armies to rescue us. We can confidently sing and dance, even as we march toward the enemy. We know God will show them his power.

69. "Help, Lord! I'm drowning! I can't find my footing, and my throat hurts from calling out to you. It's hard to count the people who want me dead. I feel a great responsibility to handle their insults with dignity because when they mock me, they mock both of us. You love me, and I know you'll answer my prayer when the time is right. Their sharp words break my heart, and you are the only one who comforts me. I'm in so much pain that I want them to suffer and die

for what they've done. Along with the oppressed and all the creatures on earth, thank you from the bottom of my heart for looking out for us.

70. "Confuse and shame the people who want to kill me, and bless all the poor and weary souls who come to you. Save us, and make us happy!"

71. Good Father, you shield me from danger. I've trusted you my whole life, and you've never let me down. Others see how you've blessed me, and they are inspired. Now that I'm old, my enemies see me as vulnerable and plot against me, so now I need you more than ever. Stay close! Your goodness stretches across the sky, and I love to sing about it to anyone who will listen.

72. Solomon writes "Now that I'm king, help me rule this land with fairness and justice. Let me be a champion for those in need, and let me inspire the people to worship you forever. Let me nourish the land like rain and help it blossom. When other nations see our success, they will send lavish gifts and bow in respect. Bless our land and our people! Give me a long, healthy life, and let everyone see that my blessings come from you."

73. Asaph writes "I used to be jealous of the success of sinners, but now I know God is good to the good-hearted. It gets under my skin when I see arrogant men whose strong bodies hurt weaker people and whose words mock and manipulate. They act as though God can't see them, and it makes me feel like my good efforts are for nothing. I know they'll fall eventually. I can be angry and stupid sometimes, but I try to stay close to you. Your guidance makes me strong.

74. "Why are you hiding from your people, God? Will you be mad forever? Remember that you chose us long ago and rescued us from slavery. It makes me sick to see your enemies disgrace the holy Temple and smash all our sacred objects against the wall. You've been our King forever. You created the stars, the rivers, and the seasons. You crush sea monsters with your bare hands, and you can crush these enemies too. Stop letting them insult you. Remember to protect your people like you promised.

75. "Thank you for being amazing and doing such amazing things! One day you will judge the world, and every creature will tremble in reverence for you. Arrogant people with finally stop their boasting to see our praiseworthy God pour out his anger."

DAY THREE - SONGS OF HOPE
PSALMS 76-150

BIG IDEA

In the darkest chapters of life, our beautiful God still deserves our worship and trust.

SONG THEMES

- **No one is greater-** God is bigger and smarter than any of us, so we should honor his power and obey his commands. With him in our corner, we can't lose. False idols and prideful kings are no match for him.

- **Sometimes God feels silent-** In our darkest hours, it may be hard to hear God's voice. Just remember he forgives and loves us regardless of our circumstances.

- **Sing with happy gratitude-** God is impossibly beautiful and blesses us much more than we deserve, so we should worship him with passion and joy.

- **Life isn't fair-** The world is full of poverty and oppression, but in the end, our just God will make all things right. He loves even the tiniest sheep in his flock.

- **God will bring us home-** In this dark time of exile, we trust that the pain will end, and God will forgive us.

- **God's always with us-** He hears every prayer and sees every move we make. We can't hide anything from him. He knows us better than we know ourselves.

- **God's goodness is overwhelming-** God fills his creation with beauty and fills our lives with good things. He teaches us to lead a happy, fulfilling life that blesses others. He crushes all evil forces under his feet.
- **He delivered our ancestors-** God performed great miracles to rescue his children and punish their oppressors. He's more than able to deliver us again.

HOW GOD SHOWS UP

Even during the dark time of exile, God still reveals his love and beauty to those who love him. God reaches out to his hurting children, even when those children cannot see him through their pain. God has always delivered his chosen children, and they must trust that he will save them again when the time is right. He has never failed them yet, and he doesn't plan to start now. God is in control even when the world feels like it's spinning out. Just when we think all is lost, he picks us up and carries us home.

PSALMS PART 2

76. Asaph continues "Our famous, majestic God dwells in the mountaintops where he devastated enemy armies and made them useless. No one is worthy to stand in his presence or talk back to him. Humbly, we bring gifts to God and keep our promises to him.

77. "All night I cry to God, and I can't find relief. My worry

keeps me awake as I dwell on the past. Is God mad at us? Does he love our nation anymore? I hear about the miracles God did for our ancestors. He controlled the storms and parted seas to help the people he loved. He led the nation through the desert like a shepherd.

78. "Our ancestors taught us great mysteries about God, and I can't wait to pass this wisdom to the next generation. God gave us the law so we would learn to trust and obey him, teaching our children to do the same. As long as we hold up their end of the agreement, God hands us impressive victories. Even after God performed great miracles for our ancestors to protect and provide for them, they complained about the manna and rebelled against him. God unleashed his anger to get their attention and led them safely through the desert despite their many mistakes. They abandoned God for worthless idols, so God allowed their country to be overrun by war. After all that, God chose an unselfish shepherd named David to be our king and lead the flock of Israel back to God.

79. "Jerusalem has been devastated by heathen invaders. They killed our people, mocked us, and brought shame on our Temple. Will God punish us with his fiery anger forever and turn a blind eye to the ones who ruined us? God, forgive the many mistakes of our ancestors and us. Hear our pitiful groans, and set us free!

80. "Strong Shepherd, have mercy on your flock! How long will you ignore our sorrowful prayers and let our enemies hurl insults at us? You delivered us from Egypt and drove other nations out of our land long ago. Save us again! Come

down from your high throne to rescue us, and we'll never turn our back on you again.

81. "Let's sing a joyful song! Beat the tambourines and blast the trumpets at this moonlight celebration! God freed us from backbreaking oppression in Egypt. He put food in our mouths and saved us from countless storms. Despite his goodness, we have turned away from him. We're a stubborn people and insist on doing things our way.

82. "Great Judge, defend and rescue the helpless children who need you. Be fair to the poor because the corrupt, stupid world will never be fair to them. Our rulers will die just like everyone else, but they think they're gods and step on anyone smaller than them.

83. "God, this is not the time to stay silent! The people who hate you are plotting to destroy us, and they are forming alliances to come against us with greater force. Scatter them like dust, and quench the flames of their fury. Reveal your supreme power to them, and make them ashamed of themselves."

84. The musicians of Korah write "I want to be in God's house all day long because he makes me so happy. I sing to him with everything I have. I journey through nature to the holy mountain, getting stronger as I go. One day in God's shadow is better than a thousand days anywhere else. The Lord is so kind and good to those of us who trust him.

85. "God, you used to pardon our mistakes and rescue us from failure. Please make our nation strong again! Remember how much you love us, and let your anger subside. I hear your quiet promise that peace will come if we **stop return-**

ing to such foolishness. I can't wait for love, goodness, and loyalty to fill our land again."

86. King David prays "Master, I trust you. I am helpless to save myself. Forgive my mistakes, and make this humble servant happy again. The whole world should recognize that you are mighty and good like none other. Teach me to be more like you. Patient, kind Father, I love you with my whole heart. Thank you for loving me even more."

87. The clan of Korah sings "God looks with fondness on Jerusalem. It's a city that welcomes all nations that obey God, and he will strengthen its citizens as they dance in gratitude."

88. A Korahite named Hemen cries out "Open your ears to me, God! I have no strength left in my body, and I feel like I'm about to die, crushed beneath the weight of your anger. All my friends have left me, and there is no escaping this pain. If I die today, will your love pull me back to life? My life has been full of suffering, and you refuse to answer me. Why do you leave me in this darkness?"

89. Ethan the Ezrahite proclaims "God, I love to sing and shout about your unending love. Loyal to your people, you chose the great King David and his descendants to lead us. The angels sing that no one in heaven compares to you. You calm the most powerful waves, and we bask in the warmth of your tender kindness. You blessed victorious King David with power and strength that could only come from you. I'm sad to say that David's descendants did not follow in his obedient footsteps to earn your blessing. They failed you, and now you have allowed our enemies to disgrace

us. Don't hide from us any longer! Come back to us while I'm still alive to see it happen."

90. I want to pray like Moses prayed, since he was such a friend of God. He used to say "God, when I'm with you, I'm home. You made the world and will rule it forever. Our human lives are short, but centuries are like a day to you. You see every sin we try to hide, and we can't escape your fearsome presence. We deserve your anger, God, but fill us with your love and joy instead. As slaves, we were miserable and sad, but you have delivered us to happiness, freedom and success. Let us continue to witness your greatness!"

91. When you turn to God for shelter, never fear! You can trust him. Armies may fall dead around you, but you will be unharmed. If you love God, he will answer your prayers.

92. It feels good to sing in gratitude to you, Lord. I joyfully remember the great things you've done. I can't stop talking about your love and loyalty. You are wiser than anyone who has ever lived, and you destroy evil wherever you see it. Your people flourish and bear good fruit their entire lives.

93. Our majestic, strong King has been enthroned since before time began. He rules the vast sky and the roaring ocean. His way will always be the best way.

94. Our mighty Judge rises up against the wicked, arrogant people who delight in destroying the lives of others. Those fools think God can't see them, but he will unleash his anger on them soon enough. God offers peace and wisdom to those who want to learn from him. He calms their worries and never abandons them. He has no patience for courtroom corruption that condemns the innocent.

95. Let's sing a joyful song to thank our mighty God. He created the whole world and still cares for each tiny sheep in his flock. Don't be stubborn or test his patience by refusing to follow him. Obey him to discover a life of peace and rest.

96. Let the whole world sing the news that our glorious God has saved our lives! He created the heavens and is surrounded by indescribable power and beauty. Bow in respect before him, and offer him generous gifts. Let all of creation joyfully shout that our God is good!

97. The earth and islands happily acknowledge the King that rules from the clouds. He rules the world with fairness. Those who choose idols over him are burnt by his lightning and put to shame. God surrounds good-hearted people with happiness and light.

98. The powerful Lord has done wonderful things, and his victories are proclaimed throughout the world. He remains loyal to those he loves. Let the band make joyful music to our King! Let the sea roar and the river clap to join in the song.

99. Above the sky, our King watches over the whole earth. He loves it when goodness and fairness win, and he forgives us when we mess up. God spoke long ago to Moses, Aaron, and Samuel, and these common men became uncommon leaders because they bravely followed God's call.

100. Let the whole world sing a happy song to our Creator who chose us as his precious flock. God is good, and his love lasts forever!

101. David writes "Loyal and just Father, I promise to live a pure, honest life before you. I promise to surround myself with

authentic followers of God and rid my palace of corrupt liars and hypocrites."

102. A weary young person writes "Lord, answer my cry before it's too late. My body is withering away, and I can't eat or sleep. I'm unbearably lonely, and people insult me all day long. I feel like you've thrown me out like a piece of garbage. One day, you'll listen to the cries of your people and make yourself known to the world. Future generations will see you set prisoners free and will shout your good name from the highest mountain. Lord, I am dying in my youth, but please turn this around and let me live a long life. You made the world long ago, and you will live long after the earth disappears. You will protect your children forever."

103. David writes "My entire soul praises my kind, loving Lord. He forgives me, heals me, and makes my life overflow with good things. God cares deeply about the rights of the oppressed and lifts them up with his justice and love. His anger does not last, and he doesn't punish us nearly as much as we deserve. He forgives our many flaws and completely removes us from our old life of sin. People come and go, but his goodness lasts forever. The strongest angels in heaven obey him and declare him King."

104. God of creation, you are covered in majesty and light. You live above the clouds and in the wind. You placed the oceans and rivers over the earth, and the water goes where you tell it to go. You nourish the land with rain to allow our crops to grow. You made all the creatures, and we all depend on you. You put food in our bellies and air in our lungs. You look upon your beautiful creation with happiness as we

tremble before you and sing your praises.

105. Let God's people spread the good news of his blessings. Let us be glad we belong to him. He chose our ancestors and made a promise to that small family of wanderers. When famine struck the land, Joseph went from slavery to leadership in Egypt, allowing him to provide for his family. As the family grew, the Egyptian king condemned them to slavery, and God sent devastating plagues upon the land to force the pharaoh to release them. He fed them with bread from heaven in the desert, and the people sang for joy to celebrate their new freedom.

106. God is good, and we can't thank him enough for his love! God has rescued Israel many times, and the people never seem to truly understand or appreciate his wonders. They quickly forgot his miracles and chose to grumble about God's heavenly bread in the desert. They became jealous of humble Moses and abandoned God to serve lifeless idols. When God ushered them into the Promised Land, they immediately married into corrupt families and killed innocent children in idol worship. God was so rightfully angry and disgusted that he removed his protection from the land, and Israel was swarmed by enemies. Even then, God mercifully rescued his chosen children each time they cried out and turned back to him. Save our nation again, Lord, and bring us back home!

107. Our good God will love us forever. He has brought us back home from the nations where we were scattered. Some of us were hungry and homeless in the desert, and God helped us find our way to a city with plenty of food and

water. Some of us were enslaved and overworked, living in darkness where no one cared about our suffering. God broke our chains and ushered us into the light. Some of us were withering away with disease, and God healed our bodies. Some of us chose a life of adventure and sailed the dangerous seas, and God quieted the hurricanes that would have killed us. Our nation was humiliated and oppressed, but now God has brought life back to our land and rescued us from our misery.

108. David writes "I have total confidence in you, Lord. My soul wakes each day with a song to thank you for your love and faithfulness. With you on our side, no enemy can defeat us.

109. "Liars attack me for no reason, even though I used to think we were friends. I loved and prayed for them, and they repay my kindness with hatred. I want them to suffer for what they've done. I want them to lose everything they care about, and I hope God never forgets this betrayal. God, show them that you love me, and let them know their punishment comes from you.

110. "God told his chosen king all his enemies would be crushed underfoot. He promised men would come from all around to follow the king, and he would belong to the highest order of the priesthood. With God on our side, victory is certain."

111. I want everyone to hear how wonderful you are, Lord. I thank you with all my heart, and I want to better understand the goodness you bring to the world. You are a kind and merciful Provider. You set us free and make us wise with your foolproof way of life.

112. If you gladly follow God's way, you and your children will prosper. If you have a kind and forgiving heart, God will light your path. If you give generously to those in need, you will be blessed and respected in your community. Keep trusting God; you have no need to be afraid.

113. Let all God's servants around the world acknowledge his unmatched glory. He covers the whole world and still notices forgotten children, lifting them from the dust.

114. When our ancestors left Egypt, God marked us as his chosen nation. He parted the sea and revealed the mountains on the ocean floor. The earth trembles before the God that has the power to do the impossible.

115. God is the only one worthy of glory. Foreigners doubt the existence of our invisible God, but he is far more real than their lifeless idols that can't even see or hear. Israel can trust our God because he offers us protection and blessing. Let us praise him forever!

116. When I was afraid, I cried out to my compassionate God, and he rescued me right away. When I felt crushed by life and trusted no one, God wiped my tears away. He mourns alongside us when we lose someone we love. No words or gifts that I offer him could ever match his goodness to me.

117. Let the whole world hear that our loyal God loves us fiercely and forever.

118. Thank you, good Father, for your never-ending love. You set me free from worry as I learn to trust you over anyone else. I was surrounded by a swarm of enemies, but I destroyed them with you on my side. I want to shout my thanks for this victory. I felt worthless, and you made me strong. Today

is a happy day! God is good!

119. I love to follow God's rules for life, and he teaches me to do this better each day. The Lord has opened my eyes to the wise words that lead me to a great life. When I'm defeated by sin, he dusts me off and helps me do better next time. I know now why each law is important, which makes me unashamed to follow him. God's law offers me a life of joy, authenticity, and freedom like I've never known. I am passionate about doing the right thing because these laws come from the God who loves me. The unspeakably wise God gave me this blueprint for life as an act of kindness. When I mess up, he helps me accept the consequences. It's hard to wait, but I trust him to answer my prayers in his time. His timeless law has brought me joy and wisdom. These words light my way so that I don't fall into tempting traps. I don't need corrupt people in my life because God is my source of hope, strength, and safety. Lord, please notice my complete dedication to you, and rescue me from oppression. Your fair and good way is like water when I'm thirsty, and I follow it with my whole heart. Show me your mercy, compassion, and unshakable love; save me from those who are trying to kill me! They are attacking me unfairly, but your words bring be happiness, gratitude, and a sense of security. Save my life, so I can live for you even more fully.

120. I hate living near the liars who are always starting fights. I can't wait to see how God will punish them.

121. I look up and know that the Creator of the world is always paying attention. He will not let me fall, and I am safe in his hands.

122. David writes "Jerusalem is a beautifully restored place where we can come together and harmoniously give thanks to God. May this city and its people be filled with peace, prosperity, and safety."

123. Merciful Master, we look up to your home in the sky and hope you will deliver us from all this oppression and scorn.

124. David writes "If God wasn't on our side, we would have been swallowed up by now, washed away in flood waters. But thanks to our God, we are free!"

125. God's trustworthy protection surrounds us like a sturdy wall of mountains. He is good to us, and when the wicked are knocked from their thrones, we will not be shaken.

126. Coming back from exile was like a dream come true! We sang for joy, and nations around us saw your blessing on our lives. Let our land become lush and prosperous again!

127. Solomon writes "If God was not watching over us in our sleep, all our efforts to build strong houses and high city walls would do no good. If God blesses a man with many children, they will defend him when he is old and vulnerable."

128. If you obey God and work hard alongside your spouse, your children and household will bear wonderful fruit, and you will live to see your grandchildren.

129. Ever since the early days of Israel, our enemies enslaved us and cruelly lashed our backs in the fields. May those who try to tear us down today wither away like weeds.

130. Lord, listen to my prayers in this dark hour. No one can escape your judgment, so let your forgiveness make us

stand in awe of you. I trust in your love and wait patiently for your rescue.

131. David writes "With a quiet heart and humble spirit, I am content to rest in my Father's trustworthy arms."

132. God, remember the hard times David went through, and remember his desire to build a Temple for you. Let your power fill this Temple, and remember your promise to bless the dynasty of David. Provide for the poor people in this city, and bless the work of our priests.

133. David writes "It is a beautiful thing to see God's people getting along harmoniously and receiving his gift of never-ending life."

134. Let all the Temple workers lift their hands to worship the Creator and accept his blessing.

135. Sing in admiration to our kind, good Creator who chose us to be his children. Unlike dead idols, he miraculously toppled great kingdoms to pave the way for Israel to rise up. Let all generations praise the God of Israel, and may idol worshippers become as lifeless as the statues they serve.

136. The Lord's love shows up through the beauty of the moon, stars, and ocean he created. It shows up through the great miracles he performed to deliver the people from Egypt. God's love could be seen in the desert and in his conquering of the Promised Land. God hasn't forgotten his people and still provides for them each day. He deserves all our gratitude.

137. Here in Babylon, we appease our captors by singing a song about the great city they stole from us. It is too painful to

sing when I am so homesick! May I never forget the joy you brought me in Jerusalem. God, make them suffer like they've made us suffer!

138. David writes "I bow down and worship you with all my heart. You answer my prayers and make me strong. You love me more than I can imagine, and you care for the forgotten people in this land. Proud kings can't hide from you and will acknowledge you in the end.

139. "Father, you know me deeper than I know myself, and you hear my words before I open my mouth. You follow me wherever I go, and even the darkest night couldn't hide me from your eyes. You designed me in secret as I grew in my mother's womb, and you know the exact moment I will leave this earth. God, help me be more like you, loving what you love and hating what you hate.

140. "Those violent troublemakers are always stirring things up with their venomous words. Shield me from their traps and bloodlust. You are my strong Defender, and you protect the rights of the vulnerable. I know you hear me. Please let these bullies be destroyed by people just as evil as them.

141. "God, look with fondness upon my sweet words of worship to you. Help me hold my tongue around deceptive people who try to woo and suck up to me. Help me avoid their sneaky traps unscathed, and make them fall into those traps themselves.

142. "I call to God from this cave and pour out my troubled heart to him. He knows how to guide me out of this mess. My enemies lay traps for me, and no one cares for me except

the good Protector who sets me free.

143. "God, I know no human being is innocent in your eyes, but take pity on me anyway. My enemies surrounded me and put me in a dark prison cell, and now I just want to die. I try to remember the days when you blessed me, and my dry soul is thirsty to feel you again. Give me hope, and help me want to live again. I trust you to guide me forward and rescue me like you promised."

144. "My General trains me for battle and shields me from nations around me. I'm so humbled that our overwhelmingly big God takes the time to notice mere humans like us. He could tear apart the sky if he wanted to. I know he can also save me from drowning in this fight. I will sing about how he saved me from these liars. May our children grow up strong, and may our farms prosper in God's country!

145. "My whole life I will thank my impossibly majestic God for his miracles. Our loyal Father looks upon his children with kindness, compassion, and mercy; his anger with us never lasts long. Let all living things acknowledge God's power and trust him to satisfy their needs."

146. I cannot trust mortal leaders who will return to dust, but I will sing to the Creator throughout my entire life. He feeds the poor, frees the prisoner, and stands up for the rights of the oppressed. We can depend on him.

147. It feels right to worship the One who heals our wounds and brings us home from exile. He named each of the stars, and he is wiser and bigger than we could ever understand. Let us make beautiful music for the God who nourishes our crops and animals. It makes God happy when we worship

and trust him. When he speaks, anything can happen.

148. Let the angel armies, the stars in the sky, the great forests, and all the animals praise the One that made them! The terrifying sharks and powerful tornadoes yield to him. Let everyone from the greatest king to the smallest child praise the God whose glory cannot be matched.

149. Let everyone in Israel dance and sing all night to God. He gave us a good king and leads our armies to put other nations to shame.

150. Let all creatures sing in admiration to our strong, supreme God who has done amazing things! Let's praise him with our loudest trumpets and drums!

DAY FOUR - FATHERLY ADVICE
PROVERBS

BIG IDEA

The wisest king in history offers excellent advice to his son and successor.

SOLOMON'S LESSONS

- **Choose your friends wisely-** Wicked advisors could tempt you to fall into corruption and could lead your kingdom into disaster.

- **Be a humble learner-** God is much smarter than you, and your mother and I have lived longer than you. Listen to our advice, and don't be afraid to admit when you're wrong. Pride prevents learning and growth.

- **Treat others well-** Lead your people with justice and respect. Work to improve the lives of others and rid the nation of oppression. Tell the truth, use kind words, and give generously.

- **Lust could destroy you-** This selfish path will cause your household to crumble. Choose a good-hearted spouse, and stay loyal to her.

- **Work hard-** Diligently provide for your family, and never let enemies catch you unprepared or complacent.

- **Money and power don't last-** God will teach you to value your character and relationships above any earthly possessions.

- **Slow down-** Take a deep breath, and think before you act. Hurry leads to mistakes, and impatience leads to anger.
- **Discipline your kids-** Give them clear boundaries, and teach them to be safe, respectful members of society.

HOW GOD SHOWS UP

When we remain close to God's heart, he blesses us with wisdom and shows us how to live. The loving Father shows Solomon and us how to enjoy a happy, full life by surrounding ourselves with good people and treating them well. He teaches us that a strong family means much more than power or wealth. God created our complex brains with a desire and ability to learn new things, and we must remain humble and patient so that we can soak up each lesson God places in our path.

PROVERBS

1. King Solomon writes "I hope that all readers young and old find value in this book of wisdom. I hope even the wisest among you find nuggets of insight here. To my dear son, I hope you will always be willing to learn from God, your mother, and myself. Stay away from thieves and murderers who may try to tempt you to join their ranks. Those fools refuse to listen to the God-given wisdom that calls out to them, and I will laugh when they fall into the traps they lay for others.

2. "God's wisdom is like priceless treasure that you should seek with all your heart. God can teach you how to treat others fairly and how to keep yourself out of trouble. Find pleasure in doing the right thing instead of falling for the smooth talk of seductive women.

3. "Son, if you stay loyal to God and people, you will be highly favored by them. Remember that our Creator is much smarter than you; trust his wisdom more than your own. When he corrects you, allow his advice to bring you healing, happiness, security, and new life. Take every opportunity to do good for people in need, and don't be jealous of people who disgrace themselves with violence and arrogance.

4. "When I was a boy, my dad taught me how to live a good life, and now I pass that insight on to you. Don't forget it! Take these words seriously, and nothing will stand in your way! Let this truth light up your path and guide you toward greater clarity. Walk straight ahead, and don't turn toward dark lies or negative patterns of thought.

5. "Another man's wife may tempt you with sweet, smooth kisses, but nothing good will come from cheating on your wife. This stupid, selfish path can only lead to pain and destruction. God is always watching, so don't let this temptation ensnare you! Find joy and contentment with the woman you married.

6. "Don't make promises that you don't intend to keep. If you remain indebted to others, you trap yourself in a spirit of restlessness. Be like the ant who avoids poverty by working hard all summer to save up for the hard winter. God can't stand those who stir up trouble through deception,

arrogance, and hurting innocent people. My son, keep my advice close to your heart, and know that it's for your own good. If you fall for the seductive beauty or flirtatious glance of another man's wife, this is like playing with fire; you will get burned.

7. "Son, respect this advice as your closest friend for it can keep you safe. One day, I noticed a bold, shameless woman throwing her arms around every man she saw. She said her husband was away on business, and my neighbor followed her to bed like a sheep walking into the slaughterhouse. If you fall for a woman who has ruined many men like this, you are asking for trouble.

8. "Wisdom is like a good, confident woman who speaks her priceless common sense to anyone who is willing to listen. She advises kings to govern well and leads men to prosperity. God created Wisdom before the birth of the earth and ocean, and she was his daily source of inspiration and joy. Listening to her will lead to a happy life and God's favor.

9. "Wisdom has built a strong house for herself and invites all in need of knowledge to feast at her table. Conceited people wrinkle their noses at her good food, while wise people happily gobble it up, knowing her nourishment can add years to their lives. Stupidity calls out to fools to eat her poisonous meal of stolen bread and water, and everyone who enters her house of lies will die.

10. "Make your mother and me proud by staying honest and working hard. If you do, God will protect you, and others will remember you fondly. Telling the truth when it's hard can guide others toward peace and new life, but when you

don't have anything kind or worthwhile to say, stay quiet. Forgive the sins of others and admit when you're wrong. If you take pleasure in doing the right thing, God will help you weather the storms of life while the wicked are blown away.

11. "God hates it when greedy people try to get ahead through deception and arrogance. Worldly wealth will do you no good on your death bed. Avoid spreading lies or talking badly about others, or no one will trust you. Let honesty, humility, and kindness guide your decisions. True beauty is seen in graciousness and good judgment. Instead of clinging to your wealth, practice generous giving, and trust God to take care of you.

12. "Accept corrective advice when it comes your way, knowing that evil thoughts serve only to endanger you, separate you from God, and alienate you from others. Be careful when choosing a spouse; a good-hearted wife could be your pride and joy. Surround yourself with honest people who treat you fairly. Work hard, and remain kind to your animals, so your land will yield plenty of food. Ignore insults that come your way, and know that eventually, justice will prevail, and the truth will come out. Words can hurt, so be thoughtful about what you say. Wringing your hands in worry can steal your joy and will do you no good.

13. "Think before you speak, and humbly admit when you are wrong. Teach your kids to accept correction too; loving discipline can help them navigate the world. Work hard for what you want, joyfully tell the truth, and protect the innocent. Don't be fooled by broke people who pretend they are rich; money and status will not last. People of

good character are like bright lights shining in this world, while arrogant, ignorant people bring ruin upon themselves. Wisdom leads to a full life of sound decisions and admiration from others. Be someone that others see as peaceful and trustworthy, and surround yourself with other wise people. Make the most of your land and resources, and you'll have plenty to leave your grandchildren.

14. "Good homes usually have wise, capable women at the helm, so be careful who you choose as a partner. Use humble, honest words that have the power to honor God, strengthen relationships, and enrich lives. Stay away from prideful fools who talk too much and think they know everything; they don't take their sins seriously. Watch your step, and don't rush into traps that appear correct on the surface. If you let anger or impatience lead you into foolishness, you will get what's coming to you. Be kind to poor people, and work for the good of the marginalized. They are God's children just like you.

15. "Gentle, friendly words diffuse anger, while careless, cruel words start fights and crush spirits. God knows all your thoughts and actions, so don't sit contently in ignorance. Be willing to learn from your elders, work hard, and always tell the truth. Relationships with God and others are far more valuable than feasts and luxuries. Respect your mom, and make us proud. Walk the road that leads to a full life under God's protection.

16. "Despite our endless lists and visions, only God knows how our future will unfold. He blesses our plans only if our motives are good and humble. Patience and self-control

will serve you better than earthly power. Do your best to follow God's way, and he'll forgive you when you mess up. Maintain honest business practices to stay out of legal trouble, and remember to give God credit for your success. Speak sweet, pleasant words that benefit others, and don't destroy relationships and reputations with poisonous gossip. Don't fall for the deception and false friendship of troublemakers.

17. "Integrity and peace of mind are tastier than the greatest feast. Let God's tests burn impurities from your heart and make it as beautiful as gold. Never take pleasure in the pain or misfortune of others; instead, treat all of God's children with respect, honesty, and forgiveness. Learn from your mistakes, and don't repay evil with evil. Stop the vicious cycle of hate before it gets too far. Let justice and common sense prevail. Bragging and planning harm toward others lead to nothing worthwhile. Raise wise, good-hearted children you can be proud of, and listen more than you speak. Remember that gratitude and laughter will keep your mind and body healthy.

18. "It's hard for selfish fools to keep friends or earn respect from others; they're always starting arguments and falling into their own traps. Be willing to ask questions and absorb the wisdom that flows your way. Listen to the perspective of others before you respond, and know that your words have consequences. Don't fall for the temporary satisfaction of destructive habits like gossip or laziness. God's protection offers greater security than wealth. If you have a great spouse and loyal friends, thank God for this blessing.

19. "Patiently educate yourself before you get excited about a new venture; if it doesn't work out, it's not God's fault. If you sleep through the workday, don't expect to get paid. Don't be fooled by fake friends who hunger for your money or power. Control your temper, and ignore people who try to get under your skin. If your friend throws a tantrum, don't bail him out of the opportunity to learn from it. Stop harmful dynamics in your family before it's too late; don't tolerate a spouse who constantly spouts negativity or children who insist on destroying themselves with foolish choices. God will smile on obedient followers who show kindness to the oppressed, but he can't stand greedy people who mistreat their parents. Regardless of our detailed agendas, God's plan will prevail.

20. "Don't start arguments or allow drunkenness to lead you toward loud foolishness. Raise good-hearted children, and work hard to feed them each day. Instead of bragging about your loyalty or honesty, prove it by your actions. Have a stable plan and solid advice from your support system before charging into battle. Don't share secrets, or you will be seen as an untrustworthy gossip. Honor your parents, and trust God to right their wrongs. We cannot hide from the God who determines our path, so if you make a promise to him, be sure to see it through. Sometimes the Lord allows obstacles into our path to change us for the better.

21. "God recognizes your true motives and sees through the walls of your house, so maintain an attitude of fairness, goodness, humility, patience, and honesty. Make pleasing God your highest priority. Stay away from crooked paths, nagging wives, and people who enjoy hurting others. Listen

to the cry of the poor if you expect your cries to be heard. If you speak kindly and fairly to others, they will respect you in return. Diffuse the anger of those who dislike you, and don't be arrogant or inconsiderate. Don't squander your wealth on meaningless luxuries, but instead find true joy by giving generously to those in need.

22. "Your reputation means more than your wealth, so avoid traps and temptations when you see them coming. Humbly obey God, and teach your children to do the same. Don't borrow money, or you will be bound and obligated to your lender. Don't oppress those less fortunate than you, but be generous to the poor. Earn influence through pure motives and graceful words. Trust God, and remember these wise nuggets of advice. If you take advantage of a poor man in court, God will defend him. If you befriend a violent, hot-tempered person, you may pick up his bad habits. If you promise to pay someone else's debts, you endanger your own household. Don't take more than your share of land, and strive for uncommon excellence in your work.

23. "Put your most dignified foot forward when dining with people of influence, but don't wear yourself out trying to get rich. You can't take it with you. Don't take advantage of vulnerable people because God will defend them. Learn all you can, but don't waste time trying to teach people who are unwilling to learn. Don't be afraid to discipline your kids; healthy boundaries will shape them into good people. Son, make your mother and I proud by taking these priceless instructions to heart, and show us a little gratitude for bringing you into the world. Follow my example, and stay away from women who tempt you to cheat on your wife.

Love God more than imperfect people. Don't surround yourself with lazy, selfish drunks who gripe all day and refuse to be responsible. Alcohol is tempting, but a bad hangover will jump up and bite you like a snake.

24. "There's no need to be jealous of lying troublemakers whose actions lead to a lonely, meaningless life; stay away from them. Build your house on a foundation of truth and common sense, which is like honey for the soul. If you have the reputation of a troublemaking fool, no one will want to be around you, but intelligent planning will bring you countless victories. Stay strong in the face of crisis, and bravely rescue people who are facing injustice. If you tell the truth, you'll be able to get up when you fall. Don't take joy in the failures of others, and above all, respect God and your elders. Let judges treat defendants without prejudice, and let courtroom witnesses avoid lying for the sake of revenge. Let friends be honest with each other, and let God's people live debt free.

25. "If a king keeps corrupt advisers out of his cabinet, his reign will be as pure and beautiful as gold. Humble yourself before the king, so you don't embarrass yourself. Don't accuse your neighbor in court unless you're absolutely sure he's guilty, and settle your differences outside the courtroom when possible. Let your carefully chosen words help those who are willing to learn from you. A truthful messenger is uncommonly refreshing, and people who break promises are as worthless as storm clouds that refuse to rain. Don't engorge yourself with sweets, and don't overstay your welcome in a friend's home; too much of a good thing will make you sick. Don't surround yourself with people

who gossip or nag, and remember that lazy, irresponsible people are worthless in a crisis. Disarm your enemies with kindness, and when a friend is hurting, don't rub salt in their wound by being overly happy and insensitive.

26. "Don't bother giving fools false praise or trust them with important tasks. There's no point in teaching people who refuse to learn. Don't listen to untrue insults that come your way, and don't be one of those lazy people who refuse to get out of bed or feed themselves. I don't understand why they're so afraid to try. People who involve themselves in other people's arguments or lie to someone as a joke are asking to be punched. Many arguments could be stopped if troublemakers stopped spreading lies. Hypocrites insincerely flatter people they don't like, but their traps and hateful motives will be uncovered in the end.

27. "You never know what tomorrow will bring, so don't brag about what hasn't yet happened. In fact, don't brag at all, but accept compliments from others. Anger and jealousy destroy relationships. A true friend may risk hurting your feelings to help you make a positive change, but don't fall for the false flattery that drips sweetly from your enemy's lips. Lean on your genuine friends when you're in trouble, and try to avoid obstacles when you see them approaching. Be careful who you marry; a nagging, belittling wife will frustrate you with her endless complaints. Good people make each other better, and loyal employees bring honor to their boss.

28. "If you are honest in all situations, you have nothing to hide. If we want our nation to last, we must have wise leaders

who open their eyes to the pain of the poor and treat them with dignity. Good leaders cause us to celebrate and live fearlessly. Sometimes, wealthy people think they know it all, but poor people have stronger character from enduring more of life's tests. God sees who you really are, so stop trying to hide from him; God will forgive your mistakes and reward your innocence. Lying and violence lead to disaster, and selfish people who trust themselves more than God will be humbled.

29. "Don't stubbornly refuse good advice, but accept it as it comes. Be a good king who helps lower crime rates and leads your people toward happier lives; value justice above personal gain, and don't worry about what anyone thinks of you. Don't waste your money or your integrity on prostitutes; this cycle of sin is hard to escape. Let your heart value the rights of the poor, and protect innocent, honest people who need help. Patiently hold back your anger to outsmart your enemies. Set healthy boundaries for your kids and servants. Think before you speak, and remember that a humble attitude will help others respect you."

30. A humble man named Agur writes "Lord, I am helpless, and you feel silent. I don't even feel human right now, and I feel like I know nothing. You hold the wind and waves in your hand and protect those who come to you. You keep your promises and reveal liars for who they are, so keep my heart honest. Bless me with enough wealth to meet my needs, but don't make me so successful that I forget about you. I promise to never dishonor my parents or take advantage of vulnerable people. When I see a flying eagle, a majestic king, a powerful lion, or two people falling

in love, it's hard for me to comprehend your mysterious, beautiful creation. When I see a formation of hard-working ants or unified locusts, I see that there's beauty and order within even your tiniest details."

31. The mother of King Lemuel writes "Dear son, don't waste your money and energy on lust; shallow relationships have ruined many great men before you. Don't let alcohol cloud your judgment or make you ignore the people you are responsible for. Speak up for people whose voices aren't easily heard, and protect their rights. When you decide to seek a wife, know that a worthy partner will be hard to find but well worth the wait. She will earn your confidence and work hard all day to benefit your household. She will be wise with money and generous to the poor. She will take care of her family's needs and become a respected leader in the community. You will love and appreciate her, and your children will respect her."

DAY FIVE - ALL THAT MATTERS
ECCLESIASTES-SONG OF SONGS

BIG IDEA

Even if you have all the wealth and fame in the world, it means nothing without love.

SOLOMON'S VULNERABLE TRUTHS

- **I can't do it all-** Solomon is the richest and most influential king ever. He longs to spark lasting change and end the world's injustices, but he can't do anything worthwhile without God.
- **Shallow pleasures fade-** Money can buy tasty food and beautiful luxuries that satisfy us temporarily, but that kind of happiness is empty and meaningless.
- **God knows the future-** We don't know how life will unfold, but God can predict every detail. We must trust in his plans and his timing.
- **Self-care is essential-** Don't be a workaholic who wastes your life chasing money or power. Choose work you love, and take days off to enjoy your blessings. You can't take a single cent into the grave.
- **Struggle strengthens-** If your life revolves around fun, you learn nothing. If you experience challenge and struggle, your character has a chance to grow.
- **Bad things happen-** You can try to prepare for struggle,

but you cannot avoid it completely. Don't place your hope in earthly things that fade, but trust the God that never fades.

- **Love is beautiful-** God created us to worship him fully and love each other fearlessly. God smiles when two people find joy in each other, depend on each other completely, and spend their whole lives making each other better.

HOW GOD SHOWS UP

Life is complicated, but God is always good and always bigger than our problems. We may get distracted by work responsibilities and financial stresses, but God longs for us to take a step back and focus on him. He knows that if we remind ourselves that worship and love are the only worthwhile things in this world, we will save ourselves a great deal of heartache. God wants us to be happy, and he rejoices with us when we find someone to love and share life with.

ECCLESIASTES

1. King Solomon writes "We work diligently our entire lives, and what's the point? Days and generations pass, and history keeps repeating itself. The wind still blows, and the rivers still flow into the ocean. No matter how much I see and hear in this life, I'm not truly satisfied. In all my searching and studying about the ways of the world, so many ventures seem futile and impossible. God has granted me with unmatched wisdom, but the more I learn, the more

I worry and hurt for the human race.

2. "I searched for happiness but came up disappointed. I tried to enjoy partying and wine, but that didn't satisfy me. According to the world's standards, I am as successful and wealthy as they come. I have built beautiful houses, planted massive gardens, and hired numerous employees, but none of that really matters. I can't take it with me when I die. My sons will inherit my wealth, and they might blow it all. I have toiled my life away, and it has only brought me worry and weariness. All I can do is enjoy the food and happiness that God gives me today, and I should do my best to please him. No other goal has any meaning.

3. "God orchestrates the timing of everything. He determines when we're born, when we die, when we fight, and when we work for peace. There are sad times of loss and joyous times of healing. There are quiet times and noisy times. We long to know our future, but God hides the answers from us until the time is right. All we can do is enjoy today while we are still alive and stand in awe of God's unchangeable plan. God will judge those who bring injustice into his perfect creation. God humbles and tests us to remind us that we are mere mortals who will return to the dust.

4. "I look at all the injustice and oppression in this world, and no one ever makes it better. It disgusts me and makes me wish I were dead. I see families toiling to become richer than their neighbors, and I see lonely workaholics with no family or contentment. This is a futile, miserable way to live. There is strength in numbers, so don't go through life without a support system. No matter how rich a man gets,

he is a worthless fool if he becomes too proud to accept advice.

5. "Think before you pray, quiet your worried mind, and don't fill silence with foolish words and rash promises to God. No matter what you accomplish in your work, your most important task is to stand in awe of your Creator. Lovers of money will never be satisfied because more wealth means more responsibilities and worries. Workaholics sometimes lose it all before having a chance to pass it on to their children. You can't take a single cent into the grave, so just enjoy the short life you've been given, and try not to worry about things that don't matter.

6. "God blesses some men with vast riches, many children, and long lives, but many of them never take time to rest and enjoy it. Be satisfied and content with what you have, or no lavish blessings will ever be enough for you. Arguments and power struggles are meaningless; God has already determined the plan.

7. "I prefer funerals to weddings because they remind me that life is short. Sadness may feel unpleasant, but it can lead to deeper understanding. Instead of partying my life away, I will work daily toward wisdom, integrity, honesty, and patience. Let's keep our temper in check, and don't grumble longingly for the "good old days". There's no going back, so stop dwelling on the past. God knows what will happen next, but we can only guess. Bad things happen to good people, and wicked people succeed sometimes. This is discouraging, but I will pursue wisdom anyway. In my search for knowledge, I learned that it is a painful, bitter

experience to be trapped by a seductive, untrustworthy woman. Don't beat yourself up for mistakes, and ignore insults that come your way.

8. "Wisdom brings a smile to my face and clarity to my spirit. I won't make thoughtless promises to God or disrespect the laws of our nation's king. I mourn to see wicked people praised at their funerals and poor people oppressed by the powerful. Sinners get away with crimes left and right. All we can do is take care of ourselves and try to find happiness each day. There's no point trying to determine the future; God is smarter than the wisest man on earth, and his plan will remain a mystery.

9. "No one knows what lies ahead, and we all die eventually whether we follow God or not. Find passion in your work and relationships. Don't put it off until tomorrow because tomorrow may never come. The good don't always win, and bad luck happens when we least expect it. When you are surrounded, quiet wisdom will serve you better than strength or riches.

10. "Wise people do their best to make the world better, but one fool can undo a great deal of good. If your boss gets mad at you, don't panic or quit right away. Stay calm, and solve the problem. Some fools have been put in a position of authority, and it's not fair. Work hard to meet your needs, but don't wear yourself out in the process. Save some energy to enjoy life. Speak only words of respect for your leaders so that you stay in their good graces.

11. "You never know what the future will hold, so diversify your investments and don't let unanswered questions

paralyze you into a state of inaction. Maintain a grateful attitude about these pleasant, youthful days, and don't waste precious time worrying about circumstances you cannot control or understand.

12. "One day your mind will become cynical, and your body will lose many of its strengths and abilities; enjoy your youth while it lasts. When we die, our bodies will return to dust, and our breath will return to the God that put air in our lungs. These words may seem brutally honest, but they will guide you toward the right path like a sharp stick guides a flock of sheep. Son, above all, remember that you were made to obey and worship God, and he will judge the dedication of your heart.

SONG OF SONGS

1. A woman says to her lover "Your kisses cover me, and I can't forget your intoxicating fragrance. Let's run away and lose ourselves in each other's arms. Women adore you, and I'm afraid you won't think I'm as pretty as them. My skin is dark and leathered from working in the sun, so I have no time to keep up my appearance. I want to know where you and your sheep will be today, so I can keep my eye out for you." The man responds "Lovely lady, I hope you will follow my sheep so that we can spend time together. Your beautiful hair falls softly around your face, and you deserve the finest jewelry around your gorgeous neck. Your eyes sparkle with love."

2.   The woman declares "To me, you are more special than any other man, like a lush apple tree in a forest of ordinary trees. I love to sit in your shade and eat your sweet fruit that strengthens and nourishes me. I am weak from passion as you caress me, and I hope we won't be interrupted." The man responds "You are like a beautiful flower among thorny women. Come with me into the beautiful spring weather. Let me admire your beautiful face as you admire the blooming flowers and singing birds." The woman sings "We belong together. When you leave me early in the morning to feed the flocks, I can't wait for you to hurry back to me.

3.   "I dream every night that I'm searching the streets and houses for my sweetheart, and I finally find him in my mother's house. He is already like family to me; let no one interrupt our love. I see King Solomon parading down the street with his impressive throne and battle-hardened soldiers. All the women come out to see the king and his beautiful crown."

4.   The man says "I can't take my eyes off you, my love. Your eyes shine, your hair dances in the wind, and your perfect teeth sparkle. When you speak, I can't stop looking at your soft, red lips and your glowing cheeks. Your smooth tower of a neck leads down to your fragrant twin breasts. As you descend from the mountain with me, my bride, your glance steals my heart and delights me. You are like my own private garden filled with the most intoxicating fragrances and the most luscious fruits." The woman replies "Sweet love, come enjoy the fruits and fragrances of your garden."

5.   The man enjoys his sweet bride and gets drunk with love.

The woman says "I dreamt that my love knocked on the door while I was comfortably in bed. My heart leapt as he drew near to my room, but then he disappeared. I couldn't find him anywhere and longed to hear his voice. The other women didn't understand what made my lover so special so I told them that his bronze body and wavy hair are as handsome as they come. His shining eyes and luscious lips draw me in, and his strong hands and legs protect me. He enchants me like no other.

6. "The women of town try to help me find my sweetheart, and we find him feeding his flock in a meadow of flowers." When she finds her husband, he shouts "I'm over here, breathtaking love. Your eyes and dancing hair captivate me. You are beloved by your mother and praised among women. Your glance is as beautiful and bright as the dawn. As I notice new blossoms on the trees of your garden, I tremble in anticipation for your touch, watching you dance in the street.

7. "You are the best woman in the world! Every curve of your body is like a work of art. Every detail of your face charms me and draws me in. You are so beautiful! Your love delights and completes me. I can't wait to taste your sweet breath again." The bride responds "Let sweet wine flow from my mouth to yours. I am yours, and I am delighted that you want me. Let's spend the night in the country and wake up early to admire the growing vines and blooming pomegranate trees.

8. "Sweet husband, you feel like family to me, and I wish I had known you my whole life so that we could have learned to

love each other even sooner. As the villagers see us emerge from our hiding place under the apple tree, we walk proudly hand in hand. No flood could drown the passionate fire of our love. No other woman could ever turn your love away from me. I am content and safe in your arms." The man responds "I just bought a vineyard of my own, and I long to share that land with you. I long to share my life with you and make you a part of my family forever."

WEEK THREE REFLECTION

Wisdom

DISCUSSION QUESTIONS

- Early in my faith walk, I spent a lot of time wondering why God allows bad things to happen to good people. Maybe you have too. After reading the story of Job, what new thoughts and perspectives have you gained regarding this difficult topic? Where do you notice God's love in this story despite the tragedies that occur in Job's life?

- Have you ever experienced a difficult season that allows you to relate to Job in some way? Are you still in the middle of that storm, or has it mostly passed? Did God or your support people assist you in getting to the other side of that obstacle? Did you gain new wisdom or strength despite that time of struggle?

- David played the harp and wrote many of the songs recorded in the first half of Psalms. How do you suppose David's love for music helped him as a king and as a person? How has music helped or enriched your life in some way? What is your favorite song, artist, or musical genre, and why?

- What do you learn about David's heart from the music and poetry he writes? What do you learn about Asaph and the people of Korah from their songs?

- If Solomon's son only learns five lessons from the book of Proverbs, what do you think Solomon would want those lessons to be?

- What does the book of Ecclesiastes say about the satisfaction worldly wealth can offer? According to this book, how might a person find true happiness?
- What are the most beautiful qualities of the relationship described in Song of Songs? How does this book mirror God's love for us?

MUSIC MEDITATIONS

- **Job-** Consider the wisdom and comfort this hurting man may have found within a song like "Praise You in This Storm" by Casting Crowns.
- **Psalms-** Listen to "Your Name" by Paul Baloche to inspire yourself to worship with the authentic emotion and passionate reverence found throughout this great songbook.
- **Proverbs-** Listen to "It's Your Life" by Francesca Battistelli, and think about any positive changes you'd like to make in your own life based on Solomon's wisdom.
- **Ecclesiastes-** Listen to "More to Life" by Stacie Orrico, and explore the idea that God's priorities and guidance matter more than temporary, earthly pleasures.
- **Song of Songs-** Listen to "When I Say I Do" by Matthew West. Reflect on how your own relationship or potential future marriage might reflect the beautiful love and intimacy God designed us to experience.

APPLICATION IDEAS

- Identify a person in your life who seems to be experiencing great pain or difficulty like Job. Find the courage to reach out to that hurting person and comfort him or her through your words or actions. Sometimes just bringing a meal, offering to babysit, or letting a person rant can be just what he or she needs to feel less alone.

- Choose a few psalms that you relate to the most. Try to combine the spirit of these songs with your own experience, and write your own heartfelt song to God. It doesn't have to be perfect, but it needs to be genuine.

- Make a list of the most critical lessons that stand out to you in Proverbs and Ecclesiastes. Rate yourself on a scale from 1 to 10 regarding how consistently you apply each of these lessons to your life. If you see that you're already doing well in an area, pinpoint the helpful habits that could help you stay on the right track in that area. If you're struggling with one or several of the lessons, make a list of some action steps and support people that could help you make small, manageable changes in those areas.

- If you are married or in a relationship, let Song of Songs inspire your next date night. Talk to your significant other about the sort of attitude each of you should have during this date. Remain focused and fascinated by the other person throughout your time together. No looking at your phones during dinner.

WEEK FOUR

Prophecy

ISAIAH-MALACHI

DAY ONE - IGNORING HIS GLORY
ISAIAH

BIG IDEA

When Isaiah warns the prideful people of Israel to turn around, they choose to stay lost and set themselves up for disaster.

WHY JUDGMENT IS NECESSARY

- **Plenty of Warnings-** God longs to bless his people and change their hearts, but they blatantly ignore his miracles and prophets. Perhaps a loss of wealth and security could humble them and remind them what's truly important.

- **Self-Destruction-** God loves his children too much to let them permanently disrespect their bodies and disregard their spirits. The coming time of judgment may interrupt their harmful habits and wake them up.

- **Worshiping Idols-** God made the universe and every person in it, but Israel chooses to openly disrespect God and trust false gods of their own making.

- **Oppressing Others-** The Hebrews steal from the poor, bully those who are already hurting, and kill innocent people out of self-interest.

- **Prideful Hearts-** The people adorn themselves with beautiful jewelry, but their hearts are ugly and selfish. They think they are smarter than God.

- **Silver Lining-** There will be a time of pain and destruction, but it won't last forever. God is too beautiful and good to let the story end there. God will bless his children again and will send a Savior to set their hearts free.

HOW GOD SHOWS UP

God could easily wipe out his rebellious nation with a wave of his hand, but he loves them too much to make it that simple. His heart is hurt and disgusted by how far they've fallen, and he sends Isaiah as one of many prophets to compel them to change. He creates miracles and small removals of protection to wake them up, and when that doesn't work, the saddened Father knows it will take a time of exile and disaster to turn his children back around. After this chapter of judgment and exile is over, God plans to send his own Son to defeat death and rescue broken hearts once and for all.

ISAIAH

1. During the time of King Uzziah, the Lord says "Isaiah, pass this message along. Rebellious children of Judah, you have forgotten who you belong to. You have defiled your bodies and infected your hearts by turning away from me. Jerusalem is being overrun by foreigners because you no longer have my protection and approval. I have no use for your sacrifices, prayers, and festivals because you're complacent about all of it. Let me turn the evil in your hearts to compassion. You were once like precious silver to me, but not anymore. I will

save those who turn back to me but will crush those who stubbornly refuse.

2. "My Temple will **one day** be lifted high for all the world to see. You will long to be in my presence and hunger to learn my ways. I will settle your disputes and bring you peace." Well, that time has clearly not yet come. Judah has households full of idols and witchcraft that don't deserve God's forgiveness. He will destroy our arrogance, sink our ships, and shake the earth so that we will be overwhelmed by his glory and power. After that, we'll discard our idols at last, knowing he is the only real God.

3. Since Judah refuses to acknowledge our Provider, he will remove our abundance and political security for a time, allowing us to be governed by immature, selfish boys. Our nation will collapse under the lack of leadership. Judah, you have brought this destruction on yourself by oppressing the poor and openly insulting God. You women of Jerusalem strut around proudly, flashing your stolen jewelry and flirting with everyone you see. God will make your appearance as repulsive as your heart.

4. When you women are finally humbled, you will have to beg men to marry you. **However,** the righteous among you will survive the judgment and enjoy God's renewed blessing and protection over the land **as he makes it lush and beautiful once more.**

5. God planted the vineyard of Judah on a fertile hill, caring for it and protecting it, hoping it would bear good fruit. But you have produced the sour fruit of murder, oppression, and injustice instead. God has understandably removed

his wall of protection, and now you are doomed! You buy big houses you don't need and take your lush fields for granted, but soon your houses will be destroyed and your vines will dry up. You party and drink your days away, but you will soon die of thirst. You refuse to recognize the evil taking root in your heart, and you think you are smarter than God. God will shake your land and allow enemies to swallow you up.

6.   After King Uzziah dies, I see our beautiful God on his throne. He's surrounded by mysterious, majestic creatures of heaven who worship him at the top of their voices. I stand humbly overwhelmed, and one of the angels burns the sin from my lips, assuring me that I'm forgiven. I volunteer enthusiastically to be God's messenger. He asks me to warn you of what's coming, but he knows that your stubborn hearts will refuse to see and understand the truth. Until your cities are ruined, you will refuse to change.

7.   When Uzziah's grandson Ahaz rules Judah, a great war breaks out, and the king trembles as Syrian armies enter our land. My son and I approach King Ahaz in the street to tell him "Stay focused, calm, and unafraid of pompous Syria. They are not as strong as they think. Assyria, on the other hand, will soon swarm and humiliate Israel, taking down the entire royal family. The lush vineyards in the land will become overgrown with thorns." After Syria and Assyria are destroyed, a young virgin will give birth to a descendant of David who will bless the land and be called "God with us".

8.   Before my baby boy learns to speak, the Assyrians will

loot the capital of Israel. When Judah refuses to listen to God's quiet warnings, he'll let Assyria attack us like a great flood. May God stay with us and **spoil the evil plans of** our enemies! God warns me "Isaiah, don't be like everyone else who fears these enemy nations. I am the only one worthy of respect and fear. My holiness trips up all who fall short." I want to reveal God's message to the people, and I place all my hopes in him. Children of God, stop consulting useless fortune tellers, and listen to what your Father is trying to tell you!

9. When your hungry bodies and hopeless spirits break, you will refuse to lean on God. There will be no escape from pain. But one day, God will bring light, hope, and joy back to our land. We'll thank God as our harvests become rich and our burdens become light. God will come to earth as a baby King who will rise up as a righteous Savior, Counselor, and Peacemaker. For the time being, God will humble the arrogant people of Israel through this time of destruction. Our angry God cannot continue to watch his chosen children destroy themselves with wickedness.

10. You people of Israel have oppressed the poor and stolen from orphans, and now you cannot hide from God's angry punishment. God says "I will allow Assyria to beat you senseless, and your worthless idols will be destroyed in the process. Your bodies will be burned up with disease, and very few will survive. When I'm done punishing you, I'll also punish Assyria for thinking they have won without my help. Years later, a few survivors will finally return to me and learn to trust me again. Don't be afraid of these arrogant Assyrians because their power and oppression

won't last forever. They are wreaking havoc today, but I will cut them down in the end."

11. The dynasty of David has been cut down like a mighty tree, but a great new King will sprout from the stump. God will grant him uncommon wisdom and skill. He will joyfully obey God and defend the rights of the defenseless. All people and animals will live together in peace and safety under his leadership. God will bring his scattered people back home, and Israel and Judah will defeat its enemies as one unified people.

12. When we come back home at last, the people will sing "Thank you, great Savior for comforting me, forgiving me, and making me strong again. Your nourishing water refreshes me. Let my grateful song be heard throughout the world!"

13. Let Babylon hear these words of warning. God is preparing the world's armies to devastate your evil nation. You will be overcome with pain worse than childbirth, and your faces will burn with shame. God will darken the stars and shake the earth as he humbles all the sinners of this earth and scatters his enemies. Babylon's beautiful land and arrogant people will be destroyed with no mercy.

14. God will show mercy to his chosen children when they return from exile. God will relieve their pain and let them mock the cruel king that once oppressed them. They will enjoy peace, rest, and joy as the proud king of Babylonia is struck to the ground like the cities he mercilessly conquered. God will free his children from the oppression of the Assyrians, and the Philistines will cry out in pain and

hunger.

15. The cities of Moab will be destroyed in a single night. Wails of grief and fear will echo through their streets.

16. Moab sends a gift to Judah to beg for advice and protection, but it's too late for this conceited nation. The Moabites will weep as their luxurious lifestyles and carefree parties come to an end. No matter how hard they pray to their false idols, they cannot escape God's humbling judgment. But one day, all suffering will end, and David's chosen descendant will rule will loyalty, love, goodness, and justice.

17. God will reduce Syria's strong capital to a deserted pile of ruins. Israel's prosperity will turn to poverty and famine. Only then will they stop relying on their own efforts and finally return to their Creator. God's children plant gardens for idols made by their own hands, and they forget that their true Father is the one who has protected them all along. Powerful nations will capsize them like roaring tidal waves.

18. The proud, beautiful people of Ethiopia are feared all over the world, but God will allow their enemies to sneak up on them. Ethiopians who survive this merciless attack will learn to humbly worship God instead of their own strength.

19. The idols of Egypt tremble before the one true God as their cities crumble in civil war. Their proud leaders fight each other for power and ask fake gods for guidance. Egypt's most clever scholars will spout foolish advice as the Nile shrivels to dust. They will embarrass themselves in this time of failure, but eventually some Egyptian cities will build altars to God and receive his blessing on their land.

20. God instructs me to boldly walk around naked and

vulnerable for three years as a sign of how the mighty nations of Egypt and Ethiopia will be humbled and shamed by their enemies. Those who trust in these proud nations will have their hopes shattered.

21. People of Babylonia, a whirlwind of disaster will soon strike you. Friends will betray you, and you'll experience such intense pain that you'll beg for each day to end. Our lookouts observe happily as your idols and cities shatter. Let Israel hear the good news that our enemies will fall! Good days will come to Edom for a time. Citizens of the barren land of Arabia will be able to care for refugees that flee all the disasters in surrounding lands.

22. Jerusalem is a noisy city of celebration whose soldiers were able to flee from capture in the last war. Even so, don't try to stop me as I weep bitterly for those who have died. This is no time to relax; it's a time of panic and confusion as God judges all the nations. Judah's defenses are crumbling as our enemies find the weak spots in our wall. You fools pay no attention to the God who allowed all of this to unfold. You celebrated when you should have mourned the sad state of our nation. Who do you think you are to pat yourselves on the back for your fancy chariots? Your arrogance is disgraceful.

23. The merchant sailors of Tyre will cry out as they return from afar to find their ports and houses in ruins. Other nations will be shocked to see this imperial city fall. They have overcome many nations to establish colonies, but God will weaken and humble them. When God allows trade and commerce to return to the city of Tyre, the wealth of

the city will be used to benefit God's most needy children.

24. Ultimately, God will have no choice but to punish the whole world for its out-of-control corruption. The earth will shake and split, and the world's kings will fall into a pit. Light, music, and happiness will disappear as God delivers his justice. People have defiled his land and broken his laws again and again, and this has naturally led the world into chaos and self-destruction. Those who survive will sing with joy and gratitude to our powerful God.

25. Praiseworthy God, I stand in awe as you destroy enemy cities and humble powerful nations to fulfill your plans. Our cruel oppressors will fear you, and poor, helpless people will find shelter in your arms. The storms of our enemies can't touch us with you on our side. One day, God will prepare a great feast for all nations and destroy death forever. Sadness, shame, and suffering will be gone as everyone worships the trustworthy God who offers us safety and joy.

26. One day, the people of Judah will sing "Our strong city is full of good, loyal followers of God. We trust our Savior to give us peace, lift up the oppressed, and humble the proud. We long to be near the God who shows his love for us by making our path smooth. We were in pain and agony, but he brought us back to life, granting us victory and joy that we couldn't have achieved by ourselves."

27. When God's justice is revealed, even the most terrifying enemies will not escape his grasp. Only those under God's protection will be able to make peace with God and enjoy his forgiveness. Israel will produce good fruit when her people finally discard their idols and return to their Creator.

28. The irresponsible leaders and prophets of Israel are too drunk to recognize the disasters that are careening their way. People of Israel, pay attention to God's warnings and stop pretending everything is okay!

29. Disaster will fall on Jerusalem in the next two years. The city of David will be filled with crying and blood as God judges his fallen people. Later, God will use great storms and earthquakes to take down those who took pleasure in attacking Jerusalem. Children of Judah, wake up from your drunken stupor and listen to the prophets that speak the truth. Stop going through the motions of religion, and put your heart into it. Stop hiding, and give your heart back to the One who made you! If you love to oppress others and spread injustice, your days are numbered! True followers will be lifted up as they stand in awe of God.

30. God told me "Those rebels in Judah layer one sin on top of the next. They trust unreliable Egypt over their Father. They refuse to listen to the truth of my prophets. Children, come back under my merciful wings that can protect you. You cannot defeat these enemies on your own, but if you cry out to me, I will answer you with compassion. In times of testing, I will stay by your side and help you learn from these challenges. Throw away your worthless idols, and I will make your harvests rich and your paths clear. I will wipe out your enemies with the great tempest of my breath, and you will celebrate with festivals of music and worship. The sun will feel warmer and brighter than before."

31. Egypt may look strong with its vast military resources, but they are no match for God. People of Israel, throw away

your idols, stop trusting in human power, and turn back to God!

32. One day, kings of this world will rule with integrity, honesty, and patience; they will not be hoodwinked by selfish fools. Materialistic women of Judah, you are spoiled with a worry-free life of luxury, but God will take it all away. Once you have been humbled, God will return peace and plenty to your land.

33. Thieves and traitors who ravage Israel will soon get a taste of their own medicine. Great King, fight for those of us you still trust you, and bring stability back to your nation. Crime tears up the streets, and our brave peacemakers desperately need your help to return order, integrity, and justice to the land. God replies to my cry, "The evil plans of your enemies will turn to dust under the weight of my power. My fire will burn up all injustice, and there will be no need to fear those who once oppressed good people. My presence, safety, and leadership will return to Jerusalem."

34. Let the whole world hear of God's anger. Every sinner on earth deserves to die as the Creator rolls up the sky and make the stars fall like leaves. Edom will become a barren wasteland, overgrown with thorns. God will give the nations back to the wild animals, since human beings have disappointed him every step of the way.

35. Let the desert sing with joy as beautiful flowers bloom in the wilderness sand. Let weak, exhausted hands applaud as God comes to the rescue. Let the blind, deaf, lame, and mute celebrate as God heals their bodies and nourishes their spirits. No sorrow, foolishness, or violence will enter

God's kingdom. Those rescued by God will shout with happiness forever!

36. When the arrogant Assyrian emperor captures over a dozen cities in Judah, he sends his chief official to deliver this message to King Hezekiah's officials. "Tell your king that his confident words are no match for the military strength of Assyria. It's time to give up. When Hezekiah destroyed all those altars and demanded that you only worship one god, how do you know he chose the right one? Your pitiful God isn't strong enough to stand up to the god of Assyria. Let me talk a little louder for you peasants sitting up there on the city wall. You will all be reduced to drinking your own urine once Assyria is done with you! Your king and your God can't possibly save you, so you may as well surrender. At least then you might survive."

37. King Hezekiah is troubled by the abusive Assyrian message and sends me this message: "We need your help, Isaiah. The Assyrian emperor has deeply insulted our God, and our armies are too weak to defeat them." I respond "Don't be afraid. God will chase the emperor back to his country and kill him there." When the Assyrian emperor hears a false rumor and sends Hezekiah a final threatening letter, our good king prays "Creator and King, your throne is higher than any other. Rescue us from these godless terrorists, so that the whole world will give you credit for our unlikely victory." God responds "Bullies of Assyria, who do you think you are? How dare you insult the Creator of the world! You brag about your past victories, but I planned those victories to carry out my larger plans. Go home, and leave my people alone!" The next day, God proves his

power by killing 185,000 Assyrian soldiers and allowing the emperor's power-hungry sons to assassinate him.

38. When King Hezekiah nearly dies of an illness, God answers his passionate prayers for healing. This good king sings "I thought my days were nearly over, and my thin, weak voice cried out in pain. My heart was bitter and restless as I begged for God's help. Lord, thank you for healing me! I will sing to you as long as I live!"

39. When the Babylonians bring Hezekiah a "get-well-soon" gift, the king happily gives them a tour of the palace. When I inform Hezekiah that these visitors will one day carry off his treasures and capture his descendants, he's just happy this disaster won't happen during his lifetime.

40. God calls me to comfort and assure his forgiven people that their pain and punishment will soon end. Clear a path as our glorious God reveals himself to the whole world! People last no longer than withering grass and fragile flowers, but our Sovereign King and his message lasts forever. Our good Shepherd will gather us and lead us safely home. Can anyone scoop up the earth and oceans in his hands? Can anyone tell God what to do? No! No golden idols, powerful nations, or wise men could ever compare to the One whose throne sits above the clouds. He knows each star in the galaxy by name. Only he has the power to strengthen the weary and make them rise up like majestic birds.

41. God says "All you who feel you have a case against me, listen up! I am the author of history. I planned the victories of great conquerors and kings. I was there at the beginning, and I'll be there at the end. Craftsmen congratulate

each other as they build worthless idols, but I chose you children of Israel for greater things. You have no need to fear because I will crumble mountains for you as I have many times before. I will feed you and nourish your land. All you false, foreign gods, what do you have to say for yourselves? Come tell us what the future holds! If you're real, **prove** it! Let me be clear. You fake, powerless idols are as worthless and disgusting as the people who worship you.

42. "I'm giving you a Spirit-filled servant who will bring peace and justice to all nations. I will give him great authority to renew my covenant with Israel. Through him, I will bring light to the world, making your vision clear and your hearts free. I am the one true God, and I've been silent long enough. It pains me to do this, but I will destroy rivers and mountains in this time of judgment. I will disgrace those who trust idols and will help blind people see the path before them. I am eager to save those who are willing to see and hear my truth." Let all the sea creatures, desert dwellers, and mountain dwellers praise our warrior God from all corners of the world!

43. The Creator says "Don't be afraid, my precious children. I know each of you by name. When you face the deep waters and harsh fires of this life, I will never leave your side. I will take down strong, oppressive nations to bring my scattered people back home from exile. I created you to bring me glory, but you must open your eyes and ears, knowing that I'm the only real God. Don't cling to the past because I am doing a new thing. I bless you with living water in the desert wilderness you're facing. I don't ask much of you,

and I forgive all your wrongs, but still you reject me. You have fully earned the time of shame and destruction that comes your way.

44. "I created and chose you, children of Jacob, so there's no need to fear. I will pour my spirit on your thirsty soul, and you will proudly declare that you belong to me. I am the Lord who was there at the beginning of time, and I do what no one else can. But all those idiots who choose to worship idols are merely praying to lifeless blocks of wood. Open your eyes and see these idols for what they are! Come back to the God who saves you. The mountains and trees shout in joy to their maker. My wisdom is unmatched, and only I know the future. I will lift up a great king who will allow you to come home and rebuild Jerusalem.

45. "A king named Cyrus will conquer many nations. Although he won't know me, I will strengthen him in order to fulfill my plans and bring my children back home. Clay pots don't question the methods of their sculptor, so why do you question my plans at every turn? I control the moon and stars and filled the earth with living things. I also pave the way for Cyrus and ensure that nations will bow to Israel once more. Your enemies won't be saved by the blocks of wood they worship.

46. "The idols of Babylon cannot even save themselves from capture, so they obviously cannot compare to your Father and Nurturer. Set aside your stubbornness, and acknowledge that I never fail to carry out my plans. Trust that your day of victory is near.

47. "Babylon, you were once a beautiful, delicate flower, but

now you are a sweating slave stripped naked for the world to see. I put my people in your merciless power to humble them, and you thought your power trip would last forever. You thought of yourself as an unshakable god, but the real God of Israel has decided to swiftly take you down and free his people. Your magic tricks and astrologers won't help you now!

48. "People of Judah who claim to follow me, I know you don't really mean what you say. You proudly put on a show, but I don't buy it. You turn to homemade idols and think you know everything, and sadly, your rebellion is not a surprise to me. I will punish and humble you to protect my good name, but I will let you survive these tests and give you another chance. I laid the earth's foundations and can do anything I want, and yet I long to bless you, free you, and help you learn the right way to live."

49. God chose me before my birth to serve him and speak his sharp truth to the world. When I use up all my strength and feel discouraged, I must trust that God will reward and defend me. He strengthens me so that I can call his scattered people back home. Everyone hates me now, but eventually, royalty will respect me as God keeps his promises and sets me free. God will bring favor back to this wasteland, feed the hungry, and bring light to those who dwell in darkness. God will comfort small people as great mountains sing his praises. He will not forget the children he molded with his own hands.

50. God says "I am not abandoning you like a deadbeat dad who sells his children as slaves; rather I am thoughtfully

punishing you to turn you back toward my strong arms."
I eagerly listen as God teaches me to speak strength to the
weary. When I'm abused and insulted, God gives me perspective and doesn't let me quit. He helps me endure, and
I know he'll defend me in the end. All you who face dark
times as you follow God, trust that he will make it right.

51. God says "If you want to be saved, listen as I remind you
of your foundation. Abraham was childless, but I made
his descendants into a great nation. If I can do that, I can
certainly turn the desert of Jerusalem into a lush, happy
garden again. My good laws bring light to the world, and
my victory will last longer than the earth. Write my advice
on your hearts, and don't be afraid when your perishable
enemies insult you. I am the strong Creator who can dry
up seas and tear apart the monsters that lie within them,
and I offer that impossible strength to you. I will finally
remove this cup of anger and turn it toward those who
oppressed you."

52. Jerusalem, be the city God created you to be! Shake yourself
free of heathens that pin you down, and rise to greatness
once more. You are slaves to the arrogant Babylonians, but
it's time to show them that you belong to me. Shout the
joyful news of peace and freedom as you carry the Temple
treasures back home and begin to rebuild. God's servant
will be beaten so badly that he'll longer look human, but
the nations will stand in awe of his restoration.

53. The people will hardly believe it when God allows his
servant to flourish like a healthy plant in dry ground. He
won't look especially attractive or memorable, but he will

endure the punishment that we sinners deserve. Our perfect Savior will suffer humbly without saying a word, and his precious sacrifice will bring forgiveness, purpose, and life to God's people. As God's devoted servant rises again with joy, the Father will give him the highest seat of honor at his table.

54. Barren Jerusalem, you will once again shout for joy as your boundaries and population expand. Your Creator will care for you tenderly like a young wife and remove the shame of your past unfaithfulness. He will renew his wedding vows to you as he carries you back to his loving, peaceful home forever. Helpless Jerusalem, you will be rebuilt more beautifully than before, standing strong against all weapons that try to pierce you.

55. The Lord says "Let all hungry, penniless people enjoy my free food and blessings. I turned David into a great leader, and I will make you great and glorious as well. Draw near to me in prayer. Allow me to forgive you and change your thoughts to match my thoughts. My words of wisdom nourish the earth and never fail. The mountains and mighty trees can't hold back their joyful praises to me. Return home from Babylon with joy, and trust me to guide you."

56. The Lord calls his people to return to righteousness and enjoy the refreshment that comes from Sabbath rest. It doesn't matter if someone has a deformity or comes from a foreign land; anyone can become part of God's family by loving and serving him. Israel's leaders drunkenly ignore my warnings today, but when God's children return from exile, all nations will be invited to pray in God's Temple.

57. God says "When good people die, they rest in peace, free from further harm. But you idol worshipers disgust me, and I refuse to save you from yourselves. You worship fertility gods by having sex ceremonies and sacrificing your children, hoping these fake idols will give you strength. These lifeless statues can't hear your prayers, but humble people who trust my way more than their own will be healed.

58. "The people of Israel claim to obey and worship me, but they are only going through the motions of religion. Fasting should be an act of reverence and humility that instills compassion for the poor, but you get irritable and whiny whenever you do it. How could I possibly see your half-hearted worship as pleasing? If you learn to joyfully give to those in need, my favor will shine on you and protect you on all sides. Honor the holy Sabbath by being still and joyfully refraining from your to-do list."

59. Some of you think that God is too weak to answer your prayers, but in reality, your sin makes him refuse to hear you. You hurt innocent people with violence and lies, leaving destruction in your crooked wake. You stumble along in fear and distress, crying out to God, but he frowns on you in silence. Crime and injustice fill the streets, and God rushes to our defense like a mighty wind, saving those who turn back to him.

60. God's glory will shine on Jerusalem, and the kings of the world will be drawn to his light. God's people will come home at last and rebuild the great city with silver, gold, and strong wood donated by foreign nations. Kings will respect us, and God's renewed mercy will protect us. Jerusalem will

be a joyful, beautiful city once more.

61. God's Spirit has enabled me to encourage the poor, heal the depressed, free the prisoners, and comfort the grieving. I come to joyfully announce that God's rescue is coming soon. We will praise him as he allows us to rebuild our ruins. Foreigners will work in our fields, and our disgrace among the nations will end at last.

62. I will encourage Jerusalem endlessly until the world declares her victorious. God's city is like a beloved bride that delights him with her beauty. Let all the guards sing from the city walls that our Beloved Lord provides for us and keeps his promises.

63. Our Warrior God singlehandedly crushes enemy nations like grapes. God would do anything to rescue his beloved children, but they sadden him continually with their rebellious hearts. We long for the great miracles of the past, when God parted the Red Sea to deliver Israel out of slavery, but our Father feels silent and treats us like strangers in this time of suffering.

64. Lord, make the mountains shake under the weight of your power. Make enemies tremble in awe of your miracles like you did before. Help us turn from our filthy sins and joyfully do the right thing. Maybe then your anger will subside. Have pity on the children you molded from clay, and free us from this suffering!

65. God replies "I reveal myself to my children and answer their prayers, but they don't even try to reach out to me. They consult mediums and insist on going their own way. I can't overlook that, Isaiah. I will bless those who

worship and serve me, but those who abandon me for idols will get what they deserve. I am wiping away the past to make all things new. My children will live long, full lives and enjoy the fruits of their labor. Wild animals will live in peace, and no danger will exist anywhere.

66. "I created the universe and could ask anything of you, but all I ask is that you obey me with humble hearts. Those who don't take my worship regulations seriously bring disaster on themselves. My followers will be mocked by those who don't understand the truth, but all will see the truth eventually. Let those who love Jerusalem rejoice as she is reborn into a new life of lasting prosperity. I defend her with fire and burn up pagan worship in this land. Many idol worshippers will die, but some will escape in order to proclaim my power in foreign lands and turn the world toward me."

DAY TWO - DISASTER STRIKES
JEREMIAH-LAMENTATIONS

BIG IDEA

A big-hearted priest tries to stop the most tragic chapter in Judah's history, but the corrupt nation is too far gone.

WHAT JEREMIAH WITNESSES

- **Encouragement from God-** God calls young Jeremiah to make bold warning statements that could save Judah if the people choose to listen.
- **God's love for Judah-** God has come to their rescue many times, and all they need to do for continued protection is trust God to forgive and change them.
- **Corrupt people-** They worship false idols, oppress the poor, kill children on pagan altars, and repeatedly ignore every true prophet God sends. The stubborn Judeans trust in their wealth more than the One who made them.
- **Personal protection-** Innocent Jeremiah earns God's miraculous protection as everything around him falls apart.
- **Last chance for peace-** As Babylonia swarms the cities of Judah, God gives his people a chance to surrender peacefully, but prideful Zedekiah refuses.
- **God's justi ied anger-** Our Lord made the earth, and he has every right to shake it up and allow this time of deserved disaster.

- **Tragic ruins-** In the aftermath of war, overwhelming famine and disease ravage the land. As their wealth and pride turn to dust, the broken people finally cry out to God for help.
- **Words of hope-** Jeremiah's heart breaks to witness the great unraveling of his nation, but God assures him that some will survive the time of exile. Their oppressors will be punished, and the people will enjoy a new chapter of peace and prosperity. God can't wait to bring his children back home!

HOW GOD SHOWS UP

God saw enemy nations closing in on his people, and he wanted to offer his protection. All he asked was for the people to trust in his help and accept his advice. Unfortunately, the people chose to rely on themselves and ignore God's passionate warnings. They allowed their hearts to grow evil, and God couldn't bear their self-destruction anymore. When disaster finally struck, God continued to protect and forgive the few who finally turned to him.

JEREMIAH

1. When good King Josiah rules Judah, I'm working as a small town priest in the territory of Benjamin. God says "Young man, I choose you to speak my truth to the world." At first this mission strikes me as impossible, but God assures me

"Don't worry about how others will respond to you. I will give you the words to speak and the authority to uproot entire nations. Enemies will pour through Judah's northern border like boiling water because Judah has abandoned me to worship idols. Don't be afraid to tell my people the truth, Jeremiah! I'll give you the strength to face them.

2. "Jerusalem, you once followed me like a young, trusting bride, and I punished all who tried to hurt you. I delivered your ancestors safely to a fertile new home, but they abandoned me for idols. Even idol worshippers are loyal to their false gods, but Israel has exchanged the one true God for lifeless statues. I will shake the sky and allow your enemies to hunt you like the slaves you once were. You lose your voice crying out to fertility gods, but you refuse to turn back to me.

3. "A man shouldn't divorce and then remarry a wife who's been with other men, so why do you crawl back to me after giving yourself to countless idols? Do you think you are immune from my anger? Judah, you have mirrored your prostitute sister Israel, but I still long to wrap you in my merciful arms. All you have to do is admit your sins and give your hearts to me.

4. "If you keep sowing seeds of worship among thorny idols, you'll feel the heat of my anger. Run away as enemies devastate your cities!" Upon hearing God's harsh words, I cry out "Lord, I thought you were bringing us peace, but instead your knife is on our neck!" As God blows our enemies toward us faster than eagles, we must cleanse our filthy hearts before it's too late! We have brought this suffering

on ourselves. My heart hurts to watch God turn our home into a wasteland that even animals flee from!

5. People of Jerusalem, look around you! Even the priests' worship is insincere, and you refuse to learn from your mistakes. God says "I took care of these children, and they betrayed me with lust and idol worship. Isn't it fair that I punish them for that? Jeremiah, they refuse to take my warnings seriously, but your words will be a powerful fire they can't ignore." An ancient army will strike our land without mercy, but God will still allow some of us to survive. The Creator of the earth and sea says "Foolish children, can't you see that I deserve your respect? I bless your harvest every year, and you don't even say thank you. You've let deception, injustice, and oppression corrupt the land, and you will be shocked as it all comes crashing down."

6. Jerusalem's streets are filled with oppression, and now God will allow it to become a wasteland! These warnings should motivate Judah to save itself, but the people laugh at me and stubbornly refuse to hear the truth. God's anger for them is starting to burn in me too! God says "Pour my anger on these liars. Let them lose their houses and be forced into exile. They have no shame or self-awareness about their sins, even though I keep warning them to turn around to avoid my judgment."

7. At the Temple gate, I declare "If you want to stay in this land God gave you, start treating each other fairly, and stop killing those weaker than you. Stop worshipping false gods, and stop believing lies that everything's okay. It's not okay! God will remove you from this land if you don't listen!"

God says "Jeremiah, don't pity these people. They burn their children on those disgusting pagan altars and bring pain and shame upon themselves. They could choose to obey me and live, but they insist that their way is better than mine. They rebel worse with each generation, and faithfulness is now a foreign concept to them.

8. "Jerusalem graves will be dug up, and survivors will wish they were dead. It makes no sense that they stubbornly cling to their idols. Even animals know how to switch direction after making a wrong turn! My people claim to know my law, but dishonest scribes have written corrupt laws I never intended. Temple priests cheat, lie, and harm others without shame. Their enemies will strike like poisonous snakes!" My heart is inconsolably sick as I see God's anger poured on my people.

9. I want to cry all day for those who have died. I now see that dishonesty, violence, and betrayal have completely overwhelmed the land. No one can be trusted. Our plants are drying up and turning to poison. Animals are fleeing, and the people will soon scatter as well. Let us sing a mournful song about our lost homes and dying children. We cannot boast about our strength or riches anymore; we can only boast that our good God wants us back.

10. Stop lifting up lifeless idols for we have a mighty, living God who stretched the sky, controls the wind, and created everything that exists. People of Judah, it's time to pack up and escape this ruined land if you can. Our stupid leaders were deaf to God's warnings, and now Jerusalem is in chaos! God, spare us from your wrath, and punish those

who destroy our land!

11. God says "When I rescued your ancestors from oppressive Egypt, they promised to obey and worship me, while I agreed to safely deliver them to this fertile land. They have fully broken this promise by dedicating their hearts to evil, and their idols cannot save them from my punishment. Don't feel sorry for them, Jeremiah! Some of them are plotting to kill you to silence the truth you speak." I respond in prayer "Lord, I trust you to judge and test people as you see fit. I put my work in your hands." When my enemies later try to kill me, God punishes them and protects me.

12. I pray "God, your ways are always right, but I don't understand why some wicked liars succeed when they deserve to be taken down. How long will our fields and animals die because of their stubborn wickedness?" God responds "Jeremiah, don't give up now. It's about to get even harder. Your family will betray you, and you won't be able to trust anyone. My chosen people have turned on me, so now I am allowing their nation to become an unsafe, chaotic wilderness. But later I will have mercy on those who return to me, and I'll bring them back home."

13. God tells me to buy a pristine new pair of white shorts and leave them among the muddy river rocks. When I return to find them filthy and ruined, God says "I created my people to be clean and beautiful, fitting perfectly around my waist. But they have made themselves useless and stained with sin. I am so angry at their self-destruction that I will smash them together like wine jars." Israel, humble yourselves and turn back to the Lord before he brings darkness on the land! I

weep bitterly as I see my fellow Judeans ripped from their homeland and the crown snatched from the king's head. Those we thought were allies are now stripping us bare, bringing intense pain and shame upon our bodies.

14. Judean people and animals pant in thirst as the grasses and crops wither away. God says "I cannot forget how these people ran from me and refused to turn from evil. I have given them plenty of opportunities to change, and now it's too late. The false prophets spread lies that all is well, but disaster will strike them deeply." I can't stop crying as I see my people dying of war and starvation. Lord, we beg for healing and peace, but there is no relief. We confess that we have sinned deeply. Please remember your love for us and have mercy. You are our only hope, Father! Please send the rain!

15. God answers "Even if Moses himself were pleading for me to spare these people, it would still be too late. The wheels are already in motion for disease, war, hunger, and exile to strike this land. No one should pity them because they've earned every bit of my anger." I am so depressed that I wish I had never been born. I've done my best to deliver God's message, but everyone hates me. Lord, punish those who torture me for following you. You are my only source of guidance and joy. God responds "Jeremiah, I will protect you with impenetrable bronze armor so that no one can harm you. Just keep speaking my worthwhile message to the people.

16. "Jeremiah, this is no time to get married or have children because this disease-filled land would be too unsafe for

your babies. Don't get caught up in the mourning around you; remember they have brought disaster on themselves. People will ask what they've done to deserve this, and you can say that I am throwing them out of the land due to their stubborn, evil, idolatrous hearts. They cannot hide their sins from me, but eventually, I will bring the survivors back home." Lord, thank you for strengthening and protecting me in this troubling time. The world will soon see your power.

17. God says "Judah, idol worship has permanently defaced your hearts, and you deserve to lose all your money and land. You trust in useless human strength, but those who trust fully in me are like a resilient, beautiful garden that bears plenty of good fruit. Only I can heal your sick hearts." Praiseworthy Lord, heal me and protect me from those who refuse to believe your message. Please notice that I have not sinned against my enemies. Punish them and spare your blameless servant! God says "Jeremiah, go to the city gate and command the people to honor the Sabbath day as a restorative day to rest. This act of obedience will strengthen them and remind them of my good law. These stubborn children need to stop thinking their ways are better than mine.

18. "Jeremiah, go watch the potter work at his wheel, and notice that he discards imperfect creations to make something new. I molded my people from clay, and I have every right to discard those who refuse to live the good lives I created them to live. They have abandoned my good path to create crooked, dangerous paths for themselves. They have turned the Promised Land into a despicable, horrifying place, so

I will scatter them like dust in the wind." Upon hearing these words, the people laugh at me and plot to take me to court. So I pray "God, do you see how my enemies are digging holes for me to fall into? I defended them in your presence, but now I see how corrupt they are. I understand your anger with them and will be happy to see their lives destroyed."

19. God tells me to bring a clay jar to a valley to give this message to the priests and elders. "Gentlemen, the people have abandoned our Lord for false gods and have spilled innocent blood on pagan altars. God would never require such horrifying sacrifices. Enemies will soon slaughter your armies in this valley, and survivors of the siege will die of desperate hunger." I smash the clay jar on the ground and continue "Judah will be broken like this jar, and the pieces will be impossible to put back together."

20. Upon hearing my message, Temple officials have me publicly beaten and arrested. When I am released, I tell them "You terrorize everyone around you, but God will terrorize you. Babylonia will soon loot this city, kill its citizens, and carry the survivors into exile. Your families will be among the prisoners, and you'll die far from home." I pray "Father, you allowed my enemies to mock and overpower me. They hate me when I speak the truth, but when I hold back, the fire of your message burns within me. Mighty God, I know you will defend me and disgrace my enemies eventually. I sing praises to the God that rescues the oppressed! My work is in your hands."

21. When King Nebuchadnezzar begins overtaking Jerusalem,

King Zedekiah hopes that it's not too late for a miracle. I tell him "Zedekiah, you are about to lose this war because of God's intense anger. Those who survive this siege will die of hunger and disease that will follow. At this point, you can surrender to the Babylonians and survive, or you can stubbornly fight them and die."

22. God tells the king "I command you to do the right thing. Protect vulnerable people from injustice, and stop killing innocent people. If you turn back to me, David's descendants will continue to rule this land, but if you ignore me, this palace will soon fall to ruins. This beautiful land will wither, and foreigners will wonder what happened here. The king of Judah will be carried away to Babylonia, never to return." King Jehoiakim gets rich by lying and withholding pay from honest workers. He kills and oppresses innocent people to serve his own selfish purposes, and no one will grieve at his funeral. God first warned us of these disasters when the nation was thriving, and we refused to listen. God says to the king "I can't stand the sight of you, and soon you will die in Babylonia. You are like a broken jar that no one wants. You are the end of David's royal line."

23. God says "Leaders of Israel, you were supposed to take care of my children, but instead, you scattered them and led them to destruction. You will pay for this evil, but I will eventually lead my children home and free them from worry and oppression. I will lift up a descendant of David who will rule with peace and justice." My heart is crushed as I witness our wicked leaders abusing their power and bringing God's curse on our land. God will make the corrupt priests trip along the slippery paths they've made for themselves.

They spread false hopes throughout the land and close the people's ears to the truth. None of them truly know God's good, fierce heart, and they twist his message to suit their purposes. God is all around, and no one can hide their evil thoughts and actions from him.

24. After Nebuchadnezzar takes the king and many others to Babylonia, the Lord shows me a basket of ripe, juicy figs alongside a basket of rotten, inedible figs. God said "Those in exile are like the good figs. I will watch over them with kindness and help them return to me. As for corrupt King Zedekiah and others who stubbornly stay in Jerusalem to fight, I will throw them out like the worthless figs and bring hunger and disease on their homes."

25. Back when Nebuchadnezzar first takes over Babylonia, I tell the people "I have passionately preached God's truth to you for twenty-three years, but you insist on ignoring me. Since you refuse to change your evil ways or discard your idols, you have brought ruin upon yourselves. Northern enemies will destroy this nation as Babylonia rules the world for seventy years. After this, God will punish Babylonia, making them slaves to those they once oppressed. All nations who reject God will feel his anger and hear his voice roar from heaven. Weep, people of Judah, as God turns our great nation into a ruined wasteland!

26. In the Temple court, I declare "Pay attention to God's commands and warnings! You continue to ignore and disobey them, but God still longs for you to turn back and be saved." Outraged by my words, the priests demand that I be sentenced to death. I respond "God himself sent me

to share these difficult truths to motivate you to change, so that he might spare your city. If you kill me, God will hold you responsible for killing an innocent man." Other true prophets had recently been killed by the king's officials, but thankfully, I convinced them to spare my life that day.

27. I make a wooden yoke for myself and declare "The powerful Creator will soon put many nations under Nebuchadnezzar's thumb. Those who fight him will be destroyed, while those who surrender will be allowed to survive in Babylonia. Don't listen to false prophets who say our Temple treasures will be brought back soon."

28. The false prophet Hananiah publicly argues with me, saying "The king of Babylonia will soon fall. Our king and treasures will soon be brought back to this land." I respond "While I certainly wish that were true, God has revealed a different plan to myself and many others." Hananiah angrily breaks the wooden yoke on my neck and shouts "God will break Babylonia's yoke around our necks in two short years!" I respond "Actually, God will replace that breakable yoke with an iron one. And since you keep lying to the people, you will die later this year."

29. After King Jehoiachin and many others are taken to Babylonia, I write to King Zedekiah, saying "The Lord wants to encourage those in exile to start peaceful, content lives in Babylonia. Plant gardens there and have children. Work diligently to help your new cities prosper. Then after seventy years, God will bring you back home, filling your future with hope. But those who stubbornly fight against Babylonia in Jerusalem will die of war, starvation, and disease." More

false prophets angrily try to stop me from speaking, but I respond confidently that God will punish these liars.

30. God encourages me to write all this down for future generations, and then he says "You will survive this time of great distress, my children. I will remove the yoke Babylonia has put on your neck, and I will let you come home in peace and fearlessness. Right now there is no relief from the wounds you have brought on yourselves, but eventually, those who hold you down will fall, and you will rebuild Jerusalem with a spirit of joy.

31. "I have always loved you, dear children, and I can't wait to fill your land with lush vines and joyful music again. I will make smooth paths for disabled and vulnerable people, and they will sing and cry to me in gratitude. I will set you free and provide all your needs. Your ancestor Rachel cries for you, but her tears will dry when hope is restored in God's chosen nation. It will be like waking up refreshed after a long sleep. My law will transform the hearts of my people, and I will forgive their mistakes, so Israel will survive as long as the sun shines in the sky."

32. God leads me to buy a field, even though I'm sitting in prison, and Jerusalem will soon fall into Babylonian hands. I pray "Powerful Creator, nothing is impossible for you. You performed wonders in Egypt to deliver your people, but they didn't obey you and have earned this time of destruction. I buy this field trusting that this dark time will not last forever. The people of Israel will once again honor and respect you, and you will gladly bless them in this land."

33. The Creator responds "Hear this wonderful truth! When I

bless my people with peace and security, I will forgive their sins and give them a fresh start. They will be my pride and joy, restored for all to see. My people will bring me offerings of gratitude as I multiply their population and appoint a good, just king from David's family.

34. As Jerusalem burns, the Lord tells King Zedekiah "I will soon hand you to the king of Babylonia. You will live peacefully in his land, and when you die, your people will fondly remember you." Zedekiah promises to free the Israelite slaves in Judah, but then forces them back into slavery. God says "When I rescued my people from Egyptian slavery, I told them to honor this deliverance by freeing slaves every few years. Because you have refused to free my children, you will die of starvation and disease instead of receiving my protection."

35. When I invite the good clan of Rechab to the Temple, they decline my offer for wine, saying that their pure diets and modest possessions help them focus on God. I tell the people "This fervent obedience to God inspires me. God will surely protect these Rechabites through the dark days to come. I wish you would follow their lead and turn your eyes back to God, but you refuse.

36. I write about my many conversations with God, hoping to inspire the people to accept his forgiveness. I dictate this book to my assistant Baruch, and he reads it in the Temple, since I can't safely show my face there. Upon hearing these words, the king burns the scroll and tries to arrest me. But God allows us to hide while we rewrite the scroll.

37. As the Babylonians start to take over Jerusalem, they retreat upon hearing that Egypt is coming to Judah's defense. I tell King Zedekiah "When our Egyptian allies leave, the Babylonians will return to brutally defeat you. You can't beat them." As I journey back home, a soldier arrests me, assuming I'm fleeing to join the Babylonians. After nearly dying in prison, I beg King Zedekiah for help, and he moves me to the more humane palace courtyard.

38. Outraged by my words, several officials throw me in a muddy well with no food or water. King Zedekiah doesn't even try to stop them. It's only when an Ethiopian palace employee begs the king for mercy that Zedekiah rescues me from the well and places me back in the more humane courtyard. Another time, King Zedekiah asks for my advice, and I reveal that the only way he can survive the exile is through surrender. Fearing the truth as expected, the king returns me to my prison cell.

39. The Babylonians overtake Jerusalem and burn it to the ground during Zedekiah's eleventh year as king. Zedekiah witnesses the execution of his sons just before being blinded and dragged away by his captors. A Babylonian official frees me from prison and escorts me to the home of Judah's new governor. The Ethiopian that rescued me from the well also survives the siege but witnesses the horrors that strike the city.

40. My Babylonian rescuer says "Your God is punishing the sins of your people, and you warned them all along. If you decide to stick with me, I'll take care of you. You may stay with the new governor that Nebuchadnezzar has appointed,

or you can go wherever else you'd like to go. You are free."
Governor Gedaliah offers plenty of food and freedom to
the Judeans, and he refuses to believe rumors that some of
his officials are plotting to assassinate him.

41. Gedaliah invites eleven Judean officials to dinner, and during
the meal, the assassins stab the governor and many others
in and around the palace. They capture many hostages and
murder even more people while fleeing the nation. The
Judean survivors fear that these crimes will cause Nebuchadnezzar to wipe them out, so many Judeans flee to Egypt.

42. The humbled military leaders of Judah approach me and
say "So few of us survived this brutal war. Pray that God will
show us the way forward. We want to obey him to earn his
favor back." The Lord answers "If you will peacefully live
here under Babylonian rule, I will build you back up and
eventually make you a free nation again. It saddens me to
see your pain, and I want to bless you. But those who flee
to Egypt and refuse to trust me will face the very disasters
they think they're running from."

43. A few arrogant bystanders respond "You're lying. If we
submit to the Babylonians, we don't stand a chance. We'll
be much safer in Egypt." They capture me as a hostage
and finish the journey to Egypt. God reveals to me that
Nebuchadnezzar will soon conquer Egypt, and many in
that land will die of war and disease.

44. God tells those traveling to Egypt "You just saw me destroy
Judah because of their sins, and you still haven't learned
your lesson. Why do you bring further destruction on
your families by worshipping Egyptian gods and rejecting

me? None of you who fled to Egypt will survive." These stubborn people respond "Actually, we were quite prosperous back when we worshipped many gods and goddesses. Until Babylonia ruined our home, we had no troubles at all. No thanks, Jeremiah. We'll keep doing things our way."

45. A few years before the Babylonian attack, my secretary Baruch becomes restless and hopeless after hearing the troubling prophecies I dictated to him. God tells Baruch "I created the world, and I have every right to tear it down now that my people have completely turned from me. Baruch, try to find some peace and gratitude in knowing you will survive the disasters to come."

46. When Nebuchadnezzar overtakes Egypt, God says "Egyptian officers confidently prepare their battalions, but when they see the army I'm sending their way, they'll trip over each other as they flee in fear. They'll die in shame, and their brilliant medicines won't save them. But my people of Israel will survive this darkness and return home in peace."

47. God says "Philistia will be covered in a great flood, and I will not let up on these sinners, even when the world mourns for them and prays for my judgment to stop.

48. "The sparkle will disappear from the cities of Moab, and children will run in fear as enemy armies invade this land. Moab places great trust in its wealth, but money won't save them in the end. These arrogant people have lived untouched by trouble and testing for many years, but God will humble them with poverty and sorrow.

49. "The Ammonites that defiled Israel with their idols will scatter in confusion as their villages are destroyed. They

arrogantly assume no one can harm them, but they're wrong. Edom repeatedly rejects my wisdom, but I see right through their stupidity. I will care for their widows and orphans, but all nations will lose respect for prideful Edom as its leaders are ruined. The people of Damascus anxiously anticipate that their city will burn, as Nebuchadnezzar turns all the powerful nations to dust.

50. "Finally, the Babylonians will face the same destruction they brought on the world. Roaring armies will surround and destroy proud Babylonia, and no one will help them. They gladly humiliated Judah, but their idols will be shattered as my people return home with tears of joy in their eyes. My lost sheep will renew their relationship with me, and I will forgive them.

51. "The tornado of my judgment will blow Babylonia away like straw, and I will show them no mercy. I commanded the earth to form and the sky to roar with thunder. Those who choose lifeless idols over me should look at my creation and recognize their foolishness. I used Babylonia as a weapon to judge great nations, but now they will pay for the ruin they've brought to my people. The children of Israel will know I'm on their side when they see Babylonia drop like a rock in the ocean."

52. King Zedekiah takes over Judah at age twenty-one and turns against God like his brother and nephew before him. For the last two years of his reign, famine ravages the land, and Babylonia attacks Jerusalem from all sides. They finally break through the city wall and capture the king as well as many Judean officials. The Babylonians burn the Temple

and leave the cities of Judah in ruins, as they carry 5,000 Judeans into exile.

LAMENTATIONS

1. The mighty city of Jerusalem was once honored by all, but now her splendor is gone. Her tears fall endlessly with no one to comfort her. Her children are enslaved, and her Temple is empty. Jerusalem's sins have made her filthy, naked, and shameful. Her people cry out in pain and hunger, while enemies laugh at her sorrow. Lord, my heart is sick and broken as I endure this punishment for my sin. Please punish those who destroyed this nation.

2. God angrily tore down every city, village, and fort in Judah. He strengthened our enemies and shattered us without mercy. Our enemies shouted in victory on top of the Temple ruins. Our leaders are now captured, and our prophets are blind to the future. Children die in their mothers' arms, and the mothers are so desperately hungry that they eat the bodies. We are exhausted with grief and beg God for mercy.

3. I sink deeply into a pit of misery and darkness, and my bones break as I struggle against the endless blows to my spirit. I am imprisoned in hopelessness, and God feels agonizingly silent when I cry. God used me for target practice and left me for dead. I've forgotten what it's like to be happy and alive. Even so, I cling to my Father's love and mercy, which arrive fresh with every sunrise. I wait patiently for my trustworthy God to turn things around. I have fallen,

but I know this is not how my story will end. I refuse to believe that God enjoys crushing our spirits. He will bless those of us who turn back to him, and he'll punish our enemies eventually. God sees our tears and eases our fears.

4. I am horrified as the glittering streets of Jerusalem grow dim around me. People paw through the garbage for food, and mothers refuse to share crumbs with their children. Our noble leaders shrivel and die in the streets. No one thought Jerusalem could fall this hard, but God allowed it because our leaders were murdering and oppressing innocent people. We stumble aimlessly, searching for the help that never seems to come. I can only hope that this dark chapter won't last much longer.

5. Lord, look at us! Remember that you once loved us. Our families are murdered, our property is stolen, and our bodies are shutting down from hunger. We are violated and over-worked, and our lives are constantly at risk. Happiness and music no longer exist for us, and we can't see through our tears. Eternal King, bring us back to you, and restore our ancient glory! Don't be mad at us forever.

DAY THREE - LIGHT IN THE DARK
EZEKIEL-DANIEL

BIG IDEA

During the time of exile, God does impossible things to reveal his glory and save the lives of his children.

MIRACLES AND VISIONS

- **Heaven opens-** God reveals his awesome beauty to Ezekiel and inspires him to speak courageously to the people.
- **Oppression ends-** Enemy nations terrorize the vulnerable Hebrews, but God punishes corrupt leaders and turns their impenetrable cities to dust.
- **Dry bones coming alive-** Ezekiel watches in astonishment as a field of dusty skeletons turn into a living army. God assures him that the Hebrew nation will return to life and prosperity as well.
- **Vision of the Temple-** Ezekiel witnesses a dazzling and detailed vision of the Temple that will be rebuilt when the exile is over.
- **Interpreting dreams-** Daniel is the only man who accurately describes and interprets Nebuchadnezzar's dreams, which earns the king's favor and trust.
- **Surviving the furnace-** Daniel's friends refuse to worship the king, and an angel protects them in the heart of a blazing fire.

- **Humbling a dictator-** God removes Nebuchadnezzar from society for seven years to humble him and change his heart.
- **Shutting lion mouths-** Daniel is thrown into the pit, but the hungry lions can't touch him.
- **Vision of the end-** Daniel sees symbols of future empires and fierce holy judgments, and he learns that God's faithful children will survive it all.

HOW GOD SHOWS UP

After Babylonia crushes Judah, God continually reminds his children that he's stronger than any enemy. God reveals his breathtaking beauty to Ezekiel and his saving power to Daniel and his friends. God even takes down the fearsome emperor of Babylonia and humbles his heart. Even though the exiled nation deserved to be abandoned and destroyed because of their past sins, their Father shows extravagant love and promises new life to the nation.

EZEKIEL

1. Before the fall of Jerusalem, I lived with a group of Jewish exiles by a Babylonian river. One day, the sky opened with a great lightning storm, and I saw an enormous creature with the four majestic animal faces and a curious flame dancing around its wings. I looked above the creature and saw a sapphire throne containing a dazzling bronze-skinned person who radiated a beautiful rainbow of light. I knew

in an instant that this person was God himself, and I threw myself on the ground in worship.

2. God lifted me to my feet and said "Ezekiel, I have chosen you to deliver my truth to the stubborn children of Israel. They will resist you as they have resisted me, but don't be afraid, and don't follow their wicked example." Then the Lord gave me a scroll predicting the future grief of the people and asked me to eat it.

3. When I ate the scroll, it dissolved in my mouth and tasted as sweet as honey. Then God said "I will make your skin as tough as a diamond so you can speak my truth with courage. Keep my words in your heart and memory, even if my stubborn people ignore you." The winged creature roared praises to the mighty Lord in a voice as loud as an earthquake, and just like that, the heavenly vision vanished. All I could do for the next week is sit by the river bank in shocked silence. God said "I am appointing you to guard my people and warn them of the disasters to come. If they listen, I will honor you for saving their lives. For now, I will silence your voice so that you may listen and learn from me.

4. "Get a brick to represent the city of Jerusalem, and surround it with miniature military camps and battering rams to act out the coming siege of the city. Lie down for 390 days in silent suffering to represent the 390 years Israel will live under my punishment. Then lay there another 40 days to represent the four decades I will punish Judah. You will have limited water and unsanitary bread at this time to represent the intense famine that will strike my people during this time."

5. God told me to cut my hair and scatter some of the strands to demonstrate how he would scatter his people. He had me burn some of the hair in the fires of Jerusalem to represent the hunger and disease that would soon strike the ruined city. Judah has disobeyed her Father even worse than foreign nations, so the whole world will see her collapse.

6. God said "I will smash the pagan altars in Judah to show that I am much more powerful than these false gods. The people will mourn the disgusting sins that brought such widespread destruction on their land. When they remember me, they will feel ashamed for choosing idols to take my place.

7. "Ezekiel, the end is coming! Israel's appalling behavior has angered me and led to this time of crippling disaster. Their wealth and pride will dissolve as they focus on surviving the chaotic violence and disease that fills the streets. They will grieve as they realize that their gold can't save them. Only I can save them."

8. During my sixth year of exile, a vision of God overwhelmed me as I sat at home with friends. His legs shone like fire and his torso like polished bronze. He plucked me out of my house and showed me the ruined Temple that even the high priests were desecrating. God's house was full of sickening idols, and its walls were defiled with graffiti drawings of snakes and fertility gods. God said "They think that if they worship idols in the dark, I won't see them. They fill their streets with violence, and now they insult me deeply by corrupting my own Temple! I will no longer listen to their selfish prayers."

9. God gathered a team of angel warriors around his throne and said "Sweep through Jerusalem and release my anger on them. Wipe out those who have corrupted the land, but spare all those who are troubled by the disgusting sins of the people."

10. God instructed one of his angels to collect burning coals from underneath the mysterious four-headed creature and toss the coals down onto Jerusalem. The dazzling presence of God left his throne to stand beside the creature at the Temple gate, and each of the four majestic heads faced straight ahead, ready for the task at hand.

11. God showed me two of Judah's leaders and said "Those evil men fill the people with false hope that this time of destruction will be short-lived. Tell them I have seen their wicked hearts, and I have seen their murder victims lying in the streets. They will fall on my punishing sword and finally recognize that I am the only true God. The sinners in Jerusalem think I have abandoned those of you in exile, but assure your fellow exiles that the opposite is true. I will protect the scattered people who turn to me with obedient hearts, and I will bring them back home to rid my land of disgusting idol worship." Then I saw the dazzling glory of God leave Jerusalem and settle on surrounding mountains.

12. God said "Ezekiel, my rebellious people refuse to see or hear the plain warnings I place before them. Get their attention by packing a bag like a refugee and wandering around the city at night. These leaders will become refugees as well, trying desperately to escape their enemies in the dark. Babylonian enemies will capture them easily and leave few

survivors. They will tremble in fear as their land is stripped bare. They think my predictions never come true, but the time has come for my warnings to become reality.

13. "Those foolish false prophets claim to speak my truth, but their lies and pretend visions are useless. They say all is well, but all is definitely not well! The people follow superstitions to try to defeat death, but I will soon reveal the truth to the good people they have deceived.

14. "Idol worshippers pray for answers, but I will hide true wisdom from them until they discard those idols and come back to me. I'm telling you, Ezekiel, even if great men like Noah and Job lived among the people today, I still wouldn't change my mind about the coming punishments. This destruction is justified, and I stand by my decision.

15. "I planted the vines of Israel to bear fruit and bring me glory, but they have shown that they are useless and can only be used for kindling.

16. "When Jerusalem was a baby, worthless parents abandoned her in a field. I rescued her, washed her, clothed her, and helped her become a healthy, prosperous woman. I made her beautiful, but she misused her beauty by prostituting herself to everyone who came along. She didn't even do it for the money. She was happy to pay others for the opportunity to betray me. Now she is even more evil than corrupt foreign cities I destroyed in the past. She proudly fills her belly while poor innocents starve in the streets. When I forgive her and lead her back to prosperity, she'll feel ashamed of the evil decisions that led her to ruin.

17. "When the helpless vine of Judah rebels against the powerful

eagle of Babylonia to grow toward Egypt, Babylonia has every right to pull Judah up by the roots. Judah cannot break its treaty with its conqueror and go unpunished. But one day I will plant my vine high on a mountain where all other trees will witness its comforting shade. The most vulnerable sprout will become the mightiest tree of all!

18. "Each person will be judged individually, regardless of the sins of his parents or children. If a good-hearted man worships me faithfully, treats others fairly, and gives generously to those in need, he will earn my favor even if his father is the most corrupt man in the land. Children, turn away from the evil that rots you from within, and I will give you a new mind and a clean heart."

19. God asked me to sing this song to mourn the fall of Israel's royal family. "Little cubs, your mother was a fierce, roaring lioness who raised you to be strong, capable hunters. Some of you exceeded your mother's expectations by conquering other nations, but others let themselves be caught in enemy traps, allowing the good fruit in your land to burn and wither into dust."

20. In my seventh year of exile, Israel's leaders asked me for advice, and God encouraged me not to hold back the difficult truth. God said "I chose your ancestors to be my children, and I delivered them from Egyptian slavery to a safe, fertile land. I asked them to honor this deliverance by obeying me, but they followed Egyptian gods instead. I patiently taught them to care for each other, hoping my laws would guide them toward good, meaningful lives. Still they ignored and defied me at every turn. Their wicked hearts

and habits led each generation further from me, and now, I can't stand the sight of them. I can no longer watch as my children destroy themselves with sin. Great destruction is the only thing that could possibly wake them up and remind them that I am the only God worthy of worship.

21. "Since my children treat me like an enemy, I will declare war on them. Their misguided confidence will wane, and they will tremble in fear before me. The king of Babylonia approaches with his battering rams, and when he seizes Jerusalem, the world will know the depth of your sin. Wicked king of Israel, take that crown off your head, and give it to the poor people you've oppressed.

22. "People of Jerusalem, you murder your own people and destroy your hearts with idolatry. You cheat vulnerable women and children, and you have no respect for your parents or my holy laws. You commit adultery without a second thought and get rich dishonestly. You are like metal waste that I must melt and burn in order to remove your impurities and make you like pure, valuable silver.

23. "There were once two sisters named Israel and Judah that I loved deeply. I rescued them from forced prostitution in Egypt, married them, and took care of them, but they both insisted on continuing their lives of prostitution to foreign idols. Their foreign lovers shamed them, and Israel was beaten nearly to death by her former lover Assyria. I wish Judah would have learned from her sister's tragic example, but she betrayed me even worse than Israel. I will divorce and punish her in my anger.

24. "My city is like a rusty pot that turns every dish into inedible,

filthy poison. This city of murderers is doomed! I will empty the corroded city and burn it until its impurities are gone. It will become a useful, sanitary place through this time of refining judgment. Ezekiel, your wife will soon die, and I will ask you not to mourn for her, even though that seems impossible. This is because my people will respond numbly and without emotion when my Temple and their families are destroyed.

25. "People of Ammon, you laughed as my Temple fell, so I will let desert people plunder your land and steal your food. Moab underestimates my people, and Edom and Philistia bring cruel revenge on them, so these enemy nations will also feel my anger.

26. "The wealthy, arrogant tycoons of Tyre are thrilled that my people will no longer be business rivals. They cheer as Jerusalem falls, but I will humble them with Babylonian armies and economic collapse. Their trade ships will be swept away, and their island cities will crumble into the sea, never to be seen again.

27. "Ezekiel, sing a funeral song for the fallen city of Tyre. Beautiful city by the sea, you had spotless linen sails, and your strong wooden ports. Your mighty soldiers, talented craftsmen, and clever business men were unmatched in their success, and other nations clamored to buy your high-quality exports. Your beautiful ships are now empty, and the world mourns as your sailors and riches sink into the sea.

28. "King of Tyre, you puff your chest and think you are smarter than everyone else. You look down on poorer nations for their lack of business sense, but when enemies come to

destroy you and your beautiful city, will you still claim to be a god? You shined like a spotless jewel, but when you're beauty is reduced to ashes, you will finally realize that you're a mere mortal, and only I am God. None of Israel's enemies will escape my punishment, as I lead my children back to their homeland.

29. "King of Egypt, you are a monster crocodile swimming in the Nile, and I am your hunter. I will hook your jaw and let the small fish gnaw your thick skin. I will throw you into the desert where you will be vulture food. You were once a mighty predator, but I will make you the weakest nation of all.

30. "I will bring storm clouds and war on bully nations that brag of their success. Their cities will crumble, their rivers will dry, and their wealth will disappear. I will break the arms of Egypt and strengthen the muscles of Babylonia.

31. "Egypt, today you are like a powerful tree with beautiful leaves and plenty of shade. Rivers help you grow and birds find safety in your branches. You grew arrogant as you became the tallest tree in the forest, so now I will cut you down, and those you oppressed will rejoice.

32. "Egypt, you're like a crocodile terrorizing all the fish around you and polluting your river home. I will catch you and toss you on the ground for smaller animals to consume. I will darken the sun and stars in your sky, and jaws will drop when the world sees your colossal fall.

33. "Ezekiel, I am placing you on the city wall to warn my people of the powerful enemy charging down the hill. Warn my children that they are destroying themselves with sin. I

want them to repent, so I can forgive them and restore their lives." In my twelfth year of exile, we learned that mighty Jerusalem had fallen, and God returned my voice to me. Then God said "My people sit in the city ruins, and they still haven't learned their lesson. They still worship idols, murder innocents, and rely solely on their own strength. I will make their country a desolate wasteland. They enjoy listening to you, Ezekiel, but your words do not inspire them to change their greedy ways."

34. "Leaders of Israel, you are like shepherds who enjoy the wool and meat of your flock but refuse to take care of your sheep. You abuse them, starve them, and hand them to wild animals, even though they depend on you for protection. I will take my flock away from your greedy hands, and I will be their good Shepherd from now on. I will lead them to fertile meadows, heal the sick, and seek out the sheep that wander away.

35. "Mighty mountains of Edom, you will flatten and crumble to ruins. You refused to help as my people were slaughtered, and now your land will be filled with death and destruction. You boasted that my people belonged to you, but when you fall, the world will know I am God.

36. "Israel, your neighbors plundered and controlled you. They mocked your destruction with glee, and now they will pay for their cruelty. Their cities will fall as you rebuild your homeland and grow more prosperous than before. You felt my anger when you defiled the Promised Land, but I will give you a new heart and mind that longs to obey me. You will finally realize that my law leads to happiness and

prosperity."

37. God took me to a valley of dry skeletons that appeared to have died long ago. God said "I will breathe new life into these bones. I will cover these skeletons with tendons, muscle, and skin, and this whole valley of death will come alive." Right before my eyes, the rattling bones came together to form an army of able-bodied men. God said "Israel is dried up and lifeless like a graveyard of bones, but I will breathe hope into their spirits and bring them back to life. I will unite Israel and Judah as one nation, and they will be my protected covenant people once more.

38. "Ezekiel, tell the foreign dictator Gog that his time is coming to an end. His battalions are massive, tough, heavily-armed, and full of strong allies. They will invade Israel like a great storm, but I will punish Gog's army with a mighty earthquake, and they will turn swords against each other in confusion.

39. "I will disarm Gog and strike his colossal army dead in the mountains of Israel. Their bodies will become food for wild animals, and their abandoned weapons will become firewood for my people. I will bless Israel with prosperity, mercy, and protection as I pour my spirit on their land.

40. Fourteen years after Jerusalem's fall, God lifted me onto a high mountain, and I saw a bronze angel standing next to the future restored Temple. The angel went through the eastern gate and measured the dimensions of the gateway, guardrooms, and entrance room in that part of the Temple. He measured four courtyards in and around the Temple gates as well as a separate building designed

to wash and prepare animal sacrifices for the altar.

41. The angel guided me toward the Temple's holy inner room, and as he measured this room, I noticed beautiful wooden carvings on the walls and noticed the design of the altar and doors.

42. We entered a three-story building on the north side of the Temple with many small rooms. The angel showed me an identical building on the south side. He explained "These holy buildings allow the priests to eat the sacred offerings in a spirit of worship, reverence, and gratitude."

43. We saw God's dazzling presence swooping through the eastern gate. His voice roared like the sea, and the whole earth glowed with his glorious light. I threw my face on the ground in worship, and the Lord lifted me up so I could witness his light filling the Temple. God said "Ezekiel, my throne now sits in this Temple, and I will live among my people to remind them to respect me and each other. Explain the design of this Temple to the people so that they will rebuild it correctly when the time is right. When my altar is built, dedicate it to me with a reverent week-long ceremony. Purify my altar with the blood of flawless animals."

44. We left the Temple through the eastern gate where God had entered, and the Lord shut the door behind us, saying "Since I entered the Temple through the eastern gate, no one will use that door except the king. Ezekiel, tell my rebellious people I will not tolerate my Temple being defiled by unbelievers and half-hearted worship. The Levites who worshipped idols will not be allowed to work in the Temple. My

priests must faithfully teach the people about my commands and our sacred traditions. Priests must keep their bodies and their marriages holy and may eat sacrifices offered to me by the people."

45. When we return from exile and divide the land among the tribes, we should dedicate the Temple area to God and set aside a fair amount of land for the ruling prince. The Lord says "Rulers of Israel, stop governing my people with violence, oppression, and deception. You need my guidance just like everyone else. Your sacrifices will allow me to forgive you and favor your people. Lead the way in celebrating the sacred festivals each year.

46. "On the Sabbath and the New Moon Festival, the king may walk through the east gate to offer his sacrifice to me. Offer a sacrifice each morning as a reminder to stay close to my heart. The king must never exploit his people or claim a citizen's land for the royal family." Then the angel showed me several small rooms near the inner courtyard and said "This is where the priests may bake the meat and grain sacrifices before consuming them. These offerings must never leave the Temple once they have been given to God."

47. A river began flowing out of the east gate and on for miles. The angel led me into the water, and it got deeper the further I waded in. The angel said "This vibrant stream flows to the Dead Sea and freshens the water within. This living water allows fish to thrive and plants to yield good, healing fruit." God outlined the nation's new boundaries and said "Divide the land fairly among the families that return from exile, and offer a reasonable portion to

foreigners who live among you and obey our laws.

48. Once the land is divided evenly among the twelve tribes, the center portion will contain the Temple and the Levite homes. The tribes of Benjamin and Judah will reside close to this holy center section. Jerusalem's wall will have twelve entrances dedicated to each tribe of Israel, and the Lord will dwell there among the people.

DANIEL

1. King Nebuchadnezzar overthrows the king of Judah and selects the best and brightest Judeans to serve him in Babylonia. He instructs his chief official to train the most handsome, clever Judeans for palace responsibilities, and among that group are four friends named Daniel, Shadrach, Meshach, and Abednego. Daniel and his friends convince their guard to give them ritually clean food, and God blesses them with great wisdom and the ability to interpret dreams. These four men impress the king more than any other Judeans.

2. The king asks his fortune tellers to interpret a mysterious dream but rashly orders their execution when they can't help. God reveals the dream's meaning to Daniel, and he proclaims "Powerful God, you are in control. Thank you for revealing this secret wisdom to me." Daniel explains to the king that Babylonia and three other earthly empires will rise up but eventually fall under God's eternal kingdom. Impressed by God's answer to Daniel, the king makes

Daniel his chief royal advisor.

3. The king commands everyone in Babylonia to worship an enormous gold statue, but Shadrach, Meshach, and Abednego will only worship the Lord. The angry king orders them to be thrown into a furnace so hot that even the guards around it are burned. An angel protects the men in the heart of the fire, and when the dumbfounded king releases them, they don't even smell like smoke. The king says "These brave men risked their lives to show deep trust in their Rescuer. **The God of Israel** has earned **my respect and** the respect of this nation." The king then promotes these three to positions of great influence.

4. Nebuchadnezzar proclaims "The King of heaven has revealed miracles to me, and it all started with a dream only Daniel could interpret. I now trust him more than any other advisors, and now I need his help again." Daniel explains that the king's empire stretches across the world like a fruitful tree, but God will cut it down. God will remove Nebuchadnezzar from society for seven years to humble him. This prediction comes true less than a year later. After seven years, Nebuchadnezzar declares "Praise God whose glory can humble any king! No one can stand against his power. From now on, I will rule with justice and humility according to his guidance."

5. Nebuchadnezzar's son becomes king of Babylonia, and a strange vision happens at a royal banquet. Daniel explains "King Belshazzar, God let your father rule many nations, but when he became arrogant and cruel, God humbled him in the wilderness for seven years. You have not learned

from his experience, and you arrogantly serve party drinks in Temple cups stolen from Israel. Your empire will soon be divided among Medes and Persia." The next day, Belshazzar is assassinated.

6. The new king Darius appoints Daniel as governor, and Daniel works harder than anyone to impress the king. Jealous officials suggest to Darius that the people should worship the king above all gods. As expected, Daniel will only worship God, so to uphold the proclamation he was tricked into, the king reluctantly throws Daniel into a lion pit. God protects innocent Daniel from the lions all night, and Darius joyfully rescues him in the morning. The king condemns Daniel's accusers to the pit, and the lions pounce before they even hit the floor. Darius proclaims "The living God produces awesome miracles throughout heaven and earth, and his power has no end. Praise the Lord who saved his servant Daniel from the lions!"

7. Daniel dreams that the glowing King of heaven strikes down four terrifying beasts that rise from the ocean. God explains that four large empires will emerge from chaos, and the last of these empires will cause widespread destruction, with a leader more proud and corrupt than any before him. Fortunately, no earthly kingdom can stand up to God's eternal kingdom.

8. In another dream, an arrogant ram strikes everyone around him and is defeated by a four-horned goat that brings even greater destruction to the earth. An angel reveals "The horns of these powerful animals represent the current empire and the destructive empires that will follow. The

final king of this age will defy God, deceive many, and destroy without warning, but his reign of terror will not last."

9. While reflecting on the seventy-year exile Jeremiah had predicted, Daniel prays "Honorable God, your love remains steady for those who obey you. None of us follow you perfectly, and our sins disgrace us at times, but you always do the right thing. You punished and scattered your people, and many still refuse to listen to you. Even so, please restore your land and your Temple. God of mercy, forgive our many sins!" The angel Gabriel responds "God will indeed free Jerusalem from sin and injustice, **rebuilding the Temple** stronger than before. **Unfortunately,** his chosen leader will **later** be killed unjustly, and Jerusalem will face war and destruction yet again."

10. While Daniel mourns, he sees a dazzling angel dressed in white with eyes like fire. The angel says "Daniel, your body is weak from trembling. Don't be afraid. God loves you and has heard your humble prayers all along. Evil forces kept us from answering right away, but now I have important words for you.

11. "Four more kings will rule Persia, and the fourth will be the richest and strongest of all. A Syrian king will invade the Promised Land and oppress Israel with unfair taxes. Another will seize the Syrian throne through deception, and this evil king will kill God's church leaders and proclaim himself higher than God. When he is overthrown, this Syrian dictator will die completely alone and unloved.

12. "Around that time, the angel Michael will guard God's

people as the Lord judges all nations. The dead will rise to eternal life, and followers of God will live close to God's shining glory forever. Stay faithful, Daniel, and when you rise to life on that day, you will be richly rewarded."

DAY FOUR - RELENTLESS GOD
HOSEA-JOEL-AMOS-OBADIAH-JONAH-MICAH

BIG IDEA

God is fed up with corruption and offers a series of profound wake-up calls to change the hearts of his people.

SIX UNIQUE PERSPECTIVES

- **Hosea-** A good man marries a prostitute who hurts him over and over, but he forgives her every time and invites her to come back home. Likewise, God's people don't deserve forgiveness, but he removes their shame anyway.

- **Joel-** The people panic during a time of famine, but God promises that this isn't the end of their story. God will return the nation to prosperity, and in the end, all evil will be destroyed.

- **Amos-** Materialism and pride are rotting the hearts of Israel, and God plans to put a stop to it. He will drastically humble the nation with a time of poverty but will return security to the land once hearts begin to change.

- **Obadiah-** The nation of Edom oppresses Israel and puts itself on a pedestal. God will humble these arrogant bullies and bring his nation's glory back.

- **Jonah-** He tries to run away from God's call, but God relentlessly uses a storm and a whale to get his attention and hold him accountable. God happily forgives Jonah and an enemy city, offering both another chance at life.

- **Micah-** Those who torture innocents and steal from the poor will not win. Our Warrior Father will fight to destroy wickedness and win back the hearts of his children.

HOW GOD SHOWS UP

God loves us too much to let us run away and hide in our shame. He calls us to take a hard look at our brokenness and offers to free us of that burden. He never gets tired of rescuing us from ourselves. Our good Father cannot stand the sight of evil and will not let oppressive forces win. All we have to do is trust that he's bigger than our pain.

HOSEA

1. Before the fall of Israel, God says "Hosea, your future wife and children will be unfaithful and difficult to love, just as my people have been unfaithful to me. I cannot claim them as mine in their current state of wickedness, but eventually they will unite with Judah, turn back to me, and gain prosperity again." Hosea marries a woman named Gomer and has three children whose names speak of Israel's sin.

2. Gomer is a prostitute who openly cheats on Hosea and shows no gratitude to him. God says "My wife Israel cheats on me with idols and refuses to acknowledge the harvests I so generously provide, so I will destroy her fields and punish her shameful idolatry. But later I will

woo her with loving words in the desert, and her loyalty will return to me. I will provide generously for her and show her love and mercy forever.

3. "Hosea, go love your adulterous wife to mirror how I faithfully love my undeserving nation." So I bought my wife back from her pimps and allowed her to slowly earn back my trust during a time of celibacy.

4. God says "The people of Israel refuse to acknowledge and love me. They destroy each other with murder, theft, adultery, and dishonesty. Crime fills the streets, and the priests refuse to set a decent example for the people. The priests will starve for leading the people into senseless idolatry. They beg for answers from a piece of wood!

5. "Leaders of Israel, listen up! I will punish you for the injustice you've brought on this land. Idolatry ruins the hearts of my people and puts them under a powerful spell difficult to break. They continuously stumble but stubbornly refuse to change. To make matters worse, Judah has stolen land from her sister, Israel, so I will punish her as well. As my chosen nations fall, I hope they will reach out to me for help."

6. The people say "God has wounded us, but surely healing will come in a few days." God responds "Your cities are full of murderers and robbers who disgrace my name with disgusting idol worship, and you think this is all going away in a few days? I have given you plenty of warnings of what's to come, but you refuse to listen. Your love for me disappears as quickly as the wind.

7. "I would love to bless my people, but I can't look past their evil hearts and actions. They steal and lie without a second

thought. They betray leaders with assassination plots and power plays. Worthless, half-baked Israel relies on foreign allies but refuses to turn to me. I wish I could save them, but I won't answer their half-hearted prayers.

8. "Israel claims to follow me, but they break our covenant and reject all things good. They trust their own judgment as supreme. My stubborn people abandon their Creator for homemade statues, and they wonder why their harvests have been small lately! Soon their ally Assyria will turn against them and oppress them."

9. People of Israel, you gleefully dance at pagan festivals, but you have no reason to celebrate. You sell your soul to worthless idols and abandon the God that loves you. You will be removed from this land God gave you, and you'll wither like a rootless vine. Honest prophets warn you to repent, but you call them fools and refuse to listen.

10. The vine of Israel was once prosperous, beautiful, and full of sweet grapes, but their wicked hearts earn God's destruction. These lying idol worshipers will be humbled and disgraced as their king is carried into exile. Maybe then they will finally awake from their sinful stupor. Israel once worked hard and bore good fruit for God, but now their fruit is utterly useless and inedible.

11. God says "When young Israel was enslaved in Egypt, I rescued and adopted him. I taught him how to live, but instead he trusted useless idols to provide for his needs. I must severely discipline my child to get his attention and turn him back to me. I love him too much to watch while he destroys himself.

12. "My people destroy each other with constant violence and treachery. Judah betrays Israel like Jacob fought Esau in the womb. Children of Jacob, wait patiently for my plan to unfold like your ancestor did. You love to get rich by cheating others, but I will make you live in humble tents again. Your disgraceful acts make me fume with anger."

13. Those who kiss homemade silver idols will disappear like the morning mist. God says "I am the Savior who led you out of Egypt and took care of you in the desert. I led you to a good land, and as soon as you found success, you forgot about me. I will devour your kings like a hungry lion to remind you of my fearsome power. You could receive new life from me, but you're too foolish to listen. You have lost my pity, and your doomsday has come!"

14. Let all who stumble over sin return to God and pray "Forgive our mistakes, merciful Lord, and we will worship you with trust and gratitude. No idol or ally could ever protect us like you." God will respond "I lovingly draw you back to my heart. I will nourish your land like a spring rain. You will bloom like beautiful flowers, grow as strong as cedars, and bear sweet fruit as you live under my shelter and care. I will be the source of all your blessings." May God's wise people take this good message to heart.

JOEL

1. As Judah faces this time of national disaster, we cry like a young bride mourning the loss of her groom. Swarms of

locusts devastate the land and destroy the livelihood of our farmers. We cannot feed ourselves or our animals, and we have nothing to offer the Lord. Our hearts hurt with worry and sorrow.

2. God's time of judgment will be far more terrifying than this locust storm. The earth will shake, the stars will darken, and the land will burn. But it's not too late for our broken hearts to return to God. Our patient God is ready to forgive us and bless us with abundance once more. When Judeans of all ages finally unite in prayer, God will answer "Have no fear! I will remove the locust swarms and make your fields overflow with food and wine. You will joyfully praise me as the source of all blessings, as I cover you with my protective Spirit and grace.

3. "On that day, I will restore Judah's prosperity and judge the oppressive nations who sell young children as slaves and steal my Temple treasure. My thunderous voice declares war on these wicked enemies, and I will crush them like grapes."

AMOS

1. A humble shepherd named Amos warns prosperous Israel that a dry spell is coming. God says "Syria oppresses other nations with savage cruelty, and Philistia and Tyre sells countless innocents as slaves. Edom shows no mercy to their Israelite cousins, and Ammon slices the bellies of pregnant women. These enemy nations will

come to ruin because of their horrifying sins.

2. "I condemn Moab for defiling a king's corpse, and I will punish Judah and Israel for abandoning my laws. Israel tramples the weak and sells honest people as slaves. You were once slaves, and I rescued you from that life; shame on you for bringing that life on others! I set you apart to bring me glory, but you have failed. Even your bravest, fastest warriors cannot outrun my judgment.

3. "I chose you to be my children, so I hold you to a higher standard than other nations. I am giving you fair warning of what's to come, like a lion roaring before attack or a war trumpet blowing before battle. You decorate your homes with stolen goods and rest on your luxurious couches without guilt, but your mansions and pagan altars will crumble to ruins.

4. "You women of Israel drink all day and mistreat anyone weaker or poorer than you. I will hook you like a fish and toss you out of the city. You proudly sin and then boast about your generous offerings to me. I'm not impressed. You fail to thank me for good times, and you fail to turn to me in dark times. I made the mountains and wind. What does it take to get your attention?

5. "Israel, when you fall, no one will pick you up. Your only hope is to return to me and stop stealing from the poor and oppressed. I control the stars and could pour the ocean out like a jar of water. Learn to treat others with respect, and perhaps I will have mercy on you. I can't stand your insincere worship. Darkness and mourning will soon fill your streets."

6.   You feel so safe in the lap of luxury, but God is disgusted
     by you. He will tear you down as he tore down worthless
     pagan nations. Pride and greed rot your hearts, but your
     gluttonous feasts will soon come to an end.

7.   Amos sees a vision of locust swarms and volcanic lava
     destroying Israel, and he begs for God's forgiveness. God
     responds "Amos, my people are running out of chances
     to come back to me. I will spare them from my anger this
     time, but I won't spare them again. Soon their cities will
     crumble." An influential palace priest denounces Amos for
     his prophecies of destruction, but Amos responds "No one
     is paying me to speak the truth to you. I'm just a humble
     shepherd obeying God's orders. Since you are trying to
     silence me, you and your family will be destroyed."

8.   God says "Amos, I will not change my mind again. The
     boasting songs of Israel will soon become cries of mourning.
     They rejoice at the end of the Sabbath each week, eager
     to cheat their customers at work again. I cannot ignore
     evil hearts that gleefully destroy the poor. Those arrogant
     snobs will soon learn what it's like to go hungry like those
     they've oppressed.

9.   "I will smash the defiled Temple and kill those whose hearts
     are already dead. These sinners cannot hide as I shake the
     earth and place my throne above the sky. But those with
     worthy hearts should not fear because Israel will ultimately
     survive this. I will rebuild your ruins and make your fields
     flourish even better than before."

OBADIAH

1. God says "Prideful Edom, you think you are as strong and solid as a mountain. You think you're smarter than everyone else, but I will pull you off your high perch and declare war on you. Former allies will turn against you and wipe you out. You robbed and killed your Israelite brothers and laughed at their distress. You will drink from the bitter cup you've happily given to others. My **Hebrew** children will rise **up to** consume you like a fire, and I will be the new King of your land."

JONAH

1. God says "Jonah, go to Ninevah and warn the wicked Assyrians that my punishment in coming." Jonah ignores God and boards a boat to Spain. A violent storm threatens the boat, and the crew throws Jonah overboard when they learn he is attempting to run from God. The storm calms instantly as a great whale swallows Jonah whole. The shaken crew promises to serve the mighty Creator from that day on.

2. In the belly of the beast, Jonah prays "Lord, I called for help, and you answered. The waves sucked me far under the surface of the sea, and I nearly drowned, but somehow, I'm still alive. Some choose to abandon you for worthless idols, but I will sing grateful songs to you. I will keep my promises to you from now on." At that, God orders the whale to spew Jonah onto the beach.

3. With a new lease on life, Jonah passionately warns the wicked citizens of Ninevah that destruction is coming, and amazingly, they take Jonah's warnings seriously. The Assyrians mourn past sins and completely change their lifestyle. Delighted at their repentance, God decides to spare the city.

4. Jonah prays "Lord, I suspected you would change your mind, and that's why I tried to run away in the first place. These people have done terrible things to Israel, and they don't deserve your mercy or patience." As Jonah finds a quiet place to pout, the ever-patient Father says "Regardless of their past, I delightfully show mercy to anyone willing to repent. Remember how I saved your life when you ran from me? I would much rather spare these 120,000 innocent people than destroy them, and honestly, you have no right to be mad about that."

MICAH

1. The mighty Judge can melt mountaintops like wax, and he will soon turn Israel's idols to dust. Samaria will be a city of ruins, and I mourn bitterly to learn that Jerusalem will also be destroyed. People of Judah, weep for your beloved children who will soon fall into enemy hands.

2. God will ruin all of you who get rich by stealing from the poor, and then you won't strut so proudly anymore. You refuse to take your sins seriously, and you condemn my harsh words for making you uncomfortable. You rob innocent women and children, and you honestly think God

has something nice to say to you? Only the humble among you will survive the exile and come safely home.

3. You leaders of Israel are supposed to love justice, but you brutalize innocent people and let desperate people pay you for false hope. You tell them whatever they want to hear, but God's spirit gives me the courage to speak the truth about your sins. You've built Jerusalem on a foundation of murder and injustice, and such a city cannot stand.

4. One day, the Temple will be lifted high for the world to admire. We will gladly follow God's guidance as he helps us find peace in our neighborhoods and abroad. We will worship and obey our God forever. God says "Your broken bodies will be far from home, but I will **guard you like a tender shepherd and** give you a fresh start. The enemies that crush you will be crushed."

5. When Jerusalem falls, don't lose heart! The tiny town of Bethlehem will one day bear a peaceful ruler who will reveal God's majesty to the people. All idols will be struck to the ground, and those who survive this dark time will trust in God alone.

6. The ultimate Judge makes his case against Israel, saying "Children, I delivered you from slavery, sent good leaders to guide you, and rescued you from many enemies through the years. I did so much for you, and all I ask in return is that you love each other and follow me. But those of you who get rich exploiting the poor will lose everything you have."

7. The corruption in this land is beyond hope or repair. These worthless people don't know how to be loyal or honest. They have no respect for the dignity or safety of others, and

they cannot be trusted. While they ignore God's warnings, I wait patiently for my Savior. God will defend his children and bring us into his warm light. It will soon be time to rebuild and enlarge our nation alongside the good Shepherd that works miracles for us. He tramples our sins under his powerful, merciful feet.

DAY FIVE - PROTECTIVE FATHER
NAHUM-HABAKKUK-ZEPHANIAH-HAGGAI-ZECHARIAH-MALACHI

BIG IDEA

God overcomes mighty enemies and protects a vulnerable nation as they rebuild.

SIX UNIQUE PERSPECTIVES

- **Nahum-** Those who crush God's children will be crushed. He is too good and too powerful to let evil oppressors win.
- **Habakkuk-** When violence and chaos overwhelm Judah, God assures them that this is not the end. Those who terrorize God's chosen nation will not remain victorious for long.
- **Zephaniah-** God has given his corrupted people plenty of warnings, but they continually reject and ignore him. God must remove their comfort to change their hearts, but then he will usher in a new chapter of peace and prosperity.
- **Haggai-** As the Hebrews rebuild the shattered Temple after exile, God encourages them to persevere. The Lord assures his children that he'll strengthen and protect them as they work together.
- **Zechariah-** God longs to bring his exiled people home. The powerful Father will protect his children as they rebuild a stronger nation. One day when corruption infects the land

again, God will have the final word.

• **Malachi-** As the rebuilt nation lives under God's protection, the people grow complacent once again. Their worship becomes insincere, and God mercifully plans to send a Savior who will change their hearts for good.

HOW GOD SHOWS UP

This is a war for our hearts, and our Father will not back down from the fight. When darkness surrounds us, he offers promises of hope and relief. When we try our hardest, he strengthens our efforts. When we grow complacent and forget how much he has blessed us, he sends his own Son to enter our world and show us how much he loves us.

NAHUM

1. No one can sneak past our powerful Lord when he's angry. With one word, he can kick up mighty storms, dry up the sea, and shake the mountains. Our good God destroys those who destroy others, and he rushes in like a mighty flood to protect his children. You strong, numerous armies of Assyria scheme against God and oppress his people, but God will destroy you. Judah will celebrate as it escapes your crushing grasp.

2. Prepare your armies, Assyria! Your best efforts to guard your great city will be useless. Your battalions will stumble and dart around in chaos. Your enemies will burst through the city wall,

steal your palace treasure, and take your queen as a hostage. You gobbled your enemies like a hungry lion, but now your knees will tremble before the Almighty God.

3. You murderous liars of Ninevah will be robbed of your vast wealth in the chaotic siege of the city. Once so attractive and enchanting to many, Ninevah will finally be seen as the filthy, shameful prostitute she is. You Assyrians once swarmed your enemies like cruel locusts, but the world will rejoice as your nation crumbles.

HABAKKUK

1. Violence, injustice, and destruction fill the streets of Judah. Babylonia advances like a pack of wolves to terrorize and devour us. With armies too large to count, they sweep through the land like a great wind. They laugh at our king and think their strength makes them gods. Lord, you are the one true God, and only you can protect us. I don't understand how you can let these wicked idol worshippers hunt us without mercy.

2. God answers "Habakkuk, write this down for future generations. Wait patiently for me to destroy evil people and save my followers." Wealthy nations, you restlessly conquer others with ever-increasing pride and greed. No level of power or success will ever satisfy you. Your victims will soon plunder you, and your idols won't be able to help you. God's wisdom and justice will reign as you stagger around

like a shameful drunk.

3. Lord, I am awestruck by your miracles and mercy. Your glory covers heaven and earth with overwhelming light. The earth trembles in fear of your mountain-crushing power. You surf on the clouds to rescue your children from their enemies. My knees collapse as I witness your impossible greatness. Our fields are barren, but I will joyfully and patiently wait for you to save us from this mess we made.

ZEPHANIAH

1. During the reign of King Josiah, God says "Humans corrupted my beautiful creation, so one day I will put this broken world out of its misery. I will wipe out those who betray me for false gods. Doubters will realize their wealth cannot save them from my power. War cries and mournful wails will echo through the land."

2. Come to your senses before God blows you away like straw in the wind. Escape his anger by humbly repenting and learning to do the right thing. If you do this, God will destroy and empty enemy nations for us to inhabit. Arrogant bullies will disappear as God brings prosperity back to his chosen nation.

3. You corrupt Judeans oppress your own people and refuse to trust your Father's guidance. Priests twist the sacred law for their own benefit. God says "I thought you would learn from my destruction of other wicked nations, but

your behavior is worse than ever. When I reveal my power to the world, you will finally humble yourselves under my protective wings." God will delight in us as he gives us a fresh, new life of peace and prosperity. Friends, his protection deserves our celebration.

HAGGAI

1. As the exiled Jews reclaim the shattered nation of Judah, God says "My people build houses and plant fields for themselves while my Temple still lies in ruins. They reap smaller harvests than expected, and I will not allow them to fully prosper until they start rebuilding the Temple." The people take these words seriously and begin to work. God promises to protect them with his presence throughout the project.

2. The next month, the Lord says "I know the Temple is still under construction, but keep up the good work. Don't give up, and don't be afraid. I have always been by your side, and I'm with you still. Soon I will shake treasures loose from the nations to fill the new Temple with riches, and my house of worship will be even more splendid than the old one. Peace and prosperity will reign in Judah. Because of your dedication to this good work, I will bless your harvests and protect your leaders."

ZECHARIAH

1. After seventy years of exile, God says "Your ancestors angered me when they rebelled against my law and ignored my warnings. Don't be like them. Return to me, and I'll return to you." In a mysterious series of dreams and visions, God reveals to me "I have allowed my people to sit helplessly in exile, but I deeply love them and will mercifully restore Jerusalem until it is more prosperous than before."

2. I see an angel measuring the dimensions of Jerusalem, and he says "Soon there will be more people and animals here than the city walls can contain. God will fill Jerusalem with his glory and build an invisible wall of fire to protect it." The Lord says "Come home, my scattered children! Anyone who tries to hurt you will have to go through me. I will fight for my beloved people, and the world will know I'm on your side. Sing for joy as I dwell among you!"

3. I see the high priest Joshua clothed in dirty rags, and God says to him "Watch as I turn your dirty rags of sin into clean, new clothes. I will save you from any fire Satan attempts to bring upon you. If you obey me, I will bless your work and allow you to bring peace and security to the people."

4. I see seven watchful eyes of God alongside two olive branches. The branches represent two servants anointed by God. God tells one of these servants "Faithful Zerubbabel, my spirit will allow you to lead the reconstruction of my beautiful Temple. The process will be slow, frustrating, and rife with obstacles, but your hard work will encourage the people not to give up."

5. I see a flying scroll, and the angel explains "God has written a curse on that scroll for the thieves and liars he will remove from the land. They will fly away to Babylonia where they'll worship their own wickedness like an idol."

6. I see angels driving chariots around the earth to inspect it, and they notice that Babylonia's punishment of Judah has calmed the Lord's anger toward his people. God says "I will crown Joshua as high priest and allow the people to work together in perfect harmony as they rebuild the Temple."

7. The people ask if they should continue to mourn the destruction of the Temple with a bi-annual fast, and God responds "There's no point in going through the motions just to appear holy. Whatever you do in worship, do it with a sincere heart. Show kindness, mercy, and justice to one another. Take care of the orphans and poor people among you. In the past, you hardened your hearts to this good message, and that's why I turned your nation into a wasteland."

8. God says "I will soon make the streets of my beloved Jerusalem safe enough for old men to walk and children to play. I know this seems impossible, but have no fear as a new age of peace and plenty comes to Judah. All I ask is that you treat others with honesty, justice, and dignity. Turn your mournful fasts into vibrant celebrations, and foreigners will flock to Jerusalem to worship me and share in your prosperity."

9. Tyre and other foreign cities have piled up ridiculous heaps of wealth, but God will throw it all into the sea. This will wake up these oppressive nations and teach them to respect our good Father. Shout for joy as the peaceful King of the earth rides into Jerusalem on a donkey! God frees his covenant

people from exile and offers them a beautiful new life of hope and safety. God guides his people like a gentle shepherd and defends them like a mighty warrior.

10. God is the One who sends the spring rain and nourishes the fields. Those who consult idols for advice only hear nonsense and lies. They wander like lost sheep with restless, worried hearts. God says "I am angry at the foreigners who misled my people for so long. I want to reclaim my children and give them good leaders who will strengthen them. I will compassionately listen to their prayers, multiply their population, and humble enemies around them.

11. "Watch as the mighty foreign cedars fall! I will mercilessly silence their oppressive roaring. They killed and exploited my people like an abusive shepherd, so I will reclaim my flock, bring them together with unity, and heal the wounded among them. I will feed and take care of them as long as they live."

12. The great Creator says "Jerusalem will be like a strong wine that causes enemies to stagger like aimless drunks. My people will be like a heavy stone that breaks the backs of any who try to lift it. No armies can threaten my chosen city as I strengthen even the weakest among them. The hearts of my people will fill with compassion for others as they draw close to me in prayer.

13. "I will pour a mighty fountain of purity into the sinful hearts of my people. They will forget the names of all false gods and lose their desire to worship idols. Survivors of this judgment will be like refined gold, purified by fire. Their tests and challenges will strengthen them and pull them closer to my heart."

14. On Judgment Day the people of Jerusalem will be looted and abused. Neighbors will turn against each other in confusion,

and disease will devastate the people and animals. Time will no longer matter as God erases the difference between day and night, summer and winter. All who survive will worship the great King, and all the nations will celebrate him without any trace of corruption.

MALACHI

1. God says "Children of Israel, I have always favored you over Esau's descendants, yet you doubt my love for you. Kids honor their parents, yet you question why you should respect your heavenly Father. Would you walk into the governor's house with the spoiled meat you sacrifice on my altar? I will not answer your lukewarm prayers or accept your stolen offerings.

2. Start taking my commands seriously, and I will give you a full, happy life. My law will allow you to live in harmony with others and always do the right thing. Your priests should spread my wisdom, but they neglect their responsibility and lead you to a cursed life apart from my presence." We all have the same heavenly Father, so why do we turn against our brothers so easily? We defile the holy Temple, break our marriage vows, and then wonder why God doesn't listen to our prayers.

3. God answers "A messenger will proclaim the truth and prepare the way for me. My presence will cleanse the impurities from your heart, and then your worship will become more sincere and pleasing to me. I will judge those who lie, cheat, and oppress others. This is not a new concept. My law has never changed, and yet you act confused that I am withholding

blessings from those who withhold offerings from me. You don't see how obedience to me will benefit you, but soon you will see how I reward my people.

4. "One day, all the arrogant sinners will burn, while my obedient followers find healing and freedom. But before that final Judgment Day, I will send a great prophet to bring my people together and save those who deserve destruction."

WEEK FOUR REFLECTION

Prophecy

DISCUSSION QUESTIONS

- What did Isaiah and other prophets reveal about the coming Messiah? How do you suppose these prophecies offered hope to a hurting nation?

- Why do you think God ultimately allowed disaster to fall on Israel and Judah? Where do you notice God's love even in this dark chapter of Hebrew history?

- How is God's awesome power evident through books like Ezekiel, Daniel, and Jonah? How do you see his mercy and love through these miracles? Was there ever a time when the Lord protected you in a way that can't fully be explained in human terms?

- The Lord uses many different prophets to warn the people of coming judgments and to encourage them with promises of blessing. As you read through the shorter Week Four books, what to these books have in common? What do they say about God and humanity?

- From what you've read in Weeks One through Four, why do you think Jesus needed to come into this world? Why did Israel so desperately need a Savior and a new plan? Discuss a time when you felt God preparing you for coming events. How did he speak to you? What did he say? How did you respond?

MUSIC MEDITATIONS

- **Isaiah-** Listen to "Your Glory" by All Sons and Daughters, and reflect on the unmatchable power and beauty of God.

- **Jeremiah-** This young prophet was a bit intimidated by God's call at first, so I wonder what motivation he could have drawn from a song like "Move" by Audio Adrenaline.

- **Lamentations-** Listen to "Can Anybody Hear Me?" by Meredith Andrews and try to empathize with those who feel God's silence in the midst of pain.

- **Ezekiel-** Listen to "Come Alive" by Lauren Daigle, and reflect on the powerful images and lessons within the rising of the dry bones.

- **Daniel-** Listen to "What Faith Can Do" by Kutless, and consider the powerful miracles and visions that God creates in response to the unshakable faith of Daniel and his friends.

- **Hosea-** This vulnerable story of unconditional love and forgiveness reminds me of the powerful stories found within the lyrics of "What Love Really Means" by JJ Heller.

- **Joel-** Listen to "The Cave" by Mumford and Sons, and consider what it means to learn from pain and work toward positive change during times of famine.

- **Amos-** Listen to "Price Tag" by Jessie J as you consider how our modern culture might relate to the pride and materialism in this book.

- **Obadiah and Nahum-** Listen to "Don't Laugh at Me" Mark Wills, and consider how God responds to bullying and oppression.

- **Jonah-** Consider how this runaway prophet might connect to the message within "Every Time You Run" by Manafest.

- **Micah, Habakkuk, and Zephaniah-** As you read about the battle-ready Warrior God in these books, think about how that same strong image of God shows up in "Praises and Arrows" by Trip Lee.
- **Haggai-** The rebuilding Hebrews struggle to prioritize God over lesser worries. They may have found helpful wisdom within "This is the Stuff" by Francesca Battistelli.
- **Zechariah-** Listen to "How He Loves" by David Crowder Band, and give thanks to the powerful Creator who loves and protects his people unconditionally.
- **Malachi-** Listen to "My Own Little World" by Matthew West, and consider how the people seemed to struggle with practicing generosity and service as a result of their faith.

APPLICATION IDEAS

- List several areas of your life where you may need to take a cue from Jeremiah and say yes to the Lord. Consider tangible ways you could use your authentic voice and unique gifts to even more boldly fulfill God's plans for your life.
- We live in a fallen world where many people have a hard time believing that God is real and powerful. Think about one person in your life who has doubts about God, and offer to listen to them as they share what has led to these doubts. How might your loving action and compassionate attitude help this friend be more open to the possibility that a loving God exists?
- Is God giving you a wake-up call in one or more areas of your

life? Identify the changes you may need to make to respect God, others, and yourself more fully. Create an action plan to change what God is calling you to change. Speak to people in your life who can help and support you with those changes.

WEEK FIVE

Jesus

MATTHEW-ACTS

DAY ONE - THE GREAT TEACHER
GOSPEL OF MATTHEW

BIG IDEA

Jesus walked among humanity to change our hearts and teach us how to live as God designed us to live.

WORDS OF JESUS

- **God lifts the humble-** God is not impressed by popularity or wealth that fade eventually. God only cares whether our hearts are able to put others first.

- **Righteousness starts within-** It's hard to be obedient if your motives are corrupt. Let God change your heart, and innocent actions will follow naturally.

- **Pride is ugly-** God sees right through showy prayers and self-righteous hypocrisy. He gets angry when arrogant people feel they have a right to judge or oppress others. Jesus came to teach those willing to learn.

- **Trust God-** God is in control, and he loves us. He can get us through any storm. If we surrender our lives to him, we have nothing to fear.

- **Show compassion-** Show kindness to poor and marginalized people around you. Jesus came to heal and bless the outcasts, so he expects us to do the same.

- **Love trumps the Law-** Some churchy people appear right-eous, but their hearts are completely selfish. Jesus calls out their hypocrisy repeatedly and makes it clear that religious traditions should never get in the way of love.

- **I'm coming back**- The wicked religious leaders turn Jesus over to be executed, but death can't hold him down. Jesus proclaims that he will rise after death and will return at the end of the world to set all things right.

HOW GOD SHOWS UP

Jesus makes it perfectly clear that God designed us to trust him and love each other. The good Savior stands up for those who are overlooked and mistreated, while bluntly calling out the arrogant hypocrites of his day. He asks everyone to take a closer look at their own hearts instead of judging others. He lovingly invites us to hand our hearts to him so he can change us from the inside out. We don't have to do it on our own.

MATTHEW

1. Joseph is a good man that comes from a long line of people who love God. His ancestors include Abraham, Judah, Tamar, Ruth, David, Solomon, and Josiah. Fourteen generations after the exile, Joseph learns that his fiancé Mary is pregnant, and he prepares to break the engagement quietly to avoid shaming her. But an angel says "Don't worry, Joseph. Mary is still a virgin, and her pregnancy is a miracle. You two will raise God's son named Jesus who will save the people from sin."

2. After Jesus is born in Joseph's hometown of Bethlehem, a bright star and a prediction of a baby king leads several eastern astrologers to Mary and Joseph's doorstep. The foreign visitors worship the infant and offer luxurious gifts. Upon hearing of the wise men's journey to Bethlehem, King Herod jealously orders the murder of all the baby boys in Bethlehem. An angel warns the young family to escape to Egypt, and when it's safe, they make a new home in the town of Nazareth.

3. Thirty years later, an odd and outspoken desert dweller named John preaches "Turn from your sins! God's kingdom is coming!" When the pharisees join the crowd of people waiting to be baptized by him, John shouts "Your sinful hearts bear rotten fruit, and you must truly change to be forgiven! Someone far greater than me is coming soon to separate good hearts from worthless hearts like yours." Around that time, Jesus comes to the river, and John proclaims "What an honor! I get to baptize you, and I am so unworthy of this privilege." As Jesus is baptized, heaven opens, and God says "My dear Son, you make me so happy."

4. In the desert, Satan offers Jesus many tantalizing things including great power over the world and delicious bread to break his 40-day fast. Jesus fervently focuses on God to resist every temptation. Jesus recruits four humble fishermen to follow him and begins preaching to large crowds in Galilee. When he begins healing the sick and paralyzed, these crowds grow even bigger.

5. On top of a mountain, Jesus preaches "If you are mourning, lost, or mistreated, God will comfort and bless you. Humble,

merciful peacemakers will be lifted up. Don't be afraid to share your beautiful light with the world. I have come not to soften our holy laws but to strengthen them by writing them on your hearts. This code forbids murder, adultery, and courtroom lies, but I'll take that a step further. Don't just refrain from sinful actions; avoid sinful thoughts as well. Let your heart desire peace over anger, faithfulness over lust, and honesty over self-interest. Love those who are difficult to love, and forgive those who deserve your revenge.

6. "Don't brag about how great you are. Do good deeds secretly, and worship when no one's looking. Stop praying those long, showy soliloquies, and make your prayers simple like this: 'Worthy Lord, I trust your plans. Please provide for my needs, forgive me, and help me forgive others. Help me do the right thing.' Remember that spiritual riches last much longer than earthly riches. If you worship and depend on your wealth, you cannot also worship and depend on God. Trust God to feed and clothe you today, and stop worrying about tomorrow.

7. "If you judge others harshly, God will hold you to the same standard. Stop focusing on the flaws of others, and address your own hypocrisy first. Ask your good Father for help, and he'll happily answer you. He enjoys blessing his children. He'll teach you to lead an uncommonly fruitful life full of respect for others and far from evil influences. Get to know your Father before it's too late, and build your life on his firm foundation that will withstand any storm the world tosses your way."

8. Jesus joyfully cures many people through the power of his

touch, including a man with leprosy, a Roman officer's para-lyzed servant, and Peter's feverish mother-in-law. Jesus asks each of these people for a show of simple faith just before each restoration. When a storm nearly capsizes his disciples' boat, Jesus calmly silences the waves. When demon-pos-sessed men antagonize Jesus, he sends the demons into a herd of pigs.

9. Jesus gives a paralyzed man the confidence and courage to stand up and walk. He invites a tax collector named Matthew into his inner circle, even though the religious leaders see tax collectors as crooks and would never asso-ciate with them. Jesus tells the Pharisees "I am here to save humble people and outcasts. I have no use for you hypo-crites who think you have all the answers. If you refuse to learn, I don't want to teach you." Jesus continues to show deep sympathy to hurting people in the community, pro-viding healing and encouragement at every opportunity.

10. Jesus tells his twelve closest friends "There are many people here in Israel who need our help. Go heal them, drive out demons, and inform them God's kingdom is coming. Trust that God will provide hospitable hosts to care for you along the way, but be aware that vicious enemies will come against you as well. Those who refuse to understand the truth will try to harm and arrest you, but don't be afraid. God will protect you and will reject your enemies. Surrender your life to God, and he'll give you a better one."

11. When asked whether he is the one promised by John the Baptist, Jesus responds "I am healing the sick and disabled. I can raise the dead and encourage the poor. I may not look

how you thought I'd look, but those who have no doubts about me will be blessed. Many of you look down on me for hanging out with outcasts, but God will soon show who I truly am. Shame on you for hardening your hearts in the face of these miracles! Father, thank you for revealing your wisdom to humble people who are willing to learn. Lord, you know me better than anyone, and I will help many people know you as they never have before. If any of you folks have heavy burdens, come lay them on me, learn from me, and rest."

12. Jesus takes a Sabbath day walk with his friends and picks an ear of corn to eat. Watching pharisees shout "You're not supposed to pick crops on the Sabbath!" Jesus calmly responds "Kindness is more important than legalistic details. Watch as I heal this man with a paralyzed hand. That's technically against the law, but it's also an act of healing and kindness." At that, the fuming pharisees start plotting to kill Jesus. This does not deter Jesus from boldly continuing to spread healing, hope, and justice regardless of the day. When people accuse him of being a demon, Jesus responds "Your logic is flawed. If the Devil had sent me, I would probably be spreading destruction instead of healing people and removing demons. If you resist me, you're resisting my Father. Your wicked words reveal the character of your heart. Those of you demanding a miracle need to start paying attention. In addition to what you've already seen, I will rise to life after three days in the grave. If you turn toward my Father and stop doubting me, I will call you family."

13. As a great crowd gathers around a lake, Jesus says "I will

use stories and metaphors to reveal great mysteries to you. Listen with the ears of your heart to discover eternal truths that many religious people still don't understand. There was once a farmer who scattered seeds. Some of them took root and bore good fruit while others got eaten by birds or choked by weeds. Likewise, some of you understand God's word deeply and live a good, meaningful life. Others hear the message superficially, which leaves your faith vulnerable to temptations, worries, and difficult circumstances. God allows good and evil people to grow in this world together, but eventually he will draw his people close to his presence and burn those with worthless hearts. Faith is tiny and cannot be seen, but the faith of one small person can lift up many others. God's wisdom is like priceless treasure worth more than all your earthly possessions."

14. King Herod executes John the Baptist at the request of the corrupt queen. Jesus tries to mourn John in solitude, but a crowd of 5,000 follows him. Jesus heals the sick among them and feeds the great crowd by multiplying five loaves of bread and two fish. He walks on water to get to his disciples' boat later that day, and he shows Peter that he must replace his fears with faith in order to imitate this miracle. The group of friends heal people in need on the other side of the lake.

15. The Jewish leaders question why Jesus doesn't follow ancient traditions and teachings to the letter, and Jesus responds "Well, you're disobeying laws that are much more important. You trust yourself more than God, and you teach people loopholes that allow them to disrespect their parents. Your mouths speak the right words, but your hearts don't

know God at all." When the disciples report that these words hurt the pharisees' feelings, he responds "Don't worry about them. They are blind to the truth, and my Father will pull them up like weeds. They eat clean food but foster unclean thoughts." A Canaanite outcast later approaches Jesus and begs "Heal my daughter, please! I know you were sent to help Israel, but please give me the leftovers of your mercy." Touched by her uncommon, passionate faith, Jesus heals her daughter and then journeys forward to feed another great crowd.

16. The pharisees try to trick Jesus into performing a miracle, and Jesus refuses to appease them. He then warns his followers to beware of these evil-hearted men. He asks his followers "What is everyone saying about me?" They respond "Some say you are a prophet or a reincarnation of John the Baptist," while Peter responds "You are the Son of God." Jesus says "God revealed the truth to you, and you listened. Well done! You will provide a strong foundation for my church that not even death will overcome. As for the rest of you, listen closely. The chief priests in Jerusalem will kill me, but I will defeat death three days later. If you want to follow me, get ready to give up everything. If you trust me with your life, I will reward you with a new life close to God's glory."

17. Peter, James, and John hike up a mountain with Jesus and see the heavenly images of Moses and Elijah with their teacher. They hear God's voice saying "Listen to my beloved Son. He brings me such joy!" Jesus calms the fears of his awestruck friends and says they may tell others about this experience after his resurrection. He later heals a boy of

epilepsy and tells his disciples "With just a little faith, you could have healed this boy without my help." Jesus then pays his taxes to abide by Roman law.

18. Jesus tells his disciples "To enter God's kingdom, you must be humble and innocent like a child. Patiently teach these precious children about me. God loves each of them and would go out of his way to save even one lost lamb. If your brother hurts you, give him plenty of chances to change, but hold him accountable if he refuses to learn. Your father forgives your countless sins, so don't hold a grudge against a neighbor who owes you a much smaller debt."

19. When the pharisees question Jesus about his thoughts on divorce, Jesus says "The law allows divorce, but unless your wife is unfaithful, there's no reason you should send her away. Respect your spouse enough to remain faithful to her, or don't get married at all." When the disciples become impatient with children around them, Jesus proclaims these kids have every right to come to him. When a rich, young perfectionist asks Jesus how he can earn eternal life, Jesus says "No human can earn it because everyone has flaws. For example, you are quite attached to your money. But if you humble yourself before God, he can make it possible for you to enter heaven's gates.

20. "Once there was a farmer who agreed to pay his workers a fair wage for the day. Those hired toward the end of the day got the same pay as those who worked all day, and the all-day workers felt offended and asked for a raise. The farmer responded 'You agreed to these wages this morning. My generosity to others is none of your concern. Take your

money, and go home.'" After Jesus warns his disciples again
of his coming death, the mother of James and John asks
which of her sons will be his chief advisor in Jesus' royal
cabinet. Jesus responds "You have no right to ask that. If
you want to lead my church, humble yourselves and be
servants to the people." Just after this, Jesus takes pity on
two loud, blind homeless men and helps them see again.

21. As Jesus enters Jerusalem on a donkey, a joyful crowd proclaims "Praise God for sending this descendant of David
to us!" Jesus angrily flips Temple tables when he sees that
merchants are cheating poor people there. Jesus responds
to a pharisee trap by saying "You want to know if my
authority comes from God? Well, what do you think? You
claim to follow God, but I know plenty of prostitutes and
tax collectors who know him better. When you disrespected
God's messengers, God thought maybe you would respect
his Son, but now you're plotting to kill him. You don't
deserve any share of God's kingdom!"

22. Jesus preaches "When God sent selective invitations to
his kingdom celebration, some ignored his invitation and
others tried to kill his messengers. Now he will send a new
invitation to anyone who will listen." The pharisees ask
Jesus about paying taxes to try to trap him into betraying
God or the emperor. Jesus cleverly answers "I'll pay taxes
to the emperor and also give God what belongs to him."
When the sadducees question Jesus' belief in eternal life by
asking what marriage will look like in heaven, Jesus responds
"Marriage will not need to exist in the next life because we
will commune perfectly with God and each other. In this
life, love God with everything you have, and treat everyone

as you want to be treated."

23. Jesus says "These pharisees say the right things, but they don't practice what they preach. They place impossible demands on the people but offer themselves unfair privileges. True church leaders should be humble servants who acknowledge the Father as the one true Leader. You hypocrites think you're guarding heaven's door, but God doesn't want you in his house. You follow some laws with painstaking perfectionism but refuse to obey the heart of the law by simply treating others with dignity. You polish your appearance and act better than everyone while letting your heart rot. Jerusalem, I long to gather you under my wings, but you've closed your hearts to the truth."

24. After his final public sermon, Jesus tells his close friends "Soon this Temple will be destroyed, and battles will rage all around. When that happens, many will claim to be the Messiah, but don't buy into their lies. Opponents of my message will persecute you and harden their hearts toward each other. And then God will bring a swift end to this age that no one will be able to predict or escape. The stars will fall, and the glorious presence of God's Son will appear in the sky. Be ready because this will happen when you least expect it. Until then, be my faithful servants, and take good care of each other.

25. "Those unprepared for my return are like bridesmaids that miss the wedding when they rush to the market for more lamp oil. My faithful servants use their talents and resources wisely to grow the kingdom, instead of fearfully hiding their gifts from others. Those who risk nothing also gain

nothing. When I return, those who love and care for the needy will inherit God's blessings, while those who only care for themselves will be turned away.

26. "Friends, my time of suffering is almost here." A woman pours extravagant perfume on Jesus' head, and although the disciples condemn this as a waste of money, Jesus is touched by her passion and generosity. Judas accepts blood money from the chief priests, and when Jesus reveals that he knows this betrayal is coming, Judas says "I would never betray you!" While sharing the Passover meal with his friends, Jesus says "Enjoy this meal as you will gratefully accept the sacrifice I will soon make for you. You will abandon me to die, but then I will rise to life." Peter says "I would never leave you!" Jesus responds "Actually, you'll deny me three times before tomorrow comes. My heart is heavy with grief. Stay hear while I go pray about it. Father, this cup of suffering is too much. I will still do this if it's what you want, but I wish there was another way." While Jesus prays and his friends sleep, Judas leads a large crowd to Jesus' location, and they arrest him. Jesus remains peacefully silent before the abusive council, while Peter denies knowing Jesus as predicted.

27. As the chief priests turn Jesus over to the Roman governor Pilate, Judas realizes the depth of his mistake and hangs himself. Pilate tells the crowd "I find no fault with this man, but you continue to demand his death. I will grant your wish, but his blood will be on your hands." At that, Jesus is stripped, crowned with thorny branches, mocked, and crucified. As Jesus dies, many souls rise to life, and an earthquake shakes the city. The Temple curtain that

once separated the people from God's presence rips in two. Amazed onlookers whisper "That man really was God's Son." Remembering Jesus' promise to rise to life, Pilate orders his tomb to be guarded closely.

28. On Sunday morning, an angel rolls the stone away from Jesus' tomb, and the guards faint at the dazzling sight. As Mary Magdalene and other women go to the tomb to pay their respects, the angel says "Don't be afraid. Jesus has risen to life, and his tomb is empty." Jesus meets them along the path back home, and they run joyfully to spread the news. When the chief priests learn what happened, they pay the guards to say Jesus' body was stolen in the guards' sleep. Jesus appears to his disciples and says "Go with my heavenly authority and teach people to follow me. I will be with you forever."

DAY TWO - THE GREAT HEALER
GOSPEL OF MARK

BIG IDEA

Jesus notices those who are hurting and loves to release them from their pain.

MIRACLES OF JESUS

- **Pick up your mat-** Jesus asks a paralyzed man to trust him enough to stand up in front of a great crowd, pick up his mat, and walk home. Sometimes it takes a bit of courageous faith to tap into the blessings God has in store for us.

- **Sabbath healing-** The pharisees believe that no work or healings should ever be done on the Sabbath, but Jesus boldly corrects their rigid assumptions. Jesus heals a man with a paralyzed hand and proclaims that acts of kindness and restoration are always acceptable, regardless of the day.

- **Stopping the storm-** Jesus calms the dangerous waves and assures his friends that they can trust him in the midst of any storm.

- **Removing demons-** Jesus calms the mind of a person with intense mental illness. This person was formerly unable to interact safely with others, but Jesus allows him to return home to restore his relationships and spread joy.

- **Come alive-** Jesus overcomes death to give a young girl another chance at life.

- **Feeding 5,000-** Jesus shows compassion to a hungry crowd and multiplies a little bit of bread and fish to provide them with a delicious meal.

- **Opening eyes and ears-** Jesus heals deaf and blind people with a simple touch, and he helps willing listeners understand God's truths more fully.

- **Empowering others-** Upon healing a boy with epilepsy, Jesus reminds his followers that they have the power to heal others too. All they need to do is put their pride aside and trust God to work through them.

- **Rising to life-** Jesus defeats death and encourages his friends to continue doing miraculous and life-giving things through God's power.

HOW GOD SHOWS UP

Jesus said some great things, but he backed up every word with extravagant, kind actions. He overcame illness, disability, and even death by simply connecting with other people and asking them for a little trust. He did impossible things to enrich the lives of others and meet their needs. He then encouraged his followers to reach out and do whatever they could to help other needy people in their midst.

MARK

1. The good news begins with the desert messenger named John clearing a path for Jesus. He baptizes many, saying "Turn from your life of sin, and God will wash you clean. I baptize you with simple water, but the one who follows me will give you the Holy Spirit." When Jesus comes to the river for baptism, heaven opens and God says "You are my precious Son who brings me joy." After forty days of desert temptation, Jesus calls four fishermen to catch people with him. Jesus begins healing people with mental and physical illnesses, and he preaches in synagogues throughout Galilee. Jesus often tries to pray in solitude, but crowds seem to find him wherever he goes.

2. These following crowds grow so thick that some in need of healing can't get through. One clever group cuts a hole in a roof and lowers their paralyzed friend directly to Jesus. As Jesus forgives the man and heals his legs, the awestruck crowd watches as he picks up his mat and walks home. Jesus invites a tax collector into his inner circle and dines with many other outcasts to the horror of the religious leaders. When asked why his followers don't practice fasting, Jesus responds "There will be a time for fasting when I'm taken away, but for now, let's celebrate and feast together. I am bringing a new message with new traditions. You condemn us for picking corn on the Sabbath, but we are still honoring the spirit of the Sabbath by worshiping God and refusing to worship our work."

3. Undeterred, Jesus heals a man's paralyzed hand in front of

a crowd of accusers. Jesus says "I healed him to enrich his life. Isn't the Sabbath meant to be a day of restoration?" Many more come to Jesus for healing, and the crowds grow even larger. Jesus choses twelve apostles to learn from him and drive out demons. Some accuse Jesus of being a chief demon, but Jesus responds "Why would Satan drive out his own minions? Whoever obeys God is a member of my family."

4. On the shore of Lake Galilee, Jesus preaches "A farmer scattered seed one day, and some seeds got eaten by birds, burned by the sun, and choked by weeds. Other seeds sank deep into good soil and sprouted abundant fruit. I use this metaphor so that your heart may hear and understand the secrets of heaven. Like the seeds, some of you will be choked by temptations or burned by difficult circumstances, but if my message sinks deep into your heart, you will bear fruit. Don't be afraid to share God's wisdom and goodness with others. If you plant even a tiny seed of faith in some-one's heart, it could sprout into a giant tree." When a great storm nearly sinks the boat holding Jesus and his friends, Jesus calmly wakes up from a nap and silences the waves with a simple command. He says "Trust me, and you won't need to fear any storms."

5. Jesus approaches a strong, frightening man possessed by many demons and sends his demons into a herd of pigs. The mended man joyfully returns home to spread the word of God's great kindness. A synagogue official then begs Jesus to heal his sick daughter, and on the way to their house, a woman recovers from a blood disorder by simply touching Jesus' robe. They arrive at the official's home to find his

daughter dead, but Jesus brings her back to life.

6.   His hometown citizens only know Jesus as the carpenter's son and refuse to take his healings and miracles seriously. Without missing a beat, Jesus shakes the dust off his feet and sends small groups of his followers into surrounding villages to heal people. He asks them to trust God to provide welcoming hosts along the way. King Herod hears about this Jesus fellow and fears he is the reincarnation of John the Baptist, who the king had recently executed. After a full day of teaching, Jesus tries to find a quiet place to eat with his disciples, but a crowd of 5,000 follows him. Instead of turning them away, Jesus patiently multiplies just a few loaves and fish to feed the enormous group. Jesus sends his friends on a boat ahead of him so that he can find a quiet place to pray. He walks on water to catch up with the boat, and they heal many sick people on the other side of the lake.

7.   The perplexed pharisees confront Jesus about his refusal to obey the knit-picky food laws, and he responds "You hypocrites stay clean on the outside, but your hearts are filthy with greed, slander, and pride. You replace God's holy law with traditions of your own making." Jesus quietly slips away from the crowd but cannot stay hidden. A woman begs for the leftovers of his healing power for her daughter, and Jesus rewards the woman's persistent faith. On the road, he touches a man's ears to help him hear again.

8.   When a crowd of 4,000 gathers around Jesus, he tells his friends "I will not send these people away without food because some of them have journeyed a long way." He multiplies a few small loaves to feed them, and after everyone

eats, there are still seven baskets of leftovers. When the pharisees try to trick Jesus into performing a miracle, he says "I have no desire to prove myself to you." Jesus warns his friends to keep their guard up around these plotting religious leaders. He heals a blind man in secret, and when Peter realizes Jesus is the Messiah, he says "Keep this good news quiet for now. First, I must suffer and die at the hands of the religious leaders, but death won't hold me down. Don't try to stop God's plans from happening. Forget your plans, and give your life to God in order to find a fresh, new life. Don't be ashamed of your glorious Father."

9. Jesus takes his three closest friends to a mountain to witness Jesus' clothes transform into a dazzling white robe. On the mountain, they camp with Moses and Elijah, and God encourages Jesus' friends to listen to his Son closely. Jesus rejoins the larger group to discover his followers arguing with a great crowd. He learns that the disciples tried to heal a boy with epilepsy but couldn't do it. Jesus patiently encourages the boy's father to have faith and heals the boy. Jesus tells his disciples "If you had prayed and trusted God, you could have healed this boy yourself. I will soon be killed and then raised to life. Stop arguing about which of you is the best, and humble yourselves to serve the community more effectively. Don't try to stop anyone from joining our healing mission, and don't lead the people to lose faith in me. Do everything you can to steer clear of temptations that could make your hearts rotten."

10. Pharisees try to trap Jesus by saying "Moses allows men to divorce their wives. What do you say?" Jesus responds "God created people to partner up and take care of each other.

Humans shouldn't try to separate what God has joined together." When the disciples become annoyed with a crowd of kids, Jesus says "These children belong to my Father, and we should all be innocent like them. Let them come to me!" A rich man asks how he can earn his way into heaven, and Jesus responds "No one is good enough to enter God's kingdom. You obey the Law of Moses, but you are awfully attached to your money and resist giving to those in need. It is impossible for you to save yourself; only God can save you. Humble yourself, and follow me." Jesus speaks again about his coming suffering and tells his friends "Stop arguing about which of you will sit at my right hand in heaven. Focus instead on serving and redeeming the people." Jesus then takes pity on a loud, blind beggar and heals him.

11. Jesus borrows a young colt to ride into Jerusalem, and the people welcome him by waving branches and shouting "May God bless this man he sent! May God bless the kingdom of David!" Jesus curses a fig tree for bearing no fruit and then curses corrupt merchants in the Temple. Jesus tells his followers "You look amazed that this cursed fig tree has died, but you can do much greater things if you fully trust God to answer your prayers. He will forgive your wrongs and come to your rescue." When the pharisees ask who gave Jesus the authority to heal and teach, he responds "Where do you think John the Baptist's authority came from?" Afraid of how the people would respond to their answer, the crooked religious leaders say "We don't know."

12. Jesus says "There was once a vineyard owner who left town and trusted his workers to harvest the grapes, but they

kept killing the supervisors and even killed the owner's son. These workers are worthless and will be executed for their betrayal." The pharisees knew he was talking about them, but they continue trying to trap him into denouncing the emperor. Jesus cleverly responds "This coin has Caesar's face on it, so your taxes belong to him. Everything else belongs to God." Jesus then teaches "The one true God has the power to raise the dead. The most important thing is to love him with every fiber of your being and love each other. Watch out for these privileged priests who take advantage of the poor and give showy, heartless prayers. They will be punished while this homeless widow is lifted up for her kind, generous heart."

13. When one of the disciples stands in awe of the Temple, Jesus says "These beautiful buildings will crumble one day. Watch out for false prophets who will try to deceive you in the coming time of war. Earthquakes and famines will ravage the land as you are arrested and persecuted for speaking the Spirit-led truth. When the stars go dark without warning, I will appear in the sky and gather God's people together. The earth will end, but my kingdom and message will last forever."

14. As the pharisees plot about how to arrest Jesus without starting a riot, Judas agrees to share Jesus' location so that he can be arrested away from the crowds. A woman pours expensive perfume on Jesus' head, and Jesus thanks her for his beautiful act of worship and sacrifice. During the Passover meal, Jesus says "My body will soon be broken like this bread, and my blood will be poured out like this wine. Never forget this sacrifice that leads you to new life. I am

aware that one of you will soon betray me, and Peter, you will deny me three times this very night. My heart is crushed as I think about what's coming." Jesus finds a quiet place in the garden and passionately prays "Father, please take this pain away or give me the strength to endure it. I trust your plan." As Jesus suffers in solitary prayer, his friends take a nap. Jesus angrily wakes them up just as Judas comes with heavily armed men to arrest him. Jesus goes peacefully and discourages his men from fighting back. Jesus remains silent as he is humiliated and abused by the chief priests, and Peter nervously denies knowing his teacher.

15. The Jewish leaders bring Jesus to Pilate, and even though this governor finds no fault with Jesus, he agrees to crucify him to please a bloodthirsty crowd. Soldiers place a crown of thorns on his head, spit on him, and mockingly shout "Long live the king!" Jesus is beaten, forced to carry his heavy cross, and crucified as jeers and insults are hurled his way from all sides. Jesus feels agonizingly alone and dies with a loud cry. Jesus' mother and his friend Mary Magdalene watch the horror unfold and watch as he's buried in the family tomb of a compassionate Jewish Council member.

16. Mary and a few other women walk to Jesus' tomb early Sunday morning to anoint the body, and they find the grave empty. An angel at the tomb entrance says "He's not here, but don't worry! He's alive and will see you soon! Go spread the word!" Jesus appears first to Mary and then to his inner circle of friends, and they don't believe that Jesus is really risen until they see him for themselves. Jesus tells them "Go tell the world the good news! Those who believe this is real will do great things in my name!" After strengthening the

belief of his friends and equipping them to preach, Jesus rises up to sit next to God in heaven.

DAY THREE - THE GREAT STORYTELLER
GOSPEL OF LUKE

BIG IDEA

Jesus uses symbolic stories to open eyes and hearts to eternal truths about God and about humanity.

PARABLES OF JESUS

- **Take the log out-** We tend to stare at splinters in someone else's eye when we have a log in our own eye. We must focus on our own actions instead of judging others.

- **Bear good fruit-** Farmers have no use for rotten fruit, but good fruit nourishes others. Be a person who shows pure character through action.

- **Scattering seed-** Some seeds wither on the pavement or get eaten by birds, while other seeds find good soil and grow into strong plants. We need to sink deep into our faith and go beyond shallow understanding to survive life's tests and grow stronger.

- **Good Samaritan-** An injured man needs help, and it's the foreign outcast who stops on the side of the road to help. God doesn't care where we grew up, but he loves it when we show sacrificial kindness to others.

- **Flowers and sparrows-** God protects delicate flowers and feeds tiny birds, and he loves us much more than that. He will provide for our needs, so we have no need to fret or worry.

- **Lost coins and sheep-** God turns the house inside out to find a tiny coin and leaves the flock to find one lost lamb. We may feel small and unimportant, but we are of vital importance to the loving Father that made us.

- **Prodigal Son-** A punk kid runs away from home and returns only after squandering his entire inheritance. Instead of shaming or punishing him, his dad runs to embrace him and throws a party to celebrate.

HOW GOD SHOWS UP

Jesus really wants us to understand how much God loves us. He's the God that runs to us when we come home, even though we feel small and unworthy. He's the God that listens closely to our prayers and allows us to flourish. All he asks in return is that we trust him and take care of each other.

LUKE

1. I have interviewed many first-hand witnesses about the mysterious events among us, and I will do my best to tell an orderly account of the truth. It began with an angel startling an elderly priest in the Temple, saying "Don't be afraid, Zechariah! God sees that you and your wife have always wanted to be parents, and now you will have a beloved son named John. He will grow to be a Spirit-filled prophet, and you will be rendered speechless until his birth." A few months later, the angel tells Elizabeth's cousin "Mary, God will be with you and give you peace as you become

pregnant with God's son and chosen King. I know you are a virgin, but nothing is impossible with God." Mary visits her pregnant cousin, and Elizabeth greets her with overwhelming joy. Mary responds "I am God's humble servant. My heart rejoices as the never-changing God lifts me up and fulfills his ancient promise of mercy through me." At John's newborn naming ceremony, Zechariah's voice begins working again. He says "Let's praise the merciful God who sets us free and delivers us the promised Savior. Let's serve him faithfully and fearlessly! You, my son, will be a great prophet who will prepare the way for God's forgiving presence on earth. God will shine in all the dark places and guide us toward peace."

2. The Emperor orders that everyone journey to their hometowns for a census registration, so Joseph and Mary must travel to Bethlehem toward the end of her pregnancy. Unable to find a home to stay in, Mary gives birth in a barn and places her newborn son in a feeding trough. Celebratory angels appear to night-shift shepherds, saying "We have joyful news for you! The Savior was just born in Bethlehem. Our glorious God has brought peace to the world!" The energized shepherds find the baby with his parents and leave the barn singing God's praises. A week later, Jesus is dedicated to God in the Temple, and the priest says "Lord, you will keep your promise through this peaceful servant. You have prepared him to bring glory to Israel and your saving wisdom to Gentiles." The young family returns home to Nazareth, and Jesus grows into a wise, healthy, obedient young man who brings joy to his Father, his earthly parents, and many others. Even at the

age of twelve, Jesus engages Temple priests in an intelligent spiritual discussion far beyond his years.

3. When John grows into an adult, he begins clearing a path for the Savior and preaching "Let God wash your sins away! You hypocritical pharisees think your connection to Abraham will save you from God's punishment, but God cares much more about those who give to people in need. You tax collectors need to stop swindling people and be content with what you have. I see that you hope I am the Messiah, but he is much greater than I. He will give you the fire of the Holy Spirit and will gather all the good people together." Soon after this, Jesus comes to John to be baptized, and the Holy Spirit rests on his shoulder like a dove. Joseph's son Jesus begins his ministry at age thirty, and his ancestry leads back to King David, Judah, Abraham, and God's original son Adam.

4. Jesus fasts in the desert for forty days and endures Satan's nagging temptations to break his fast and join the Devil in ruling the earth. Jesus refuses to worship anyone other than his Father, and Satan eventually gives up. Jesus begins preaching Spirit-filled messages and gains attention throughout Galilee. In his hometown, he says "The Spirit has chosen me to encourage the poor, free the oppressed, and heal the blind." The people of Nazareth only see him as the carpenter's son and refuse to believe in Jesus' power. They angrily try to kill him, but Jesus walks away unscathed and goes to a nearby town to remove demons and heal fatal diseases. Jesus tries to find solitude to pray each morning, but he becomes so popular that crowds find him wherever

he goes.

5. The crowd becomes so thick on a lakeshore that Jesus steps into Simon Peter's fishing boat to preach from the water. To thank him for the use of his boat, Jesus leads him to a spot where he catches so many fish the boat nearly sinks from the extra weight. Simon and his awestruck friends James and John leave everything to follow this mysterious man of miracles. As they journey onward, Jesus joyfully heals a man with leprosy, and he allows a paralyzed man to stand up and walk home. When Jesus invites a tax collector into his inner circle, the religious leaders question why Jesus insists on hanging out with outcasts and why this group discards Jewish traditions regarding prayer and fasting. Jesus responds "I came to help people who humbly repent instead of people who think they have it all figured out. This is the time for us to celebrate and enjoy each other, and my friends will fast when I am taken from them."

6. The pharisees question why Jesus would pick corn for a Sabbath day picnic with his friends, and Jesus answers "David fed his men with Temple bread on the Sabbath." Jesus then boldly heals a man with a paralyzed hand and says "What are we allowed to do on the Sabbath? Help people or let them come to harm?" With twelve chosen friends by his side, Jesus heals many people and preaches "If you are poor, hungry, and hurting in this life, God will bless you in the next life. Forgive people who hurt you, and treat them with the same courtesy you would want. Even sinners can love the lovable. God is the only one worthy to judge, so he will condemn you if you think you have a right to condemn others. Stop staring at the im-

perfections of others, and address your own colossal sin of pride first. If your heart is good, your words and actions will be like the good fruit of a healthy tree. If you build your house on God's firm commands, you will be able to withstand any storm."

7. Jewish elders approach Jesus and say "We know a kind-hearted Roman officer who built a synagogue and continually helps others. His favorite servant is fatally ill and needs your help." When Jesus arrives in his neighbor-hood, the officer says "Thank you for coming, but I don't deserve for you to walk all the way to the house to heal my friend. I trust that if you say the word, he'll get better." Pleased and amazed by his faith, Jesus heals the servant from afar. Soon after, Jesus stops a funeral procession to bring a grieving mother's son back to life. As news travels about his miracles, people ask "Are you the one John the Baptist told us would come?" Jesus responds "The blind can see, the sick are healed, the poor are encouraged, and the dead are rising to life. Blessed are those who have no doubts about me! John was not what you expected, but he was a great man. Likewise, you call me a drinker and a friend of outcasts, but God will soon reveal who I really am." While Jesus dines with a pharisee, a prostitute pours perfume on Jesus' head in tender worship. The pharisee sneers at the prostitute, and Jesus says "I have forgiven her many sins, and her heart now pours great gratitude and love for me. I think her selfless gift is beautiful."

8. Several women travel with Jesus' group to learn from him, and this group includes Mary Magdalene, who gratefully follows Jesus after he removes seven demons from her. Jesus

preaches "A farmer scattered corn seed, and while some of the seed found good, deep soil, other seeds found rocky ground or got eaten by birds. I speak to you with stories and metaphors so that your heart might understand these truths in a new way. Some of you allow the Devil to snatch your heart away from me like a bird, and others let your faith wither during times of testing or worry. But those with deep understanding and an obedient heart will bear good fruit. Don't hide the truth, but share it to light the way for others." Jesus' friends panic as a storm nearly sinks their boat, and they stand amazed as Jesus calmly orders the storm to stop. On the other side of the lake, they meet a demon-possessed, naked cave dweller. Although everyone fears and rejects this man, Jesus walks right up to him and sends his demons into a herd of pigs. He then brings a Temple official's daughter back to life.

9. Jesus tells his twelve apostles "I'm giving you the power to heal others and remove demons. Trust that hosts in each town will feed and shelter you, but if a town rejects you, don't waste your time there." Herod catches wind of Jesus' healings and fears that John the Baptist has come back to life. Jesus feeds a great crowd with very little food, and Peter recognizes Jesus as the promised Messiah. Jesus responds "Soon I will suffer at the hands of the religious leaders, but death will not hold me down. If you surrender your own plans to follow me and face hardship with me, what you gain will be much more glorious." Peter, James, and John witness Jesus transform into a dazzling form alongside great leaders of the past, Moses and Elijah. They stand awestruck when they hear God saying "This is my Son. Listen to

him!" When the disciples fail to heal a boy with epilepsy,
Jesus says "Have some faith, and trust God to heal people
through your hands. I won't be around forever to remind
you how this works! Stop arguing about which of you is
the best and who should or should not be included in our
group. Become like a humble, innocent child, welcoming
everyone willing to follow me."

10. Jesus anoints seventy-two faithful men with the ability to
preach, heal, and drive out demons, saying "There are
many people who need our help. You will find peaceful
hosts to shelter you throughout your journey, but I also
want you to keep your guard up and move on if you
start to feel unsafe. If anyone witnesses my miracles and
still rejects our message, they deserve what's coming to
them." When these men return, they joyfully proclaim
"We did impossible things and removed demons just by
speaking your name!" Jesus joyfully responds "Satan is
losing ground at last! Father, thank you for opening eyes
and hearts to your great wisdom! Thank you for helping
them know you through me." Later, a priest asks who
qualifies as a neighbor, and Jesus responds "A traveling
man was mugged, beaten, and left half dead by the
roadside. Several priests and important men walked
right by without a second glance, but a Samaritan
outcast took pity on the man and went out of his way to
heal and care for him. Which of these men acted like a
neighbor?" That night, Jesus stays in the home of two
sisters. While one sister complains that her sister isn't
helping cook and clean for the group, Jesus responds
"Dear Martha, you're worrying yourself sick over mean-

ingless tasks. Your sister is choosing to be still and learn from me, and you are welcome to join us."

11. Jesus says "Keep your prayers simple. Give thanks to God; ask him to take care of you. Ask him to teach you to forgive others and make righteous choices. Any of you would gladly help a friend in desperate need, so if you knock on God's door in prayer, he will happily answer you." When some witness Jesus's power over demons and accuse him of being a chief demon, Jesus says "It would make no sense for Satan to divide his forces against each other. It is with God's power that I do these things. Some of you doubt me and beg for a miracle, but I want to turn your dark hearts into lamps that warm and illuminate the world. Some of you are overly concerned with laws that make you look good, but you hypocrites should pay closer attention to your hearts. You claim to hold the keys to the kingdom, but those you oppress will go in instead of you." Upon hearing this, the pharisees angrily begin plotting to take Jesus down.

12. Jesus continues to his inner circle "Watch out for those pharisees. Their secrets and lies will soon be public knowledge, and they don't deserve your fear. God is the only one worthy of fear, and he loves you because you are my brothers. If someone accuses you, the Spirit will teach you what to say. It's tempting to get rich and hoard your wealth without ever enjoying it, but remember that this life won't last forever, and God's riches are far more valuable. Our Father feeds the animals and dresses the flowers, so be a generous giver, and trust that God will take care of you too. The end will come when you least expect it, so let God catch you using your strengths wisely on that day. My controversial message

may start arguments in your house, but that doesn't make it any less true."

13. Jesus preaches "Innocent people die due to injustice and tragic accidents, but you who stubbornly stay in sin are the ones who actually deserve to die. A farmer cuts down fruitless trees, so it makes sense for God to cut you down if your heart only yields rotten fruit." When a synagogue official condemns Jesus for healing a chronically ill woman on the Sabbath, Jesus boldly responds "You keep your animals from starving on the Sabbath, so why shouldn't I release his woman from eighteen years of pain today? In God's kingdom, even the smallest, most unimportant person can lift up a whole community. If you refuse to humbly get to know God, he will see you as a stranger and won't open the door for you." In an attempt to shut Jesus up, the Jewish leaders say "The King is after you. You should leave town to protect yourself." Jesus boldly responds "I still have three days of healing work to do here, and I intend to stay until then. You can tell that sly fox that if he wants to kill me, I'm on my way to Jerusalem."

14. A man with terrible swelling comes to Jesus for help on the Sabbath, and pharisees silently watch as Jesus looks them in the face and says "I'm going to save this man's life now. Hope that's okay with everyone. I see that some of you are looking for a good place to watch me speak, but those who humbly offer their good seats to others will be lifted up. God loves everyone including the poor and disabled, and he happily shares his table with anyone willing to answer his invitation. Those who follow me must love God more than their families and themselves. Only those willing to

sacrifice their comfort and possessions for me will be able to endure the obstacles coming around the corner."

15. A pharisee announces "This Jesus fellow eats with outcasts!" and Jesus responds "If you had a hundred sheep and lost one, you'd gladly leave the ninety-nine in a safe area to bring the lost sheep back home. If you lost a valuable coin, you'd sweep the whole house to find it. There was once a man with a reckless son who squandered his inheritance and ended up homeless and nearly starving. The son returned home, and his father ran to him to embrace him and threw him a huge party. His older son was jealous since he had been faithful to his father all along, but the father explained that he loves both sons but feels especially happy that his dead son has come back to life. Our Father also runs to embrace the outcasts when they come home.

16. "Some employers praise their property managers for keeping 'creative' financial records, but God sees this behavior for the lie it is. You cannot serve him and also be a slave to money. You pharisees love money and know how to appear righteous, but you're not fooling the God who sees your heart. You rich men with easy earthly lives will suffer in separation from God, while good-hearted poor people will feast at God's table in heaven. God sent many prophets to warn you to repent, but not even a dead body rising to life could convince you of the truth.

17. "If you lead an innocent child astray, you are better off dead. Hold each other accountable, but if someone tries to right a wrong, forgive them as often as it takes. A little faith can equip you to do great things, but don't expect accolades

for serving God as you should. Just humbly continue doing the right thing." Jesus heals ten men on the road to Jerusalem, and only the Samaritan among them stops to thank Jesus for this miracle. When religious leaders ask when God's kingdom will come, Jesus answers "God's invisible kingdom dwells within our hearts. Some will be transformed by God while others continue going about their business and get left behind.

18. "A corrupt judge finally gave into a poor woman's wishes when she nagged him continuously, so surely, the good Judge will be happy to favor you if you reach out to him. Humbly admit your sins and imperfections as you pray, and don't act like those pharisees who pretend to have it all together. Come to God like an innocent child with pure love and no greedy motives. No human is perfect and selfless enough to earn God's favor, but fortunately, our God specializes in making impossible things possible. When enemies of God humiliate and kill his Son, not even death will hold him down." As Jesus journeys on, he shows compassion to a blind man and heals him.

19. A short tax collector named Zacchaeus climbs a tree to see Jesus over a crowd and expresses great joy when Jesus asks to stay in his house that night. As the crowd grumbles about his past sins, Zacchaeus promises to redeem himself by giving generously to the poor and paying back everyone he ever cheated. Inspired by the man's repentance, Jesus says "Salvation has come to this man's house today! Some people are afraid to turn their blessings into opportunities for positive change, but this man has vowed to bless his community and spread joy because of the second chance

I have given him." Jesus borrows a donkey and rides into Jerusalem as his followers shout "God bless this peaceful king sent by our glorious God!" Jesus refuses to quiet the celebration when the pharisees become annoyed by the noise. He weeps for the future destruction of Jerusalem and begins driving corrupt merchants out of the Temple so he can teach there. The Temple leaders want to kill him but are afraid that arresting him in front of his followers would cause a riot.

20. Angry pharisees ask "Who gave you the right to do what you do?" Jesus refuses to fall into their trap and cleverly responds "Who gave John the Baptist his authority?" The cowardly people pleasers refuse to answer so as not to turn the crowd against them. Jesus continues "There was once a vineyard owner whose highly unworthy tenants abused any messenger the owner sent to collect rent. They even killed the owner's son. Likewise, these pharisees killed many true prophets and will soon kill God's Son, so God is taking the holy kingdom from them." The pharisees try to trap Jesus again by asking about his willingness to pay Roman taxes, and Jesus responds simply "Give the Emperor the coins with his face on them, and give God what belongs to him. Watch out for those rich hypocrites who take advantage of the poor and offer showy prayers to God.

21. "I see rich people dropping their regular offerings in the treasury, but that poor woman offered two coins, which was a much bigger sacrifice and meant much more to God. You should know this beautiful Temple won't last forever. There will soon be false prophets, wars, natural disasters, and famines everywhere, but if you bravely bring light into

these dark times, I will protect you and give you the words to say. When Jerusalem falls and the sky grows strange, this will be a signal that the glorious Son of God will soon return to earth. Don't get so wrapped up in your life that you forget to acknowledge God's plans unfolding on earth."

22. Judas accepts a bribe from the chief priests and agrees to help them arrest Jesus away from his adoring crowds. During the Passover meal, Jesus says "I am happy that I get to share my final meal on earth with you brothers. When you enjoy and share this meal in the future, remember that my blood is poured out like this wine to seal a new promise with you. Stop arguing about who's the greatest among you, and follow my example of humble service to others. One of you will betray me, and even you, dear Peter will deny me three times tonight. But when you turn back to me, you must strengthen your brothers and keep your faith strong." Jesus encourages his friends to pray for strength to resist temptation. He then prays "Father, I wish you would take this suffering from me, but I will fulfill your plan no matter what. I am so unbearably anxious that I am sweating drops of blood." Jesus finds his friends sleeping and notices Judas coming with a crowd to arrest him. One disciple cuts of the ear of an enemy, but Jesus heals the severed ear and says "You could have arrested me in broad daylight this week, but you chose this dark hour to capture me like a criminal." As Jesus is mocked, beaten, and accused before the Council, his best friend Peter denies knowing him.

23. The Roman governor Pilate sees no reason to punish Jesus, so he passes the buck to King Herod who laughs in Jesus' face and sends him right back to Pilate. Pilate wants to whip

Jesus and let him go, but an angry mob demands that he free a murderous political rebel named Barabbas instead. Pilate gives into the crowd and turns Jesus over to be crucified. In the face of his killers, Jesus says "Father, forgive them. They don't know what they're doing." A criminal crucified next to Jesus mocks him while another says "We are getting what we deserve, but this man has done nothing wrong. Remember me when you return, Jesus!" Jesus responds "Today we will be together in paradise. Father, I place my spirit in your hands!" Then he dies, and the Temple curtain splits. The women followers witness Jesus' horrifying death and help prepare his body for burial.

24. After the Sabbath, the women return to Jesus' tomb with spices and perfumes for the body, but they find the tomb empty. Angels say "This is a place for the dead, but Jesus has risen to life just like he promised." The women joyfully share the news with the rest of Jesus' followers, and most refuse to believe them. Peter, however, runs to the tomb to see the empty tomb for himself. Jesus appears to several groups of his followers later that day and says "Don't be scared! Look at the scars on my hands and feet so that you know it's really me. Now that you have seen my risen presence, you must preach about the miracle of new life that anyone can receive through repentance and forgiveness." His followers watch Jesus depart for heaven and spread the news with passionate joy and gratitude.

DAY FOUR - THE GREAT SAVIOR
GOSPEL OF JOHN

BIG IDEA

God's Son forgives the entire world and takes the punishment upon himself.

LOVE OF JESUS

- **Word becomes flesh-** He existed before the world but still chooses to enter it as a helpless baby so that he can change our hearts and save our lives.

- **Loving the Samaritan-** He shares a drink with her even though she's from a race of outcasts and has an unsavory reputation.

- **Blocking the stones-** A woman is about to be stoned for adultery, and Jesus reminds the accusers that only a sinless person has a right to throw stones.

- **Tears for Lazarus-** Jesus loves his fallen friend and pauses to grieve, even though he knows Lazarus will be alive again soon.

- **Riding into Jerusalem-** Knowing the religious leaders are plotting his death, Jesus rides peacefully into the eye of the storm, ready for whatever will come.

- **Washing feet-** Before his last meal, Jesus takes the role of the servant and washes the feet of friends who will soon betray and deny him.

- **Passing the torch-** Jesus asks his friends to take care of each other and teach others to love God. He promises to send them the Holy Spirit to guide them and ease their worries, so they'll never walk alone.

- **Ultimate sacrifice-** Jesus allows himself to be arrested, humiliated, tortured, and killed so that we could be forgiven and freed of our mistakes.
- **Defeating death-** After three days in the grave, Jesus comes to life and destroys death's power over humanity.

HOW GOD SHOWS UP

Our God doesn't sit on his high throne and observe our broken world from afar. He chooses to enter it as a vulnerable human and live alongside the people he created. He notices the outcast, forgives the sinner, and puts all pride aside to lift others up. He knows what's coming, but he doesn't run away. He feels unbearable emotional and physical pain so we don't have to. He conquers death so death can never conquer us. We owe him everything, but all he wants is for us to take care of each other.

JOHN

1. The Word of Life was with God from the beginning and brings light to all the dark places of our world. A messenger named John told people about the light, but many still did not recognize God's presence on earth. The Word became a glorious, honest human who lived among us. He still blesses us endlessly with grace and truth and makes it possible for us

to know his Father. When people thought John the Baptist was a prophet or the Messiah, John said "I am preparing a way for someone far greater than me. He will sacrifice himself to wash away the sins of the world. I see the dove of God's Spirit resting on Jesus' shoulder, and I have no doubt he is the One we've been waiting for." Jesus invites a small group of men to get to know him and promises they will witness great miracles by his side.

2. Jesus invites his new friends to a family wedding, and Jesus' mother reveals that the wine has run out. Jesus turns jars of water into wine so that the celebration can continue, and this helps his new followers believe in him. Jesus finds corrupt merchants turning the Temple into a marketplace, and he angrily drives them out. As he begins performing miracles throughout Jerusalem, Jesus seems to know the hearts and thoughts of those he helps.

3. A pharisee named Nicodemus says "Jesus, I believe your wisdom comes from God, and I'm ready to learn from you." Jesus says "Then listen to this truth. Those who inherit God's eternal kingdom need to be spiritually reborn. God will give you a new heart and allow his Spirit to lead you on a great and unpredictable adventure. God loves humanity so much that he sent his Son to save anyone willing to love him more than they love darkness. Those who hate the light will be turned away from it." As Jesus' popularity increases, John the Baptist says "I told you all that my goal was to prepare the path for someone greater than me. Well, here he is, and I will gladly make myself less important to allow him to shine. Jesus speaks with the truth of God's Spirit, and those who believe in him will find a fresh, new life."

4.   The Jewish leaders become preoccupied with Jesus' success, and Jesus escapes the crowds to visit a quiet Samaritan town. He asks a local woman for a drink at the well, and she is shocked that this Jewish man would share a cup with an outcast like her. Jesus says "If you believe in the God that sent me here, he will give you an eternal spring of water, and you'll never be thirsty again. I know all about your scandalous past, and I see that you're a Samaritan, but I'd still love to talk to you about God." As the woman tells her friends she just shared a drink with the Messiah, Jesus' friends return from an errand shocked that Jesus has been talking to her. Jesus responds "Look around you! This field is full of good people ready to be harvested." Many Samaritans in that town turn to Jesus because of the woman's testimony, and he stays there to teach these eager listeners for two more days. Jesus then journeys on and heals the dying child of a government official.

5.   Jesus enters a crowd of sick and disabled people by a pool and notices a man who had been paralyzed for 38 years. Jesus tells him "If you want to get well, pick up your mat and walk." The man bravely picks himself up and shocks the crowd by walking home. The Jewish authorities stop the healed man to say "Today is the Sabbath! You shouldn't be carrying your mat today, and Jesus should have waited until tomorrow to heal you." Jesus boldly responds "My Father is always working, and so will I. The Father loves me and reveals his plan to me, and you'll be amazed as he allows me to raise the dead, bring justice to this unjust place, and bring life-giving truth to those willing to listen. John the Baptist is a great man filled with God's light, and

he can testify that I act with God's authority. I don't need human praise like you who constantly try to please each other. My only desire is to please and serve God."

6. Jesus multiplies one boy's lunch to host a feast for 5,000 followers, and they gather twelve baskets of leftovers afterward. The impassioned people try to make Jesus king by force, but Jesus escapes to a quiet place and later walks across the lake to reach the boat of his stunned disciples. When the crowd finally finds Jesus on the other side of the lake, he says "You enjoyed the bread I gave you, but you failed to understand the miracle. Bread goes stale eventually, but the eternal life I offer never runs out. God wants you to believe in me instead of asking for an even bigger miracle. I am the eternal bread that can take care of you forever." The people grumble "But aren't you the carpenter's son? How can you say you come from heaven?" Jesus responds "I'm telling you the truth. It's your choice if you want to miss out on the good new life I'm offering. The living God sent me and gives me the power of his Spirit, but I know some of you will refuse to believe me."

7. Knowing the Jewish authorities are hunting him, Jesus declines his brothers' invitation to attend the Festival of Shelters but then enters the crowd secretly. He overhears whispered compliments and suspicion about his ministry, so he stands up on the Temple steps to proclaim "Some of you question my authority to teach, but these ideas come not from my education but from God. My honest heart only wants to glorify God instead of myself. Try to see past my nontraditional actions to notice my pure motives and heart. You think of me as the carpenter's son and think you know

all about me, but you don't really know the One who sent me. Soon I will go back to a place where you cannot follow. If you're thirsty, I have eternal water for you." The angry Pharisees try to arrest him several times during the Festival but cannot quite catch him. Some in the crowd proclaim him as the Messiah while others call him a liar and a fraud.

8. When Jesus returns from a quiet time of prayer, he sees a crowd ready to throw stones at a woman caught in adultery. He says "If you have never sinned, go ahead and throw the first stone." One by one, her accusers walk away, and Jesus says "You are free, but learn from this, and don't sin again." The pharisees again question his authority, and Jesus says "I will light the way for my followers and guide you out of dark places. I know who I am, and I know I speak the truth. If you want to judge me, that doesn't affect me at all. If you really knew me, you would know my Father better. When I return to him, you will not be able to follow unless you believe I am who I say I am. You are slaves to sin, but I can set you free and make you part of God's eternal family." The pharisees shout "You have a demon in you! Who do you think you are?" Jesus responds "I seek no glory for myself. I only want to honor the Father I love, the God you claim to know. Before Abraham was born, I was one with my Father." They throw stones at Jesus, but he disappears from the Temple without a scratch.

9. When his friends ask if a blind man is disabled because of his parents' sin, Jesus responds "Sin has nothing to do with disability! Some people have different abilities and physical challenges so that God's power can be revealed in a special way through their lives." Jesus rubs mud on the man's eyes,

and when he washes his face, his eyes work for the first time in his life. Since the healing happens on the Sabbath, the pharisees question the healed man in an attempt to find and condemn Jesus. The man says "You think Jesus is not from God because he doesn't interpret the Sabbath like you do, but all I know is he healed me, and it has changed my life. How could this miracle have come from anywhere but God? You seem pretty preoccupied with him. Would you like to follow him too?" The pharisees curse the man and kick him out of the synagogue, but Jesus pulls the man aside to say "I am the one who healed you. I've come to the earth so that the blind may see and so that the blind pharisees may finally understand that they don't know everything.

10. "The false prophets and selfish leaders of the past took advantage of you for their own gain, but I am a good shepherd who will give my own life to save my flock and lead you toward a full, good life. No one can overpower me, but I will freely choose to die for you, and even then, God won't let death hold me." When some continue to doubt his identity as the Messiah, Jesus says "I have already told you the truth, but you close your heart to me. You refuse to trust me, but no one can snatch my sheep from my protective care. I have done nothing but good deeds and healing miracles in your presence, and you want to stone me. Why? You may not believe that I'm the Son of God, but you could at least believe that my actions are in line with God's heart."

11. Jesus' dear friend Lazarus becomes fatally ill, and Jesus travels to Bethany a few days later, even though the area

is crawling with Jewish authorities who want to kill him. Lazarus is already dead when Jesus' group arrives, and Mary and Martha say "If only you had been here, our brother would still be alive." Jesus weeps with the sisters and asks them to roll the stone away from the tomb. Jesus prays passionately for the Father's help, and Lazarus walks out of the tomb as healthy as ever. When the chief priests learn of Jesus' latest miracle, they plan to kill him but also say "Many people are coming into Jerusalem for Passover. Surely Jesus isn't stupid enough to show his face publicly, but let's look for him just in case."

12. Lazarus' grateful sister, Mary, approaches Jesus a week before his death and anoints his feet with expensive oil. Jesus sees this as a beautiful, passionate, and generous offering despite several disciples considering it wasteful. Meanwhile, the chief priests plot the murder of Lazarus to cover up the fact the Jesus had raised him. The next day, instead of running from his oppressors, the brave Savior peacefully rides into the heart of Jerusalem. He is welcomed by a large crowd who had heard about the resurrection of Lazarus, and the pharisees fear that the whole world will soon follow him. Jesus says "If you want to follow me, trust me to give you eternal life and don't cling so tightly to your earthly life. My light will be among you a little longer, and I want you to be people of the light after I've gone back to my Father. I speak with the Father's authority, and if you continue to stubbornly reject me, you also reject him."

13. Before Passover Dinner, Jesus washes the feet of his friends, and at first, Peter resists this humble gesture. Jesus says "You call me Teacher, and I have just washed your feet to teach

you the kind of servant leaders I want you to be. Most of you will lead and serve in my name, but one of you will betray me." He sends Judas away, and the rest of the men think Jesus is sending him to buy food for the festival. Jesus continues "God's glory will now be revealed through me, and I must say goodbye to you. You won't be able to follow me. Stay here and love each other as I have loved you. Your love will reveal that you are my people. Peter, I know you think you're ready to die by my side, but you will deny me three times before morning.

14. "But don't worry. I will prepare my Father's house to welcome you when the time is right. If you know me, you'll be able to find your way to his house. The Father lives in me and does his glorious work through me. The Holy Spirit is coming after me to live in your heart, reveal great truths to you, and enable you to obey God. Even after I leave you, I will reveal myself to whoever loves and obeys me. As I leave you, I offer you uncommon peace that will ease your worries and fears. I love the Father and must soon fulfill his plan. Let's take a walk through the garden.

15. "My Father is like a gardener who planted me in this earth like a life-giving vine. Any person that unites with the vine will be like a healthy, fruitful branch, but those who cut themselves off from me will wither and dry up. My followers reflect God's glory and maintain desires and actions that align with God's plan. If you remain connected to my love, you will be able to love each other selflessly and sacrificially. Friends, I chose you to walk with me and learn to bear eternal fruit. Those who hate me will hate you as well, but when you are mistreated like I will be, remember

I can relate to your pain. I have chosen you to spread the word about me, and I will send the Holy Spirit to help you lead with greatness.

16. "You will be kicked out of synagogues by misguided priests who think they are doing God's will, but keep your faith strong in the face of rejection. Your enemies don't know God like they think they do. Your hearts are sad to know I'm leaving, but this is for the best so that the Holy Spirit can come live among all of you forever. The Spirit will reveal many faulty assumptions humans have held about God and sin. When I leave, you will weep while the evil world shouts in gladness, but then I will return, and all your sadness will be forgotten. Your hearts will fill with unshakable gladness when you see me again. The Father loves you because of your friendship with me, and he will gladly answer your prayers. The world may scatter you and make you suffer, but trust God to stand by you as he defeats the darkness.

17. "Father, the time has come for me to reveal your glory to the world. You've enabled me to offer eternal life to all who find you by drawing close to me. They are learning to obey you and listen to your message through me. I pray for our precious people as they learn to share your glory with others. I will come back to you soon, but they will stay here. Keep them safe, and fill their hearts with my joy as they spread my message. Remind them of the truth when they are tempted to follow evil paths. I dedicate their hearts to you. I pray that their spiritual community will be one with our hearts, just as you and I are one. Let their love and unity show the world who they belong to."

18. Judas finds Jesus and his friends in the garden, and Jesus asks the Roman soldiers to take him peacefully and let his friends go free. When Peter cuts off the ear of one of the enemies, Jesus says "Put your sword away, and let me drink this bitter cup the Father has given me!" As the High Priest questions Jesus, he answers "I taught publicly in the Temple, so all my words are common knowledge. If I have said anything that deserves your abuse, just tell me what it was." As Peter and John eavesdrop in the courtyard outside, Peter denies knowing Jesus to protect himself. The Jewish authorities take Jesus to the governor's house, hoping Pilate will execute him since the Law won't allow the priests to do it themselves. Jesus tells Pilate "You ask if I'm the king of the Jews, but my kingdom is not in this world. If I was a king on earth, my followers never would have let me be arrested. My only purpose is to speak the truth to those who choose to listen." Pilate finds no fault with Jesus and offers to set him free, but the crowd yells "No! Kill Jesus, and give us the bandit Barabbas instead!"

19. Giving into the crowd, Pilate has Jesus whipped, and the soldiers mock him by putting a crown of thorns on his head. After the flogging, Pilate tells the crowd "Okay, I punished this innocent man like you asked, and now I will let him go." But the crowd screams "No! He claimed to be the Son of God and deserves to be crucified! If you set a man free who claims to be king, you're undermining the emperor, and he won't be happy." Finally, Pilate gives into the crowd's demand and sentences Jesus to crucifixion. The beaten Jesus carries his heavy cross up a hill and is nailed to the wood alongside two criminals. Jesus' mother stands

with a group of Jesus' friends during the horrifying execution, and Jesus says "John, take care of my mom for me." Thirsty and broken, Jesus cries out "It is finished!" and dies. A secret follower of Jesus buries his body in a family tomb.

20. The third morning after his death, Mary Magdalene discovers the empty tomb, and runs to tell John and Peter that the body has been stolen. The men run to the tomb, and John believes immediately that Jesus has risen from the dead. As Mary weeps for the missing body, the risen Jesus calls from behind her, "Mary, turn around! It's me! Go to my brothers and tell them that I'm back but will soon return to my Father." Later that evening, Jesus appears to his friends and says "May the Holy Spirit give you peace as you go forgive my people. Look at my scars and touch my skin if you need further proof that I'm really here. Those who believe in me without this proof will be especially blessed."

21. Peter and a few other close friends of Jesus decide to go fishing. Jesus appears on their boat and says "You haven't caught much today, boys. Put your net on the other side of the boat, and your luck might change." As the men pull up an overwhelming number of fish, John exclaims "That guy was Jesus!" When they pull the boat up to the beach, they find Jesus in front of a campfire. He grins and says "Let's eat some of those fish, friends! Hey Peter, you denied me three times before, so I will ask you three times if you love me. Take care of my flock and be ready to die for the flock like I did." I could write many more books about the great things Jesus did, but the whole world couldn't contain them.

DAY FIVE - BIRTH OF THE CHURCH
ACTS

BIG IDEA

After Jesus returns to heaven, his followers boldly spread the news that death and darkness no longer have the upper hand.

CAST OF CHARACTERS

- **Peter-** Bold leader who confronts the Jewish Council and encourages thousands to accept God's grace and guidance. After some initial skepticism, he eventually accepts Paul's ministry toward Gentiles.

- **Stephen-** Church treasurer who performs great miracles and speaks with great wisdom. He's killed for bravely speaking the truth.

- **Saul-** Pharisee who terrorizes and arrests Christians until he sees the risen Jesus and transforms so dramatically that he changes his name to Paul. He becomes a passionate foreign missionary and a dedicated follower of Christ.

- **Barnabas-** Faces many dangers alongside Paul as they share Jesus' story with Gentiles who worship false Greek gods.

- **Cornelius-** Good-hearted Gentile who helps Peter understand that God's grace is for all people.

- **Silas-** Journeys with Paul to spread God's love in Roman colonies.

- **Timothy-** a young, well-liked Christian who leaves his

comfortable home to join Paul on his dangerous mission.

- **Apollos-** Misguided but fervent preacher who humbly accepts Paul's correction.
- **Governor Felix-** Passively keeps innocent Paul in prison to avoid ruffling the feathers of the Jewish Council.
- **Governor Festus-** Honors Paul's request to appeal to the Roman Emperor.

HOW GOD SHOWS UP

God sends the Holy Spirit to guide his people toward a changed life. He allows the best friends of Jesus to spread his story with boldness. He leads a hard-hearted pharisee named Saul to dramatically transform into a man willing to go to the ends of the earth to spread the love of Jesus. God equips these leaders to handle any obstacle, and not even prison and death can silence their message of grace.

ACTS

1. My name is Luke. In my first book, I spoke of Jesus' ministry prior to his death, but that was just the beginning. For over a month after his death, he appeared frequently to his apostles and taught them even more about God's kingdom. He said "Wait here in Jerusalem, and trust in the Father's timing. When you least expect it, the Holy Spirit will fill you with heavenly power and enable you to share the truth with people across the world." As Jesus ascends into heaven, his friends stare at

the sky until two angels say "Stop staring! He'll come back when the time is right." Jesus' friends and family continue gathering regularly to pray, and the number of believers begins to grow. The community prayerfully chooses Matthias to replace Judas as an apostle.

2. During one of the early church gatherings, the sound of a strong wind fills the house, and a curious crowd gathers because of the noise. The church members begin shouting the good news, and each observer somehow hears and understands these words in his own language. Peter says "You may think we're drunk, but we are simply filled with the joy and energy of God's Spirit. The Spirit allows us to foresee that even at the end of the world, God will save those who call to him. Jesus had the authority to do great miracles, and he still allowed himself to be killed so that God could rescue us from death's power. As King David said: 'God draws close to me, removes my worries, and fills my heart with happiness. I am a mortal man who holds out hope that God will provide never-ending life.' We know that Jesus is the promised Messiah who fulfills his ancestor David's wish for eternal life. If you turn from your sins and devote your hearts to his purposes, the Holy Spirit will guide you toward a full life as God's child." That day, 3,000 people are baptized in the name of Jesus, and the church grows larger each day. The new believers gather regularly in prayer and fellowship. They humbly donate money to lift up the poor, and the apostles work great miracles in Jerusalem.

3. As Peter and John enter the Temple to pray, they notice a homeless man who was born paralyzed. Peter looks into his eyes and says "I have no money for you, but in the name of Jesus, I can help you walk again." Peter helps the man to his feet, and his initial tentative steps soon turn to celebratory, worshipful dancing. A stunned crowd gathers by the Temple gate, and Peter says "Why are you staring? This man is not walking because of my power but because of the power of God. You demanded the death of God's servant, Jesus, even after Pilate offered to free him. You killed the innocent, glorious Savior, but God raised him from death. We all saw it with our own eyes. It's through Jesus that this man can walk now. I know you were ignorant about who Jesus was when you crucified him, and God brought impossible good out of his unfair suffering. Despite your mistakes, God still loves you and longs to forgive you if you are willing to choose him over your sins. If you turn to him, he will strengthen you, bless you, and teach you to obey him."

4. Some annoyed, disbelieving Jewish leaders arrest Peter and John to shut them up, but Peter's speech still helps the young church grow to 5,000 members. The Jewish Council questions Peter's authority, and Peter responds "If you're angry that the paralyzed man is healed, you should know that the Jesus you killed enabled him to walk again. You tried to silence his good message, but he is still saving the world through those who love him." The Council members whisper "What should we do with these guys? No one can deny the miracle they did, but maybe we can command them to stop preaching in the name of Jesus." Peter and

John respond "You think you are the ultimate judge of what's right in God's eyes, but sorry. God has revealed the truth to us, and we can't help but share it!" Fearing that punishing the apostles would incite a riot, the Council members let them go with a stern warning. The church members pray "Creator of everything, the leaders of our land conspired against Jesus, but they cannot silence his message. We will speak the truth with even greater boldness. Please let your healing and miracles be seen throughout the earth!" The impassioned believers spread the word with a unified sense of purpose. They unselfishly provide for the poor people in their midst, leaving no family behind.

5. A married couple gives part of their money to the church but lets the community believe they've given all they have. Peter confronts them, saying "The money was yours to keep or give, but why did you think you could lie to God and get away with it?" When the couple tries to continue the ruse, God strikes them dead to keep their prideful, dishonest attitude from spreading like a virus through the church. Jealous of their miracles and amazing church growth, the Jewish leaders arrest the apostles, but an angel unlocks the prison doors. When the Jewish Council finds the freed men preaching on the Temple steps, they say "We warned you not to teach in the name of Jesus or spread the rumor that we are responsible for his death!" The apostles respond "We obey God, but we don't take orders from you. We can't be silent about what our eyes have seen. You killed Jesus, but God raised him from death and now offers us a new life through the Holy Spirit." The pharisees simmer with murderous rage, but one of them says "Calm down, men. When

other self-proclaimed Messiahs died, their movements died with them. Even though Jesus died, the numbers of this group seems to be growing larger every day. Let's just be careful that we don't fight these men too harshly, just in case their words and miracles actually do come from God."

6. When Greek-speaking church members claim that their widows aren't getting a fair portion of church funds, the apostles say "We need to continue focusing on delivering God's message to the people, but we want to take your concern seriously. Let's appoint a trustworthy team of leaders to manage our finances." Stephen, the leader of this financial team, performs great miracles and speaks with Spirit-filled wisdom. The Jewish leaders cannot intelligently debate with Stephen, so they arrest him and accuse this innocent man of disrespecting Moses and the Temple.

7. When asked to respond to these false accusations, Stephen says "Our people have a great and interesting history, don't we? Long ago, God asked our childless ancestor Abraham to leave home and trust that he would have an enormous family that would inherit this very land. God blessed Abraham with Isaac and blessed Isaac with Jacob. Jacob's sons jealously sold their brother Joseph into slavery in Egypt, and God used this terrible sin to lift Joseph to a powerful position that equipped him to save his family from famine. When Egypt became intimidated by this growing family, they enslaved our ancestors, and God chose Moses to set them free. Moses was the adopted son of the Pharaoh, so our ancestors fought against his leadership many times. Even after God equipped Moses to perform great miracles for their benefit, our ancestors still rebelled and made an idol for themselves in the

desert. This generation worshipped God from a travelling tent, and later, King Solomon replaced the tent by building a beautiful Temple. God cannot be contained within a man-made Temple. His throne is in heaven. You stubborn people rebel against God's true messengers just like our ancestors rebelled against Moses and the prophets. You have killed his righteous Servant and refuse to obey the very law you claim to protect!" The angry Council members cover their ears and stone Stephen as the dying man shouts "Jesus, I see you! Receive my spirit, and forgive these men for what they are doing."

8. A young pharisee named Saul witnesses Stephen's gruesome murder and sets out to destroy the young church, dragging believers out of their homes and throwing them in jail. Survivors of Saul's raid scatter to Samaria and begin teaching and healing people there. Phillip manages to convince a greedy pagan magician to change his ways and follow Jesus, and the unquenchable joy of the Lord spreads throughout the city. Phillip helps an Ethiopian royal official understand the good news of Jesus by answering his questions about Jewish prophesies and speaking of the amazing new life promised by the Savior.

9. As Saul journeys to Damascus to find more church members to threaten and arrest, a dazzling vision of Jesus stops him to say "Saul, nice to meet you. I'm Jesus. Why do you keep hurting my people? If you believe this encounter is real, I'll show you what to do next." Jesus appears to a Damascus believer and says "Ananias, I want you to find Saul and heal him of the temporary blindness I have placed on him. I know he has done terrible things to my people, but I am

trying to change his heart so that he will serve me and share my message with many nations." Brave Ananias trusts God enough to approach murderous Saul and heal his eyes. Right away, the restored Saul hops up and begins preaching powerful sermons in the name of Jesus. Saul tries to join the church in Jerusalem, and they are understandably suspicious of him at first. It's only after Barnabas vouches for Saul that they believe in the authenticity of his transformation. The church strengthens and grows during this time of peace. Peter travels to Joppa to attend the funeral of Tabitha, **a church leader** who had spent her life helping the poor. Peter raises his friend from the dead, and news of this miracle spreads quickly.

10. A Roman military captain leads his family to Jesus and shows great generosity to the poor. An angel appears to him and says "Cornelius, God has seen your good deeds and would love to answer your prayers. Go find a man named Peter in Joppa and invite him to dinner." When Cornelius passionately welcomes Peter to his home, Peter says "A Jewish man like myself is usually forbidden from entering the home of a Gentile, but God is showing me that people of all races are welcome in God's family if they have good hearts and pure actions. God's good news is for everyone. It seems that you've heard of a man named Jesus who healed the sick, removed demons, and rose from the dead after he was killed. The prophets told us he would come, and now he has removed our sins and given us new life." Peter watches as the Holy Spirit enters the hearts of the joyful Gentiles nearby.

11. When the believers in Jerusalem disapprove of Peter's meal

with Gentiles, Peter explains "I had a mysterious dream in which God invited me to eat a cornucopia of clean and unclean meats, making it clear that God can now make any person or animal clean regardless of race or past law. I was then invited to Cornelius' house and watched as his Gentile family and friends received the same Holy Spirit that we received. Who are we to stop God from welcoming them into the family?" The scattered believers begin preaching to Gentiles in their cities, and many of them gather money and food to prepare for a predicted famine.

12. King Herod executes the apostle James and arrests Peter to please the Jewish leaders. Peter's prison cell is heavily guarded, but an angel sets him free the night before his trial. Mark's mom and her servant can hardly believe their eyes when Peter shows up on their doorstep and asks them to inform the church of his escape. The angel strikes King Herod down for not crediting God for Peter's escape.

13. God chooses Saul and Barnabas to preach the Gospel in distant lands, so they immediately sail to the island of Cyprus with Mark. Saul confronts a local magician for spreading lies about God's message. The magician is stricken blind, and the governor of the island believes Saul from then on. Saul's name becomes Paul due to his dramatic transformation. In another city, synagogue leaders invite Paul to encourage the people, and Paul says "Gentiles and fellow Jews, listen up! The God of Israel delivered our ancestors from Egypt, protected them in the desert, and made them into a great nation. God chose an obedient man named David to be a great king, and many generations later, a great man named John prepared the way for an

even greater man, David's descendant Jesus. The Jewish leaders didn't understand him and sentenced him to death, but God raised him to life. He saves us from our sins in a way the Law alone never could." When the whole town comes the next week to hear Paul speak, Paul notices the Jews' jealousy of Paul's popularity. Paul says "You Jews had the opportunity to hear the good news first, but since you close your ears to me, I'll share this light with the joyful Gentiles who appear ready to listen." The Jews throw Paul out of the region, and his group journeys on.

14. In Iconium, Paul and Barnabas use miracles and bold messages to convince many Jews and Gentiles to turn to Jesus, but nonbelieving Jews try to stone them. They escape to Lystra, and Paul allows a paralyzed believer to stand up and walk. At first, the amazed locals believe Barnabas and Paul are the Greek gods Zeus and Hermes, but Paul shouts "Stop worshipping us! We are mere humans like you. We are here to turn you away from these worthless idols and toward the living God who created everything. He has let you believe in these false gods in the past, but all along, he was the one providing you with food and happy hearts." Some in the crowd continue to worship the men while others side with the Jewish persecutors and stone Paul. Fortunately, Paul survives the attack, and they journey on to Derbe to win hearts for Jesus. As they travel back home through the same group of cities, Paul appoints elders for each church and encourages the believers to stay strong through whatever testing they face.

15. Paul and Barnabas argue fiercely with church leaders who

insist that believers must follow the entire Jewish law to be saved. Samaritan believers joyfully receive Paul's news about his ministry to the Gentiles, but Jewish Christians in Jerusalem insist that the Gentiles must learn the Law and become circumcised to enter the Christian family. Peter tells the leaders "Brothers and sisters, God revealed to me his desire to share the good news with people of all races and cultures. He forgives them and equips them with the Holy Spirit just as he does with us. God's grace covers them just as they are, and we have no right to add unnecessary burdens to their infant churches." Paul and Barnabas tell of the miraculous transformation of the Gentile believers, and James responds "It's great that these Gentiles believe, but the Law has been around for a long time, and we should at least write them a letter asking them to avoid raw meat and sexual immorality. There's no need to bother them with the entire religious code, but a few regulations related to safety and respect couldn't hurt." Paul and Barnabas journey separately to strengthen the new churches in other nations and share the apostles' letter with them.

16. As they journey back to Lystra, Paul and Silas meet a young, well-liked Greek Christian named Timothy who journeys on with their group. The Spirit doesn't allow the group to enter Asia but leads them to the Roman colony of Philippi. Good-hearted Lydia opens her heart to Paul's message, and she invites Paul's group to stay at her house. A demon-possessed fortune teller harasses and annoys Paul until he finally orders the demon to come out of her. Her fortune-telling abilities leave with the demon. Her angry employers capture Paul and Silas and publicly announce

"These Jewish troublemakers are trying to convince us to abandon our customs." The authorities severely beat and arrest the men, but Paul and Silas continue singing joyful songs to God through the night. A great earthquake shakes the foundations of the prison to unlock the doors, and the trembling prison guard asks what he must do to be saved. Paul responds "Just believe in Jesus, brother." The transformed guard joyfully feeds Paul and Silas, cleans their wounds, and frees them. Paul and Silas boldly demand an apology from the local police since these two Roman citizens were publicly beaten and arrested without charges.

17. Paul and Silas spend several weeks preaching in Thessalonica, explaining that Jesus the Messiah suffered and rose from death. Many women and Greeks there believe, but the Jewish leaders incite a riot by shouting "These men have caused trouble everywhere, and they break the emperor's law by claiming this Jesus fellow is a king." Paul and Silas quietly flee to the more welcoming town of Berea. When the mob catches up to the apostles there, the church sends Paul to hide out in Athens until it's safe to return. Paul begins debating teachers in the idol-filled city, and when they express a desire to learn more, Paul says "I've noticed your city is very religious, but you have been worshipping gods that don't exist. I worship the Creator of everything who rules the world and orchestrated the timing of every event throughout history. He hoped you would recognize him through the beauty of his creation, and he forgives you for turning to idols in the past. But now that you know that your Father raised his Son from death for you, he will certainly hold you responsible if you choose to reject the

truth." Some people laugh at Paul while others become curious to learn more.

18. Paul journeys to Corinth and stays with a Jewish couple who was forced to move there from Rome after the Emperor exiled all Jews from the capital city. When the Jews in Corinth fiercely oppose Paul in the synagogue, Paul says "Fine! If you want to stay lost, that's on you. From now on, I will focus on ministering to the Gentiles." Paul baptizes many Gentiles and leads the Corinthian church for a year and a half after God tells him "Don't give up, Paul. Keep speaking with courage and boldness to this large group of believers. I'm with you and will keep you safe." Paul then passes through Ephesus, Jerusalem, and Galatia to strengthen new believers there. A smooth, enthusiastic speaker named Apollos begins preaching about being baptized in the name of John the Baptist, and Paul's companions pull him aside to teach him about Jesus. Apollos happily accepts their correction and becomes an incredibly effective advocate for the Way of Jesus.

19. Paul learns that Ephesian believers have never heard of the Holy Spirit and have been baptized in the name of John, so he patiently teaches them about Jesus and equips them with the Spirit. Some synagogue members stubbornly resist Paul's teachings, so Paul gathers the believers in town and moves onto Asia. Paul's connection to God is so strong that even his handkerchiefs have the power to heal. However, when sons of the High Priest try to use the names of Jesus and Paul to remove a demon, the possessed man overpowers and attacks the imposters. Locals learn about this and gain greater reverence for the name of Jesus.

An Ephesian silversmith named Demetrius starts a riot in Ephesus because he's afraid that the boom of Christian conversions will cause his idol-making business to suffer.

20. After reluctantly laying low during the Ephesus riots, Paul says a warm goodbye to the believers there and spends a week in Traos. During Paul's midnight farewell sermon to the believers of Traos, a sleepy young listener falls out a third story window, but Paul passionately runs downstairs and heals him. Paul tells the Ephesian elders "You witnessed our entire ministry here, and you saw the tears we shed as we humbly and passionately served God despite the plots and riots of the legalistic Jewish leaders. I didn't hold back, and I hope I made it clear that believers need to abandon their sins and turn to Jesus. The Spirit is leading me back to Jerusalem, and I don't know what awaits me there. I may never see you again, so you are now responsible for carrying on with this good work and taking care of these precious sheep. Fierce wolves will come, but you must fight to keep our flock strong. Follow my example and work not for the pay but for the people. Lift up the weak, and find more joy in giving than receiving." They share a tearful goodbye, and Paul boards the boat.

21. Paul's group sails to Tyre, and the believers there warn Paul of the dangers awaiting him in Jerusalem. They beg him not to go there. When Paul insists the Spirit is leading him to Jerusalem, the group prays for him and sends him onward. At Phillip's house, a prophet warns Paul that he will be tied up by Jewish enemies if he goes to Jerusalem, and Paul responds "You're breaking my heart with your passionate concern for my safety, but you should know that

I am ready to die for Jesus if that's what needs to happen."
Paul enjoys a warm welcome in Jerusalem and gives the
church elders a full report of his adventures. They respond
"Brother Paul, the Jewish Christians here have remained
devoted to the Law, and they've heard rumors that you are
teaching Jews in other countries to abandon our laws and
customs. We know this can't possibly be true, so could you
set the record straight by joining us in a purification ritual
in the Temple?" Paul agrees to appease the church leaders,
but a mob of Jews from Asia arrive in Jerusalem and shout
"This man has turned everyone against the Law, and he
has defiled the Temple by bringing Gentiles into this
holy place." As Paul is dragged from the Temple and
beaten, a Roman commander arrests him to keep the
mob from killing him. Sympathizing with the innocent
apostle, the commander allows Paul to silence the crowd
and stand on the steps to make a speech.

22. Paul says "Fellow Jews, let me defend myself to you. I
learned the Law at a young age from highly respected
teachers here in Jerusalem. I followed Judaism so fervently
that I arrested many early Christians and did everything
I could to silence them. But then I saw the risen Jesus. He
struck me blind with his dazzling light and sent a brave
believer to heal my eyes and say 'God is choosing you to
spread the news about what you've seen. Let Jesus wash
away your sins so you can get to work right away.' The
Spirit knew it would be hard for Jerusalem Christians to
trust me since I had done terrible things to them, so he sent
me to distant lands to preach to Gentiles." At the mention
of Gentiles, the mob begins flailing and screaming "Kill

him!" The commander removes Paul from the crowd and treats his fellow Roman citizen with respect. Eager to release Paul, he takes the prisoner before the Jewish Council.

23. Paul stares down the Council and says "You should know my conscience is perfectly clear this morning." One of the priests strikes his face, and Paul responds "You think you are worthy to judge and strike me, but God will strike you hypocrites! Did you know I used to be one of you? I come from a long line of pharisees, and you put me on trial for believing the dead can rise to life." At this, a violent theological argument breaks out between the pharisees and sadducees about weather resurrection is possible, and the commander takes Paul back to prison. The Lord encourages Paul to bravely journey on to Rome as Paul's nephew overhears the Council members plotting to kill Paul. Paul's nephew informs the commander, who greatly increases Paul's security and sends this message to the governor: "The Jews tried to kill this Roman citizen, and I rescued him and brought him before their Council. They continue to plot against him even though he is perfectly innocent, so for Paul's safety, I'm transporting him to you for a fair trial."

24. On the day of Paul's trial, the Jewish leaders say "Governor Felix, thank you for your wise, peaceful leadership. You've done such great things for our country. We hate to waste your precious time, but we have found this Paul fellow to be a dangerous nuisance who starts riots and defiles our Temple." Paul responds "I know you to be a fair judge, sir, so I am happy to defend myself before you. I have never started a riot in Jerusalem or anywhere else. They will be able to give you no proof of this lie or any of their other

accusations. I believe in the same God as these men and follow the same Law. I also follow the Way of Jesus that they refuse to accept. I was performing a purification ceremony and minding my own business when Jews from Asia started a riot and tried to kill me. I committed no crime. I'm on trial today because these men disagree that Jesus rose to life." Felix keeps Paul in prison in an effort to please the Jews.

25. When Festus becomes governor, the Jewish leaders beg Festus to transport Paul to Jerusalem so they can kill him. Festus wants to appease the Jewish Council, but Paul wisely responds "I have done nothing against Roman law or Jewish law, and you know it. If you have proof that I've committed a crime, I'll gladly pay the price, but if not, I must appeal to the emperor's court in Rome." When King Agrippa comes to town, Festus consults with him about Paul's situation, and the king is curious to meet the prisoner and hear his story. When presenting Paul to the visiting king, Festus says "This is the man that the Jewish leaders scream and complain about. They want him dead, but they have no evidence or clear criminal charges against him. I'm pretty sure we should send him to the emperor as he has requested."

26. Paul says "King Agrippa, thank you for taking the time to hear me out. The Jews who accuse me know that I come from a family of pharisees, which is the highest order of the Jewish priesthood, and I was so devoted to the priesthood that I angrily punished this movement of Jesus followers that seemed to threaten Judaism as I knew it. But when Jesus himself appeared to me and proved that he has risen from death and fulfilled a great promise to our ancestors, my heart dramatically changed. He called me to reveal

the truth of God's amazing grace to Gentiles who desperately need this good news, and I obeyed my Lord. The Jewish leaders didn't like my association with Gentiles and arrested me. Good king, do you believe me? My prayer is that this meeting might be an opportunity for everyone here to learn God's truth and turn their hearts to him." The king responds that Paul is innocent and could be released if he hadn't already requested a meeting with the emperor.

27. Festus and Agrippa agree to honor Paul's request and put him on a prisoner boat to Rome. The dangerous wind causes the journey to be slow and difficult from the beginning, and Paul suggests that they give up to voyage due to potential loss of life and cargo. The crew stubbornly journeys on and gets caught in a violent storm. After fighting the weather for several days without food, Paul says "We shouldn't have started this leg of the trip, but now that we're here, my God has encouraged us to take heart. We will lose a lot of cargo and even our ship, but he will allow us to survive this mess and get to Rome. Let's eat all the food we need with an attitude of trust and gratitude to God, and then we can throw the rest of our food overboard to lighten the ship. It sounds crazy, but if the ship's going down anyway, this decision could save our lives." The crew trusts Paul's instructions, and this allows the lightened ship to sail close enough to an island that they are able to abandon the wrecked ship and swim ashore.

28. The island natives of Malta welcome the stranded men, and Paul heals their sick chief. The grateful tribe gives the group many gifts and equips them to sail onward. Paul praises God when they finally arrive safely in Rome. Paul calls a

meeting with the Jewish leaders in the city and says "Our fellow Jews in Jerusalem had the Romans arrest me even though I did nothing wrong. They fight against me simply because I believe that God's promise to our ancestors has been fulfilled. I had to appeal to the emperor to save my life, and now I'm here to humbly ask for your support." The Roman Jews respond "We received no letter from Judea saying you were coming, but we're definitely curious about this Jesus you speak of." Paul preaches to this group with great passion and is able to convince some of them of the truth. For two years, Paul preaches in Rome with great boldness and freedom.

WEEK FIVE REFLECTION
Jesus

DISCUSSION QUESTIONS

- Jesus hung out with outcasts like Matthew and Mary Magdalene. Why do you suppose he chose them over the religious leaders? How did the outcasts respond to Jesus and his teachings? How did the religious people respond?

- From the first few chapters of Matthew and Luke, what do you know about Joseph and Mary? Why do you think God chose each of them to be the earthly parents of his Son?

- When you look at Jesus' sermons, what are the topics and lessons that he seems to focus on the most? What does this reveal about how God wants us to live?

- Which healings and miracles of Christ strike you the most? Why do these particular acts stand out to you? What do these wonders reveal about Jesus?

- Jesus enjoyed using parables in his sermons. Why do you think he used these metaphorical illustrations rather than stating his points plainly? Which parable is your favorite and why?

- John 13-17 gives us a lengthy, behind-the-scenes look at the Last Supper. What pieces of advice and wisdom are imparted by Christ during this final meal with his friends?

- What is the significance of Christ's arrest, torture, death, and victory over death? Why do you think the Father's plan includes these events? What does Jesus' sacrifice reveal about the nature of God?

MUSIC MEDITATIONS

- **Matthew-** The Christmas story reminds me of the amazing courage and love it took for God to choose to enter the world as a vulnerable baby. Reflect on this amazing truth, and listen for God's love within "I Will Find a Way" by Jason Gray.
- **Mark-** This gospel highlights many of the healings and miracles of Jesus. Listen to "The Hurt and the Healer" by Mercy Me, and consider what it would feel like to be individually healed by Jesus.
- **Luke-** My favorite parable by far is the prodigal son story. Hear this powerful story in a new way by listening to "When God Ran" by Phillips Craig and Dean.
- **John-** This gospel highlights the selfless love and deep sacrifices of Jesus. Listen to "Glorious Day" by Casting Crowns, and thank God for the powerful love he showed through the life, death, and resurrection of his Son.
- **Acts-** Listen to "Our God's Alive" by Andy Cherry, and think about where you see the life and energy of the Holy Spirit within the stories of the early church.

APPLICATION IDEAS

- One key character quality of Jesus is his compassion for the poor and downtrodden. Determine one tangible way you can reach out to such people in your community. Then, have the courage to take the next step.

- Jesus was not afraid to confront the ugly-hearted people in his path. How can you respectfully but assertively speak up against hypocrisy or pride that may exist within your own church or community?

- If you've never done so before, watch a movie that depicts the ministry, crucifixion, and resurrection of Christ. This may help you more fully understand the awesomeness of his deep sacrificial love. If you feel that this type of movie would be too triggering or difficult for you, it may be a good idea to opt out of this challenge and instead take the time to read the entire Gospel of John.

WEEK SIX

Church

ROMANS-JUDE

DAY ONE - BROTHERS AND SISTERS
ROMANS- 1 CORINTHIANS- 2 CORINTHIANS

BIG IDEA

If you want to be part of God's family, all you need to do is choose the Father and love his children.

FAMILY RULES

- **Trust his grace-** You can't earn your way into heaven, but God is more than able to save you if you accept his grace and stay connected to his wisdom.

- **Let the Spirit change you-** Honor God's gift by letting him change your heart. Put his will above your selfish desires. The heart must transform for lasting changes to show up in our actions. Willpower alone won't work.

- **It's all about love-** The Law is not complicated. If you love God and others, you're living as God intended. If you don't love, you're missing the point.

- **Welcome everyone-** Lift up the outcasts among you, and allow any grace-loving Jew or Gentile into your community. Respect each other even when you disagree about the details. It's not your job to judge each other.

- **Honor marriage-** If you choose to marry, remain faithful. Put your spouse's needs before your own.

- **Use your unique strengths-** God created each of us with different strengths, and the Spirit helps us use them to build up our churches and communities.

- **Remember Jesus-** God's Son lived among us, suffered for our sake, and defeated death so that we might live forever in God's beautiful presence. Never lose sight of this awesome truth.
- **Give generously-** Show gratitude for God's blessings by sharing your blessings with others.

HOW GOD SHOWS UP

Jesus came to earth so that we could have an opportunity to truly know God and live in loving community with each other. He invites us to accept his transformative grace, and he longs for us to trust him with all our worries. He wants us to use our passions and strengths to live with a higher purpose and bless others in this life. He loves us enough to want the best possible life for us, and that life includes the support of our church family.

ROMANS

1. Dear Roman brothers and sisters, my name is Paul, and I'd love to share some good news with you. God made great promises to his prophets long ago, and now those promises have been fulfilled through his Son who grants us grace and peace. I'm so grateful that you are already doing a great job sharing your faith with the world. You are in my daily prayers, and I'd love to meet you in person so that we can bless and strengthen each other. Many circumstances have kept me from you so far, but I hope to journey your way very

soon. I am confident that salvation is available to anyone who has faith in God. Since the dawn of creation, some have chosen to give their hearts to evil and idolatry. If they choose to trade the Creator for a manufactured statue or a beautiful marriage for meaningless sex, God will not stop them. They corrupt their hearts with pleasure-seeking greed and selfish pride. They disrespect each other with violence, dishonesty, and cruelty. They feel no reason to change.

2. We see that God judges those who make terrible choices, but it's not our job to judge them ourselves. If God blesses another sinner with mercy or patience, that's **up to him.** God longs to fill our stubborn hearts with his glory and peace, but it is our choice whether to accept that gift. Many Jews think they are better than Gentiles who have never heard the Law, but some of those same boastful Jews disobey God's commands. Meanwhile, many good-hearted Gentiles naturally connect with God and serve others, even though they've never heard the scriptures. Jewish **purification** rituals mean nothing if we don't let the Spirit purify our hearts.

3. God loves us faithfully and always does the right thing, even though humans are constantly doing the wrong thing. Our imperfections reveal just how perfect God is. Jews certainly are lucky that they grew up knowing God's Law, but that doesn't make them better than Gentiles. Regardless of race or culture, we are all imperfect humans in desperate need of God's grace. The Law helps us know the **difference** between right and wrong, but only Jesus can set us free from our past mistakes and remove our desire to sin in the future.

4. God chose our ancestor Abraham because of his faith and

not because of his works. He needed forgiveness just like we do, and he was circumcised as a humble sign of his trust in the Lord. We remember Abraham as a man of righteous actions, but we mustn't forget that his story started with his simple, humble belief in God's promises. God offers that same free gift of redemption to anyone who believes that Jesus suffered, died, and rose to life so that we might rise as well.

5. Now that Jesus has given us his grace and peace, we can proudly give him the credit for our enriched lives. His Spirit enables us to endure difficult tests with greater hope and treat others with unselfish love. We were living as God's enemies and fighting him every step of the way, but Jesus loved us enough to die so that we could become God's friends. Isn't that wild? Sin has infected the human race since the dawn of mankind, but God's gift of grace is greater than our countless mistakes. Our ancestor Adam ruined God's plan, but now Jesus is making it right.

6. Some may think that God's grace provides an excuse to keep sinning, but I say no way! When our hearts unite with Jesus, he removes our desire for old habits, and he lifts us into a new and better life. When he died for us, he nailed our broken hearts and sinful motives on the cross alongside himself. We were once completely enslaved to our selfish desires, but those choices led to death and offered nothing good. Now we are forgiven and free to dedicate our lives to God.

7. When our spouse dies, we are free of our marriage vows and able to marry someone else. In the same way, we are dead

to the old way of the Law and are now free to follow Jesus. Back when human nature ruled our hearts, our religious rules reminded us to treat others with decency and worship God with regularity. The Law is certainly a beautiful thing, but the problem is that it focuses on our actions instead of our hearts. When the Spirit replaces our selfish desires with a desire to be like Jesus, our prideful actions disappear without a list of rules spelling it out for us. The Law tells us how to act righteous, but if our hearts don't understand why righteousness is important, we are at constant war with ourselves, trying to stay sinless through our own willpower. I tried obeying all the little details on my own for a long time, but the desire to sin still existed in my heart. Thankfully, Jesus has awoken my heart and made me excited to live for him.

8. People are weak and flawed, so God no longer expects us to save ourselves through our willpower alone. He has sent his own Son to change us from within. While many people live according to their selfish human nature, our Spirit-filled minds lead us toward peace and God's favor. The Spirit that rose Jesus from the grave raises us to new life as God's children. Our suffering in this life cannot compare to the glory that God gives us in this life and the next. While the whole created world groaned under the pain of sin and separation from God, we hoped that God would bring us back to himself. The Spirit rescues us, looks into our hearts, and answers prayers we didn't even know we had. God works for our good no matter what our circumstances. The Spirit allows beauty to emerge from pain. We have nothing to fear because with God on our side, nothing can stand

against us, and absolutely nothing can separate us from his powerful love.

9. When I see my fellow Hebrews fighting the truth and living a cursed life apart from God's Spirit, my heart breaks for them, and I wish I could take their place. God chose them and set them apart long ago. God gave them the Law, protected them, and allowed Jesus himself to be born as a member of their race. But my fellow Jews mustn't keep questioning why God now opens his family to Gentiles. It's his right to save anyone he chooses. Tiny lumps of clay have no right to question which creations the potter decides to display proudly in his house. Gentiles are being put right with God through their trust in the Father, but Jews who continue to trust in their own willpower will continue to be disappointed.

10. I know that many of my fellow Jews are deeply devoted to God, but they stubbornly strive to reach God on their own. I pray that they will open their eyes to the truth that Jesus is the only way our hearts can really unite with God. All Jews and Gentiles are welcome at God's table, and anyone who accepts the invitation will be blessed. God has opened his arms to the rebellious nation of Israel all along, but now he is expanding his reach to include good-hearted people who simply never knew about him before.

11. Just because Gentiles are now welcome does not mean God has abandoned the people of Israel. I am an Israelite myself, and I am incredibly grateful that God's grace allowed our nation to survive the darkest parts of our history and emerge blessed. Nonetheless, my Gentile friends, I love instilling the

life of Jesus in people who were once enemies of God. God loves you very much, but don't start thinking you're more important than the Jews. All of you are equally capable of falling away from God and being broken off his tree like a dead branch. Our mysterious Creator gives life to everything and mercy to everyone.

12. Let our merciful God transform your heart so that you can dedicate your life to him and bring glory back to this world. Humbly remember that you can't fulfill God's entire plan on your own, but you can certainly work hard to contribute to the bigger picture. We all have unique strengths that we were designed to use in our churches and communities, and we should use those strengths to love others well. Stay hopeful and patient during rocky times, and stay peaceful and kind with others even when it's not easy.

13. Obey the laws of your nation, and you will have no need to fear the authorities. Recognize that they enforce the law for the betterment of the community, and they deserve your respect and cooperation. Remember that the whole Jewish Law boils down to love. If your heart loves and respects others, your actions will be honest and peaceful. You will have no reason to hide.

14. Welcome each other regardless of cultural or personal differences. Some of us adhere to certain food restrictions as an act of faith while others eat anything and maintain strong faith as well. We are all serving God in our own way, and we shouldn't judge each other for differences that don't really matter. Instead, let's lift each other up. Respect the cultural differences of others, and don't lead a brother to

abandon a choice that strengthens his personal sense of faith or well-being.

15. The Spirit strengthens us and enables us to lift the burdens of others. Jesus spent his life serving and healing others, enduring insults to pull others up. Let his example encourage us to do the same. God is our source of hope, joy, and peace. May he enable us to accept each other into God's family regardless of cultural differences. Brothers and sisters, I'm sure your hearts are already filled with God's goodness and wisdom, but I speak boldly in this letter because I have a passion to serve God with all I have. I want to share the good news where it would not otherwise be heard and boast about the great God that changed me. I am traveling now to serve the people of Jerusalem and give their poor people a donation from churches abroad, but then I hope to make my way to you. Please pray for my safety along the journey, and if it's God's will, I will be so happy to meet you in person.

16. Brothers and sisters, you should get to know my friend Phoebe. She has helped many people and now needs your help. I want to give a shout-out to my friends in your church who host worship gatherings in their homes and have worked hard to help others. Some of you have stood by me in prison, and some of you have risked your life to save mine. I love and appreciate each of you so much. Watch out for anyone who may try to destroy your faith in God or unity with each other. With the help of our glorious God, we will be able to stand firm and spread the truth of Jesus. Let us praise his name alone!

1 CORINTHIANS

1. Greetings to all the Corinthians who love and worship Jesus. May the peace of our Savior be with you. I'm so glad God has enriched your minds through his grace and guidance. You can trust him to hold you close and help you stand firm in the face of temptation. I hear you have been arguing quite a bit with each other, and I pray that you heal those divisions and come together as a unified family. Whether you look up to human teachers like Apollos, Peter, or myself, remember that none of us measure up to Christ. Jesus is the ultimate authority because of the power of his sacrifice on the cross. His sacrifice may not make sense to our brains, but you don't have to be a scholar or a success for it to stir your heart. In fact, God purposely calls the outcasts ahead of the scholars because outcasts seem to better understand the humility it takes to accept God's free grace and take none of the credit.

2. When I first preached to you, I was nervous and stumbled over my words, but the Spirit spoke through me anyway to bring you closer to him. Now that you're becoming more mature in the faith, it's important that you learn why we need the Holy Spirit to guide us. The Spirit can bless you with strengths and gifts that you would not be able to use by your strength alone, and the Spirit can help your thoughts and motivations more closely match that of Christ.

3. Before you had the Spirit, I treated you like children of the faith, speaking to you differently since you weren't ready for the full truth. Some of you are still living apart from the

Spirit as evidenced by your petty arguments about which apostle you like best. We're all just servants of God trying to plant and nurture the seed of faith in you. It's God that will help that seed grow, and that's all that matters. We helped lay the foundation of your church, but be careful to keep Jesus as your cornerstone as you keep building. Only he can help you weather the storms life may throw your way. Be a walking Temple for God's Spirit, and trust his wisdom over your earthly logic.

4. We apostles do our best to serve God and share the truth with his people. I answer only to his authority, and I speak this advice to you with a clear conscience. I don't care if you judge me for being poorer than you or less articulate. Jesus requires his apostles to humble themselves and experience great hardship just like he did. But where I am weak and hurt, God is strong, helping me endure every test with a gracious attitude. I hope that the leaders among you will follow my example and serve your church family like that.

5. I am told that a man in your community is tearing apart his family by sleeping with his stepmother, and he should be removed from your community before his wicked, selfish attitude spreads through the rest of your church. You should certainly minister to people who are lost in sin and do not yet know God, but we will not be a community of hypocrites who say we've been changed by Jesus while still giving our hearts to such wickedness. God will be his ultimate judge, but you do not have to tolerate a behavior that could tear your group apart.

6. The Spirit equips you to know what's right and wrong, so

why would you go to a pagan judge to settle an argument you could settle within the church community? The very fact that you bring lawsuits on each other shows that you are disconnected from the Spirit and each other. If you continue to give your heart to idolatry, adultery, theft, and slander, you will not be welcome in God's kingdom. God's grace washes you clean of the past, but that doesn't make it okay to continue down a road that is terrible for your body and spirit. Your body is meant to do God's work in the world, so disrespecting your body with sexual sin is like defiling the Temple. Remember to glorify the God who paid a price to rescue you.

7. You wrote to ask several questions about marriage, and to tell you the truth, I enjoy serving the Lord as an unmarried man. If you choose to marry, you should give yourself completely to your spouse and put each other's needs first. Keep each other happy and satisfied so that neither of you is tempted to go outside the marriage for affection. Take your marriage vows seriously and take care of each other no matter what life throws your way. Even if your spouse doesn't share your faith yet, allow the Spirit to speak through your love and change her heart. Whether you were born Jewish, Greek, enslaved, or free, God calls you just as you are and wants to bless your life. Likewise, you can serve God well whether you are married or unmarried. Society looks down on us single people, but since we are free of the worldly responsibilities that come with marriage, we can do God's work with our whole heart.

8. I detected pride in the words of your letter, so I must insist that you build each other up with love. Some of you think

you know everything, but I can assure you God knows more. You asked whether you can eat food offered to idols, and the truth is, there's no real problem with that since we recognize that those false gods don't exist. However, if you choose to eat this food, some may misinterpret this as an act of idol worship, and that may tempt them to turn from God. Don't do anything that could pull a brother or sister into sin.

9. Jesus appeared to me and chose me to spread his truth. Some refuse to accept me as an apostle and refuse to financially support my ministry, but I know that my good work has earned the church's support. The apostles and I work hard to build and protect churches like yours, and I think it's fair to ask for a reasonable living wage. That being said, I will happily continue this work for free if necessary because of my passion for the good news. I will continue to build rapport with Jewish and Gentile groups and teach them about Christ. I will continue to work with the focus and discipline of a marathon runner to share in God's intangible blessings.

10. Friends, let us learn from the mistakes of our ancestors. God parted the Red Sea for them and covered them with a cloud of protection, but somehow their hearts still desired sex, alcohol, and idol worship more than they desired the Lord. They angered God with their sins and their whiny, selfish attitudes, but let's choose to live in our Father's favor instead. When you are tempted by the world, let God equip you to resist impulses that would do you no good. Avoid idol worship, and remember to thank God regularly for his sacrifice on the cross. You are not bound by restrictive

laws, but whatever you do, do it for God's glory and the betterment of others.

11. I do my best to be like Jesus, and I hope you'll follow my example. Christ will guide you, just like a loving husband can guide his family. Men can respect God in worship by taking off their hats, and women can humble themselves by covering their heads with hats or long hair in worship. God created men and women to help each other and lean on each other, so both genders are welcome to come together in worship. I'm disappointed at how you have handled the Lord's Supper in worship. Some of you eat too much and get drunk while others go hungry, and this is disgraceful. Instead, eat and drink while prayerfully remembering Jesus' sacrifice for you, and make sure everyone gets a fair portion.

12. The Holy Spirit enables each of you to please and serve God in unique ways. The Spirit may prepare you to teach, heal, preach, work miracles, or speak effectively to people of other cultures. We all have different strengths and spiritual gifts, but the Spirit allows us to work toward the same holy purposes. The body is made up of many parts with vastly different functions, and each part needs the others in order to make things happen. An eye or a foot can't achieve much if it's not connected to the larger body, and likewise, one Christian can't do much good without the support of his church family. The church is Christ's body, and together, we can change the world. Regardless of our individual talents, the next gift is much more important

13. I could be an eloquent preacher, a master of many languages, a wise scholar of scripture, or a mountain-moving

miracle worker, but none of those gifts mean anything if I don't also have love in my heart. I could sacrifice everything I have, but if I do it with selfish motives, it means nothing. If your heart is full of love, you treat others with patience, kindness, and humility. You celebrate the successes of others and forgive others easily. True love doesn't give up on people when they are difficult to love. Sermons and books of wisdom fade eventually, but love lasts forever. As I get older, I realize I have no use for meaningless things that only connect me partially with the truth. Love connects me fully with God's truth. Faith and hope are important, but love is more vital than anything else.

14. You can love others well by helping church visitors better understand God's message. Offer words of encouragement, help, and comfort through your sermons, and make your words easy to understand. Speaking in strange tongues can be a beautiful act of worship, but if no one can interpret what is said, it carries no meaning for the listeners. Let your worship glorify God while also teaching your fellow worshippers more about God. Your worship leaders should have a wide variety of musical and spiritual gifts to reach a wide variety of people.

15. Let me remind you of the amazing cornerstone of our faith. Jesus was killed to redeem our brokenness, and he rose to life three days later. He appeared to the apostles and over 500 witnesses who are still alive and could assure you this really happened. I am ashamed to say I persecuted the early church, but Jesus appeared to me and forgave me for my crimes against his people. I don't deserve to be called an apostle, but God's grace allows me to spread the good

news alongside them. Some of you doubt that Jesus actually defeated death, but if it's not true, our entire faith journey is a delusion, and we've been lying about God all along. Jesus really did rise, and because he did, death will not be the end for any of us. I regularly risk my life for this church because I know my life on earth is just the beginning. My physical body is merely a seed encased in a dull little shell, but when that seed is buried, my spiritual self will blossom as a beautiful, strong flower much more reflective of God's glory. The power of death can no longer hurt us thanks to Jesus. Hold onto this truth, and let your work glorify God.

16. During your Sunday meetings, set aside a portion of your income to benefit poor people and new churches that need your support. I hope to spend the winter with you after I travel through Macedonia. Even though we have many enemies here in Ephesus, I will stay here a bit longer because I know God will still do something great through our work. If Timothy gets there before I do, welcome him with a spirit of peace and respect. Stay focused and brave as you serve God, and follow goodhearted leaders who will teach you to serve others joyfully.

2 CORINTHIANS

1. Timothy and I hope this letter finds you with the grace and peace of Jesus. We thank our merciful Father who helps us help others. Our suffering is worth it if it benefits you in some way. When God rescues us from suffering, we

hope that relief reaches you too. We faced great obstacles in Asia and almost died, but our Rescuer used this scary time to remind us to trust in the God who raises the dead. Hopefully, God will continue to answer your prayers for our safety. I'm happy that our relationship with your church has included a great deal of bold authenticity, and we hope these letters will make more sense when we see you in person. I had planned to see you on my way back from Macedonia, and I promise I did not make those plans lightly. Our glorious, loving God is my witness that we didn't show up because we wanted to protect you and keep you happy.

2. If I had journeyed to you as I originally planned, I would have made you sad, and that would have broken my heart. When we see each other, I want us to bring joy to each other. I wrote my last letter with many tears, not to make you sad, but to help you realize how much I love you. If someone in your community has hurt your heart, I beg you to forgive him so that he doesn't become so lonely that he gives up living. Satan seeks to divide and destroy us, but forgiveness holds our family together. When I preached the good news in Traos, God prepared the way for our success, but I became worried about our missing friend Titus, and we journeyed on to find him. Thank you, God, for allowing us to share in Christ's victory parade and allowing us to spread the good news like sweet, life-giving perfume.

3. Please don't mistake my boldness for arrogance. Timothy and I have no glowing recommendation letters, but we know that Christ recommends us for this work because we've seen many hearts transform. Despite our shortcomings, God makes us capable of serving him and sharing the new

Way of the Spirit. When God revealed the Law to Moses, the glory of God shone as a blinding light on Moses' face that the people couldn't even look at. If the glory of the Law is that powerful, imagine the glorious power of the Spirit that replaces our condemnation with salvation. We will not cover our faces like Moses did to appease closed-minded people who couldn't handle the glow of glory. We long for the Spirit to transform us into shining examples of his glory. Let no veil separate the world from the truth written on our uncovered faces.

4. Our merciful God equips Timothy and me to do this work, so we take our calling seriously by telling you the whole truth and staying away from sins we would be tempted to hide from you. As we shine God's light for all to see, some still remain in the dark because idols of this world hinder their perception of God's glory. We are common vessels, and we want to show that the glory we carry comes from God and not from us. We have faced many enemies and endured many dangers, but through it all, we have never been alone. We have survived so far, and although we still face mortal danger, we hope this is just the beginning for you. The God who raised Jesus from the grave also raises us to a life full of his grace. Our bodies grow older and weaker every day, but our souls grow stronger over time. We must remember that the unseen rewards of our faith last much longer than any tangible hardships in this life.

5. Your body is a temporary tent, but your soul is a strong house that God has built to last forever in his presence. You may groan with the pains of this life and long for your heavenly home, but that longing can help you live

with courage, unafraid to die and reunite with our Lord. Timothy and I long to please him, and that's where our passion comes from when we try to persuade others of the truth. We're not trying to brag, but we want you to see our genuine hearts and appreciate the love and service we can give you. You may think we're crazy, but we are simply ruled by the loving Savior who died to save us all. Jesus does away with our old selves and turns us into new beings. Let God change you from his enemies to his friends!

6.   Don't waste God's amazing grace. Accept his favor and help today. We apostles have been beaten, imprisoned, and faced with countless hardships while serving God and spreading the love of the Holy Spirit. Our pure motives convince some to praise and honor us while others insult and punish us. We may look like poor, sad, pitiful men, but we are richer than you can imagine. Friends, we have opened our hearts and spoken the plain truth to you, and I pray that you will open your hearts to us. Stop trying to live alongside dark-hearted pagans as if their choices are okay. Separate yourselves from wicked influences, and surround yourself with Christian brothers and sisters.

7.   Purify your body and soul so that nothing will get in the way of your love and awe for God. I hope you will open your hearts to me because I would never hurt you. In fact, you are incredibly dear to me, and I am so proud of you that I cannot contain my joy. When we arrived in Macedonia, we ran into one challenge after another, but God allowed us to find Titus. We were happy to reunite with him, and he said you treated him well. He also said you longed to mend your relationship with me. Even though my last letter made

you sad, I'm happy I wrote it because your initial sorrow turned into a determination to change. I told Titus how proud I am of you, and I hope you know that we love you and trust you completely!

8. Our hearts were stirred to see the poor Macedonian churches give all they could to help God's people of Judea. They showed their devotion to God through their generosity, and I encourage you to do the same, since God has blessed you with much more financial security. If you are eager to love others well, I encourage you to do that by helping us complete this mission we started together. I'm not trying to put an unfair burden on you, but since you have plenty to give, just do what you can. If you ever find yourself in need, I will make sure another congregation is there to help you. Titus is excited to return to you alongside his brother. Please welcome them with love, and trust them to handle your gifts according God's purposes.

9. I have no doubt that you recognize the needs of God's children in Judea. In fact, when I bragged to the Macedonian church about your eagerness to help others, it stirred up their own generosity. Please show that our boasting about you is based on truth, and give with an open and willing heart. God will allow your gifts to do great work, and he will continue to provide you with more than what you need. Giving is a way to thank God for his blessings and pay those blessings forward. When others hear of your gift, they will be inspired to pray for you and follow your example.

10. Some of you say that I am meek in person and harsh in my letters, but please don't make me be harsh with you when

I visit. Don't let your actions flow from selfish motives, but let God help you tackle lies and obstacles that come against your faith. Only allow yourself to think thoughts of love and obedience. Don't act like you're better than anyone else. We are all children of God and can only boast about his miraculous grace. If you think these words are harsh, please understand that I love you, and this message is consistent with what I've preached to you in person. We hope to continue our work with you so that we can see your faith grow.

11. I wish you would accept me because I love you more than you know. I long to see you unite with Jesus as the bride he loves, but I am afraid that you will leave him at the altar by falling for the lies of false apostles. My words may not be as smooth as those polished deceivers, but I assure you God has equipped me with sound knowledge. I humbled myself and spoke to you for free because I love you. Those false apostles claim to follow Christ, but they take advantage of you and would never sacrifice their comfort or well-being for God's family. Meanwhile, I have been whipped, stoned, and imprisoned while doing this work. I have endured shipwrecks, floods, and poverty, but thanks to God, none of it has stopped me.

12. I know a man who experienced a beautiful vision of heaven, and he witnessed things words can't begin to describe. I will brag about this man, but I refuse to puff my chest and brag about myself. When my enemies beat me down, I humbly know that God's grace is all I need to press on. When I am weak, God lifts me up and makes me strong. I am speaking like a bold fool because I must convince you that I love you

more than the false apostles you are listening to. I don't need your money if you're not ready to give. I only want you to accept how much I care. Some of you think I've taken advantage of you, but I've never burdened you for anything. I'm afraid that when I visit you, I will break down weeping when I witness your selfish quarrels and tolerance for sexual immorality.

13. During my first two visits, I mentioned that at least two witnesses must agree to accuse someone of sin, and during my third visit, I will hold you accountable so that justice will reign in your community. I will bring a strong presence this time because our Savior is strong. Examine your hearts to discover whether Christ is really living in you, and I will continue to pray for your hearts to grow strong and pure. Let God's love and peace inform all your interactions with each other, and may the Spirit fill your church.

DAY TWO - GUIDED BY GRACE
GALATIANS-EPHESIANS-PHILIPPIANS-COLOSSIANS

BIG IDEA

The Holy Spirit guides us toward true freedom by teaching our hearts to love selflessly, live courageously, and let go of harmful temptations.

PAUL'S ADVICE

- **Welcome the Gentiles-** People of all races and backgrounds are welcome in God's family, so let's love each other inclusively.

- **Let grace free you-** You could choose to enslave yourself to the Law, or you could simply accept that you're an imperfect human who desperately needs God's forgiveness and guidance.

- **Let the Spirit inspire obedience-** Grace is no excuse to stay lost. When we truly know God, he teaches us to live with love, patience, humility, and uncontained joy. He motivates us to energetically fulfill his plans.

- **Come together-** God has given each of us unique strengths and talents, so let's use them to make our world better. None of us can do it alone, so we must respect each other's differences and work as one unified body.

- **Let love guide you-** Put pride aside, and respect others in all situations. Use kind words, do your best, and seek to understand the perspectives of others.

- **Be brave-** No prison or punishment can stop you from speaking the bold truth. Even if you die, no one can separate you from God's love or force you to stop running this good race. Don't worry about what anyone else thinks of you. God's opinion is all that matters.

- **Remember the big picture**- We were lost in darkness, but God sent his Son to redeem us and pull us back to the light. When you're tempted to spit angry words, betray your spouse, or trust false idols, remember that God sees you and calls you to a better life of love and purpose.

HOW GOD SHOWS UP

God does not expect us to live a sinless life by our willpower alone. Instead, he offers to live in our hearts and guide us toward more loving choices. He forgives our mistakes and knows we'll be much happier if we accept that forgiveness and refuse to stay lost in those mistakes. When we truly connect to the Holy Spirit, we open ourselves up to a more courageous, peaceful, and joyful life.

GALATIANS

1. My name is Paul, and the risen Jesus called me to be his disciple. Jesus sacrificed himself to free us from sin, and he deserves all our praise. I am surprised to hear that you are already abandoning his amazing grace to follow a false gospel spread by God's enemies. This may not be what you want to hear, but I only care about God's approval. Many of you know that Jesus himself appeared to me to change

my heart. I was fully devoted to the Jewish Law and did my best to wipe out this Christian Way that seemed to threaten my traditions and beliefs. God forgave me for my misguided sins and chose me to serve him in distant lands. I returned to Jerusalem three years later to confer with Peter and James, and people praised God because I who once tried to destroy the church was now determined to build it up.

2. After another fourteen years abroad, Barnabas and I returned to Jerusalem to inform the church leaders about our ministry with Gentiles. James, Peter, and John shook our hands, blessed our work, and asked if we'd be willing to collect money from our churches to support needy people in Jerusalem. We happily agreed to help. Inspired by our attitude of inclusion, Peter began eating with Gentiles, but then he stopped because this angered Jerusalem Christians who wanted Gentile Christians to follow the entire Jewish Law. I publicly argued with those who refused to value inclusive love over their precious traditions. People of all races are adopted into God's family because of their faith in Christ and not by perfect adherence to the Law. I am done trying to save myself through perfect actions. I will instead honor Jesus' sacrifice by enjoying his perfect grace.

3. You have heard the truth of Christ, so why do you believe the lie that the Law can save you? Did the Law fill you with the Spirit, or did your love for Jesus do that? Don't foolishly abandon your trust in God to trust in your own actions. Even our ancestor Abraham started as an imperfect man with uncommon faith, and it was through that faith that God blessed him and blesses us. If you devote yourself to perfectionistic actions without first knowing God, you're

setting yourself up to fail. Christ knows we can't do it on our own, and that's why he accepted the curse we deserve. Abraham had transformative faith long before Moses wrote down all the rules. The Law showed our ancestors the difference between right and wrong, but now Jesus has come to transform us from within. The Law gives us healthy boundaries for living, but now that Christ has washed us clean, we belong to him and no longer have to confine ourselves by those boundaries.

4. Jews were once slaves to their Law, and you Gentiles were slaves to a different set of rules and customs. Jesus was born to a Jewish mother and lived perfectly within the Law to free us from that burden and make us his brothers and sisters. We are no longer fearful slaves but God's beloved children who will inherit his blessings. I remember how you patiently and joyfully took care of me when I was sick, and now you are suspicious of the truth I tell. How did that shift happen? Those who are trying to turn you against me don't have your best interest at heart. Please know that I worry for you because I love you. While the son of Abraham's slave Hagar was turned away, God chose the son of his free wife Sarah to inherit God's promise. Like Sarah and her chosen descendants, we are meant to be free.

5. You promise to obey the whole Law, but your quest to circumcise and save yourself causes you to reject God's grace. A few deceivers infected your ranks to lead you away from the truth, but I am confident you will return to the freedom of redemption. Don't let this freedom become an excuse to act like reckless wild animals and tear each other apart. Instead, let your love guide your interactions with

others. Our human nature leads us into selfish and corrupt decisions, but the Holy Spirit guides us toward a life of love, joy, peace, patience, kindness, goodness, faithfulness, humility, and self-control.

6.   Gently encourage each other to turn from sin, but keep a closer eye on your own actions to avoid the same mistakes. Examine whether your behavior is aligned with the Spirit, and don't worry about how you compare to others, since we all have unique strengths and challenges. Remember that you reap what you sow, and loving actions will yield eternal blessings. I hope you never grow tired of doing the right thing. Some of you have chosen to take pride in a physical ceremony, but I can only take pride in Jesus' sacrifice which transforms me more than circumcision ever could. May the grace of Jesus be with you all.

EPHESIANS

1.   Peace be with you, faithful Christians of Ephesus. I'm so grateful our Father decided to send Jesus into the world for us. His sacrifice sets us free, and his grace transforms us into his beloved sons and daughters. Our wise God knew all along that he would use Jesus to set all of creation on the right track again. Because you believe this good news, you belong to God, and he promises to guide and bless you through the Spirit. I am incredibly grateful for your great faith in Jesus and love for others. I pray that the Spirit will increase your knowledge of God's mighty power over all things.

2.	You were once spiritually dead, lost in a cycle of selfish desire and disobedience to God. But God's overflowing gift of mercy and love has brought you to life. He created each of you to uniquely make this world better. You Gentiles are not part of the Hebrew nation God originally chose, but through Christ, God allows all races to unite with him. You are now part of God's family, built on the foundation of Christ.

3.	When our merciful God chose me to spread his message, he told me the long-kept secret that all his Jewish and Gentile children can have a relationship with him. I feel so humbled and privileged to show you how much he loves you and wants to bless you. I'm happy to speak boldly and endure great suffering for your sake. I hope the Spirit further strengthens your hearts to allow Jesus to live there. Let love be your main goal in life so that you will better understand the deep, unmatchable love of God.

4.	Honor God by treating others with humility, patience, and kindness. Peacefully unite as one body doing the work of the one true God. God equips each of us with unique strengths and talents, and we come together as mature, unwavering people of God to better our churches and communities. All parts of the body fit together to do great things through love. Don't continue to live in shameless sin, dark thoughts, and stubborn resistance to the truth. Get rid of that old, selfish life, and let God make you more like himself. Tell the truth, earn an honest living, and learn to cope with your anger. Use kind words that build others up, and forgive others like God forgave you.

5. Christ's beautiful love led him to give his life for us, so we should let love guide our hearts away from vulgar words or greedy actions. Don't remain friends with fools, but live good lives as people of the light. Strive to please God, and don't do anything you'd be tempted to hide. Avoid wasting your time with drunkenness, and worship God with joyful songs of gratitude. Love, respect, and take care of your spouse, giving yourself wholeheartedly to him or her.

6. Respect the parents who raised you, and raise your children to be good-hearted people. Work cheerfully and diligently even when no one's watching, knowing that God sees every detail. Treat your employees with kindness and decency. Let God strengthen you to fight the temptations of this world with faith as your armor. Keep your hearts open to God by praying in good times and bad. Pray for your Christian family, and pray for me as I continue to boldly spread the good news. I'm sending Tychicus your way to encourage you, and I hope God will give you his grace and peace.

PHILIPPIANS

1. Friends, my heart fills with joy and gratitude every time I think about you. You stand by me whether I'm imprisoned or free, and I know God will continue to bless your work. I pray that your love and wisdom will keep growing until your life fills with good fruits only Jesus can produce. The good message is spreading throughout this prison, and my capture has led our brothers and sisters to preach with

even greater courage. Some preach from a spirit of selfish ambition, but most spread the word with a sincere heart. Either way, I'm just happy more people are learning about Jesus! I am quite eager to leave this prison so I can rejoin our exciting ministry, but if I die, I will enjoy an even better life with Christ. My hope is that God will let me keep working on this earth for now, so I can add to your progress and joy. Don't be afraid if enemies come against you. Stand firm, and know it's a great privilege to share in Christ's suffering.

2. Jesus strengthens and comforts you from within, enabling you to treat others with compassion. Put aside any selfish ambition, and place the needs of others before your own. Jesus freely left his heavenly throne to become a working class human who suffered and died to fulfill God's plan. Now he is back on the throne and deserves all our praise. Friends, you have always been so respectful to God, and I hope you'll continue that shining example of joyful obedience. If I must die to lift you up, I will gladly do it. I hope my son Timothy and I can visit you soon because we care about you so much. I will also send my friend who is recovering from a near death experience in hopes that you can ease his anxiety.

3. Maintain a joyful relationship with God, and watch out for people who trust physical ceremonies like circumcision to save them. The Spirit has changed us, and we need nothing else to prove our worth. I was circumcised as a baby and grew to be a zealous pharisee that followed the Jewish Law to the letter. I persecuted Christians who threatened my beloved traditions, but now I have thrown away that old life to accept my new life. I no longer depend on my own

righteousness but on God's righteousness. All I want is to know Jesus and be more like him. I still have a long way to go, but I'll keep running straight ahead, never looking back, until I win the race. I hope you will follow my example and remember that you do not belong to this world. You are citizens of heaven, and when you die, your life will really begin.

4.   Dear friends, I miss you so much, and I am unbelievably proud of you. Remember to find common ground with your brothers and sisters, showing a gentle attitude toward everyone. Pray with a happy, grateful heart, and God will give you uncommon peace that will end your worries. Fill your minds with honorable advice, and put those lessons into action. Thank you for showing how much you care for me, even though I was perfectly content before. I've experienced abundance and poverty, and I've learned I can face anything with the strength God gives me. You gave me generous gifts at a difficult time, and it was more than enough. Thank you so much, and may God bless you!

COLOSSIANS

1.   Dear Christians of Colossae, we've heard great things about you, and you've been in our prayers. When Epaphras told you the good news, he saw the Spirit place faith, hope, and love inside you. We pray that the Spirit will further increase your wisdom, strengthen your patience, and equip you to make this world better. Let's give thanks to the Father who rescued us from darkness and delivered us to forgiveness

and freedom. Christ is God in human form and existed before the dawn of creation. God's Son defeated death to bring us life and draw the universe back to himself. Our thoughts and deeds once made us God's enemies, but God now calls us his friends. Don't fall away from the hope this good news once stirred in you. I am happy to risk my life so the world might know the precious secret that Christ's presence lives in us and allows us to share God's glory.

2. You may not know me personally, but I work hard so that you might grow in courage, love, and assurance of the truth. Christ is the key to unlocking God's wisdom, so don't listen to lies that could enslave you and lead you away from him. Sink your roots deep into your faith, and hold on tight. External ceremonies are not necessary to unite your heart with Christ. If you simply trust him, he frees you from sin and raises you from the dead. Some people insist on particular food laws and holy days. They act superior to you, but they have forgotten to hold onto the God that nourishes you from within.

3. Set your heart on eternal things that matter, remembering that your life on this earth is temporary. Sexual indecency and greedy motives have no place in your life anymore. Swallow any angry insult or self-serving lie that threatens to escape your lips. Throw away your old self, and let the Creator turn you into something better. Treat each other with compassion, gentleness, humility, and forgiveness. Most of all, let our peaceful Savior guide you toward love in all matters. Worship Jesus with music and gratitude. Love your spouses, obey your parents, and patiently raise your children. Work hard when no one's looking, as if you

are serving Jesus himself. Trust God to judge anyone who mistreats you.

4. Be humble enough to treat your servants with fairness and decency. I am in prison for sharing the good news, so please pray that we can continue to spread God's message with clarity. When you speak to nonbelievers, make the most of these opportunities to make new friends and share a bit of God's wisdom. I am sending two of our brothers your way to give you more updates about me, and those of us in prison send you our love. Epaphras works hard for you still and wants you to know he prays fervently that God will further strengthen your faith and obedience.

DAY THREE - FEARLESS LEADERS
1-2 THESSALONIANS-1-2 TIMOTHY-TITUS-PHILEMON

BIG IDEA

Paul offers support to Christian leaders who are doing a great job, and he encourages them to stay strong.

PAUL'S ENCOURAGEMENT

- **Your strength is contagious-** The Thessalonians' persistence in the face of suffering has inspired other churches to strengthen and grow.

- **You're not alone-** Other churches and Paul himself are being unfairly persecuted like the Thessalonians, but they'll get through this together.

- **You make me happy-** Paul draws great joy from the Thessalonians' positive example, and he asks them to simply keep loving each other and working hard.

- **This isn't the end-** When Jesus comes back, God will judge those who hurt God's children and will lift up those who have endured unfair tests.

- **Stay strong-** Paul praises Timothy for his strength to resist temptation. He encourages Timothy to take care of himself and protect his heart so that he won't get broken or discouraged by the obstacles ahead.

- **Your heart is beautiful-** Paul tenderly recognizes Timothy's authenticity as rare and special. He longs for Timothy to share that beauty with the world, teaching others to strive for obedience.

- **I trust you to carry on-** Paul has faith that Timothy and Titus will set good examples for their churches by encouraging these congregations to respect each other and hold tight to the truth.

- **Keep blessing others-** Philemon has loved others well, and Paul asks him to continue this by welcoming a former slave back home as a brother and friend.

HOW GOD SHOWS UP

God loves the church enough to equip dedicated, passionate leaders to guide his people toward a life of goodness and unity. He requires leaders to maintain humble, servant hearts by putting others first and setting a great examples for others. If God calls us to be one of these leaders, he never expects us to do it alone. He guides and strengthens us through every challenge and obstacle. He puts mentors in our path to encourage us and motivate us forward.

1 THESSALONIANS

1. Dear children of God in Thessalonica, we thank God for how you continually put your firm faith into action. It's clear that God loves you, and the Spirit is with you. You have suffered much, but like us, you remain completely convinced of the truth. Your unshakable faith and joy have inspired other churches and allowed the good news to spread like wildfire through your region.

2. As you know, we were insulted and abused in Philippi before we met you, but God gave us the courage to share the good news with you nonetheless. We did not seek attention or try to flatter you. We simply loved you like a gentle mother loves her children. We worked hard for you and tried not to burden you. We encouraged you to receive God's glory and favor by obeying him. You're suffering at the hands of those who disagree with your faith, but please know that you are not alone. Hostile Jews are doing this to Christians in Judea too, and we must remember that our enemies won't escape God's anger. We have tried to return to you several times, but the Devil seems to be keeping us from you. You are our pride and joy, and we miss you so much!

3. When we could stand the delays no longer, we sent Timothy to help you stay strong through this time of persecution. He returned with great news of your love for us, and that really encouraged us when we needed a boost. We thank God for the joy you bring us, and we still hope God will allow us to come to you. We hope that your love for each other and for your community will grow even closer toward perfection.

4. You have truly done an amazing job, and I encourage you to continue allowing the Spirit to refine you. Treat your spouse with respect, and don't let lust enter your heart. Don't take advantage of your fellow man. You do a great job loving others, so I challenge you to let that love grow even more perfect. Work hard for your family without requiring attention or accolades. If you are mourning the death of someone you love, remember that one day, God will raise them to life, and you'll be reunited.

5. I'm sure you already know this, but Jesus will return when we least expect it. Those who live in darkness will be shocked, but you must live with your eyes open. Don't get complacent. Always be armed with faith, hope, and love. Keep lifting each other up, and show respect to servants like me who teach and guide you. Forgive those who hurt you, and strive to do good for everyone in your midst. Don't hold back, and see what great things happen when you let the Spirit loose.

2 THESSALONIANS

1. Peace be with you, Thessalonian friends. We thank God as your faith and love grow even greater than before. We brag about you all the time because you have truly endured many tests. I am certain that when this life is done, you will be greatly rewarded, and God will bring justice on those who hurt you. Jesus and his angel armies will punish those who reject their Creator. Those who choose to live apart from God on earth will be separated from his good and mighty presence in eternity. We pray that God will help you keep doing as much good as possible.

2. I know there is a rumor going around your community that the end times are already happening. Perhaps you misunderstood one of our letters or sermons, but let me set the record straight. The final judgment will not happen until the Antichrist performs false miracles, sits in the Temple, and claims to be God. Jesus will destroy him with a breath of fire, and everyone who delights in evil will be condemned.

Let's thank God for choosing to protect and glorify us. Let's allow our hope to strengthen our determination to do and say the right things.

3. Please pray that we will be able to spread God's message to new places while evading our enemies. I know our faithful Lord will help you resist whatever temptations come your way. Just continue to trust in the truth we have told you, and allow God to increase your knowledge even further. Follow our example, and work hard for your family and church. Don't get complacent or waste your time gossiping. I hope you never grow tired of doing good deeds.

1 TIMOTHY

1. Peace be with you, Timothy. You are like a son to me. I'd like you to stay in Ephesus for now because false teachers are spreading lies and starting foolish debates that must be stopped. Lovingly remind our people to keep their minds pure and their faith authentic. I thank Jesus for forgiving my ignorant persecution of the church and equipping me to serve him. His grace saved my life and changed me even though I was the worst sinner of all. Our invisible King deserves all the glory! Son, I trust you to keep a clear conscience as you battle the blasphemy in your midst.

2. We should pray for our government leaders to let us live quiet, peaceful lives in service to God. Let us pray for everyone to learn the truth that Jesus sacrificed himself to connect our hearts to God. This beautiful truth is the reason

I continue reaching out to Gentiles. In worship, I want men to pray with lifted hands and peaceful minds. Women don't need fancy clothes or hair to worship alongside men and receive God's protection. All they need is a humble desire to do good deeds.

3. Please encourage church leaders and volunteers to set a positive example for everyone else. They should have good-hearted spouses, obedient children, and peaceful interactions with others. They must not let alcohol or money poison their motives or behavior. Make sure they are sincerely committed to the truth that God became a man who rose into heaven and is now famous to all nations.

4. Dead-hearted liars are teaching that salvation depends on abstinence from marriage or from certain foods. However, God's grace allows all foods to be eaten if we remember to thank him for providing it. Stay spiritually fit by avoiding these lies and immersing yourself in life-giving words of truth. Let your hope in our Savior inspire you to keep diligently preaching and sharing your spiritual gifts. Don't let people look down on you for being young. Just keep setting a loving example, and I know you'll lead others to God.

5. Speak to your church members as you would speak to your own family members. Encourage grown children to take care of their widowed mothers, and let the church support elderly widows who have no family to support them. If you notice an elder doing especially good work, increase his pay to match his excellence. If two or more witnesses accuse an elder of sin, hold the sinful leader accountable. As you lead the people, don't show prejudice toward anyone, and

don't get in too big of a hurry. Take care of yourself, so you don't get sick.

6. Servants should work hard for Christian masters and love them like family. Remember that prideful false teachers don't know as much as they think. They love to stir up arguments and use religion to get rich. They don't realize that the only way to feel rich is to be content with what you have. We came into the world with nothing, and we'll leave with nothing. Putting our hunger for wealth above our faith can only result in a broken heart. I know you will stay away from all that foolishness and strive to live with righteousness and love. I trust that you'll run this race with excellence, obeying the immortal King who lives in a light too bright for our eyes to see. Tell the wealthy church members to do good deeds and generously give to others, knowing true riches come only from God. Stay strong in the truth, Son.

2 TIMOTHY

1. Timothy, my son, I hope our Lord gives you mercy and peace. I pray for you every day, and I'll be so happy when I see you again. You have a beautiful, sincere heart just like your mother and grandmother. I encourage you to share that heart without holding back. Don't be ashamed or afraid to share the good news. God's grace saves us and enables us to do this work. Even though I've suffered, I still trust the God I serve, and I hope you will hold firm as well. I am deserted and imprisoned, but one friend has really helped and encouraged me here. May God bless him!

2. Teach reliable people what you know, and entrust them to teach others. Be an obedient, hard-working soldier in God's army. Because I preach about the risen Jesus, I am in chains, but the Word is not in chains. I long for more people to hear the truth, so I will continue to live for Jesus and endure whatever I must face. Remind your congregation to seek God's approval without hesitation and avoid poisonous, divisive arguments. God knows who really belongs to him, and his foundation cannot be shaken. We must strive to live with purity, peace, and love. Be patient and kind as you encourage these folks to come to their senses.

3. In the last days, people will be greedy, conceited, rude, ungrateful, hateful, and violent. They will value selfish pleasures over God. Stay away from such people. Their tricks won't get them very far because everyone will see how stupid they are. You have followed my example, so you know that God has rescued me from every danger I've faced so far. We all face tests, but no matter what, you must hold onto the faith and wisdom you've spent your entire life building. If you stay plugged into God's scripture, you will gain helpful instructions that will equip you to serve God well.

4. I urge you to spread the good news with boldness, courage, and patience. Some may refuse to listen to you and will hear what they want to hear, but stay calm and get back to work. As my time on earth draws to a close, I know I have run this race with everything in me. I have done my best, and I can't wait to receive God's eternal blessing. People have deserted me, but God has stood by me and rescued me. Please journey to me before winter, and may God keep you safe as you travel.

TITUS

1. Young friend, you know God entrusted me to spread the
    God's promise of eternal hope, and now I entrust you to
    organize the churches in Crete. Please appoint elders with
    healthy marriages and obedient children. They must have
    patient, humble attitudes, and they must not engage in
    violence, drunkenness, or greed. They must encourage
    others with the truth of God's message and debunk hateful
    liars who spout nonsense.

2. Teach older men to set a good example for others by main-
    taining disciplined behavior and steady faith. Older women
    should teach young women to love their families well, and
    they should stay away from excessive wine and gossip. You
    must also be a good example for the people, using sincere
    words that enemies cannot argue with. Encourage servants
    to assist their employers with honesty and loyalty. God's
    grace should inspire all of us to give up our worldly desires
    to be more like our Rescuer.

3. Remind your church members to obey local authorities
    and maintain a kind, friendly attitude toward everyone.
    Remember we were once disobedient fools, and it was the
    kindness and love of God that saved us. We were not saved
    because of anything we did but because God forgave us
    and poured his Spirit on us. Encourage the people to focus
    on helping others instead of getting distracted with divisive
    arguments.

PHILEMON

1. Brother Philemon, I hope God will bless your family and the church that meets in your home. I pray for you every day, and your beautiful love for others brings joy to my heart. As your friend and fellow Christian, I have a request for you. I met and mentored your slave Onesimus here in prison, and he is a different person than he was before. When I send him back to you, I hope you will accept him not just as a slave but as a fellow brother in Christ. Welcome him like you would welcome me, and charge all his debts to my account. I trust you to do the right thing, and I hope God will allow me to leave this prison and journey your way soon.

DAY FOUR - FAITH IN ACTION
HEBREWS-JAMES

BIG IDEA

The unmatchable Savior asks us to show our unshakable faith by living with loving and courageous action.

CALL TO ACTION

- **Worship fully-** The Creator existed before the world, and Jesus suffered for our sake. God is greater than any prophet or priest. Stop doubting him, and honor his greatness through your worship.
- **Take care of yourself-** Treat the Sabbath as a weekly day of relaxation and restoration. Trust God to meet your needs as you pause your work.
- **Trust Jesus' sacrifice-** We no longer need to depend on ourselves or offer animal sacrifices. Just trust that Jesus' gift is enough to forgive and restore you.
- **Start with the heart-** Let the Spirit change you from the inside out. He will purify your thoughts so that your deepest desire is to be more like Jesus.
- **Let faith change you-** The heroes of the past were just ordinary people with extraordinary faith. They were able to do great things and endure many temptations simply because they trusted the one who made them.
- **Lift others up-** Reach out to the poor without judgment, forgive people who have messed up, and acknowledge every human as a

child of God. Set aside your selfish desires, and strive to meet the needs of those around you.

- **Watch your words-** Use honest, humble words that serve to spread peace and joy to others instead of anger and hurt.

HOW GOD SHOWS UP

God is bigger than any mountain and wise enough to set the universe in motion. He sacrificed himself to save our lives, and he deserves our endless trust, respect, and obedience. Our extraordinary God would never ask his children to live mediocre lives of complacency. On the contrary, he calls us to share in his glory by joyfully celebrating his beauty, taking great care of ourselves, and blessing others through our words and actions.

HEBREWS

1. God used to speak to us through prophets, but now he speaks to us through his glorious Son who existed before Creation. He redeemed the world and is now enthroned far above the angels. God chose his Son to rule his eternal kingdom with justice. When the world fades, Jesus will remain.

2. We must hold fast to the truth, remembering that our ancestors paid the price for their doubt and disobedience. Many witnesses can testify that God is using miracles and wonders to increase the credibility of those who spread this Christian message. We humans are far less impressive than

the angels, but God crowns us with glory and entrusts us with the beautiful world he created. Jesus became a lowly human like us, endured great suffering for our sake, and overcame the power of death by rising again. Our Savior understands any hurt or temptation we face because he's been there. He forgives us and frees us from all our fears.

3. Although Moses was a faithful servant in God's house, Jesus is in charge of God's house and deserves far more honor. Don't rebel against the Father like our ancestors did in the desert. That generation angered and tested God so much that they weren't allowed into the Promised Land. Friends, do not let sin and stubbornness lead you away from our living God. Help your fellow Christians stay firm in their belief as well.

4. God rested on the seventh day of creation and longs to give us deep and satisfying rest too. All we have to do is trust him. Some choose to believe this great news while others resist it and rely on themselves. Trust God enough to take a break from your work and take care of yourself sometimes. God's Word cuts through our walls to reach our deepest desires and thoughts. We can't hide anything from the God who made us, so don't be afraid to approach him about anything. He was tempted on earth just like we are, and he longs to help us through our struggles.

5. High priests like Aaron are appointed by God, and since they have weaknesses and imperfections, they must constantly offer sacrifices to seek forgiveness for themselves and the people they lead. Christ was also appointed by God as a priest higher than any other. Jesus wept and

prayed passionately through his suffering, but this humble servant remained obedient and fulfilled God's plan to save the world. I hope you will internalize these basic truths, so that you can mature in your faith and handle more complex spiritual matters.

6. You already know the foundational truth that Jesus defeated death so we could enjoy his eternal grace, so let's move toward more mature teachings. You have experienced the goodness of God through the Holy Spirit, so I hope you won't abandon your faith in the Messiah who suffered immensely for your sake. God rains blessings on you so that you might bear good fruit, but if you choose to bear thorns and weeds, you are useless. God certainly sees the great work you have already done for others, and we don't want to minimize that. I just urge you not to become lazy or complacent toward the God who always keeps his promises.

7. Melchizedek was an honorable king and priest who blessed Abraham after a battle long ago. Abraham was so grateful for this kind blessing that he gave Melchizedek a tenth of his battle loot, just as Jewish families give a tenth of their income to God. As much as we respect Melchizedek, Jesus deserves much more praise. Unlike any other priest, Jesus lives forever and never passes his torch to any other priest. He has no sin in his heart, so he never needed to offer sacrifices to ask forgiveness. The only sacrifice he ever offered was himself.

8. Jesus is our High Priest who sits right next to the Father in heaven. The work of earthly priests is a mere shadow of Jesus' greater work. Likewise, the covenant he arranged

between God and humanity is much better than the old one. We did not live up to our end of the original covenant, which required obedience to the Law in exchange for God's blessing and protection. This new covenant allows us to know God more deeply so that our hearts will truly desire to do the right thing. Thanks to God's new promise, he no longer keeps a record of our mistakes.

9. The first covenant was full of highly specific rules about how we should worship and what we should eat. The Temple was arranged in a certain way, and priests conducted purification ceremonies through animal sacrifices. At the time, God required these laws to keep order among his people, but now that Jesus has come, we understand that none of these external rituals and rules really required a change of heart. The Spirit writes the law on our hearts and allows us to understand God and morality in a much deeper way. The sacrifice of Christ purifies us, so we no longer need to sacrifice animals to guarantee our forgiveness.

10. Animal sacrifices within the Jewish Law certainly serve to remind people of their sins, but these rituals don't actually wash away our guilt or our desire to sin again. Only Jesus can do that. He sacrificed himself to take away our darkness in a way no animal sacrifice could ever do. He changes our hearts so that our desire to know God is greater than our desire to sin. We now have total freedom from guilt and unlimited access to God through sincere prayer. Let us respond to this gift by helping and encouraging each other. If we take Jesus' precious gift for granted and continue to rely on our own works to save us, God will surely judge us in the end. Remember all the times God allowed you to

endure suffering and come out stronger than before. Be patient, and keep living courageously. We are not people who simply quit on our faith.

11. Faith is an unshakable certainty in what we can't see. Our Creator is invisible, but we know he made every beautiful thing in this world. It was Abel's faith that made God approve of his offerings. It was faith that allowed Enoch to be swept up to heaven and escape death. Noah could not see the flood coming, but he trusted God enough to build a boat that saved his family. It was faith that allowed Abraham to leave everything familiar and follow God into the wilderness, and it was faith the allowed Sarah to become a mother of nations after years of infertility. Faith made Moses' parents disobey the pharaoh and protect the life of their newborn son. Faithful Moses gave up his inheritance as the pharaoh's adopted son to suffer alongside the Hebrew slaves. Faith allowed him to part the Red Sea and deliver his people to freedom. Should I continue? Heroes like Gideon and David started as weak nobodies, but God allowed them to win great victories and do impossible things because they had faith.

12. So many people in our midst have witnessed the power of the risen Christ, so what are we waiting for? Let's let go of every sin that holds us back, and let's run directly to Jesus. He did not give up in the face of great suffering, so don't let yourselves give up either. You may face great tests as members of God's family, but don't fall down in discouragement. Get back up, and keep running this race. Live peacefully, and don't let yourself grow bitter or poisonous to others. We don't see God's blazing presence or

hear his thundering voice like our ancestors did on Mount Sinai, but we witness the love of Jesus every day. Let's listen closely to our unshakable God and worship him with awe and gratitude.

13. Keep loving others in your church and community. Remember the homeless and imprisoned people society forgets about. Faithfully respect your spouse, and don't let yourself become preoccupied with money. Be content with the blessings God has given you. Imitate the Christian leaders you look up to, and don't let false teachers lead you astray. Remember that God's grace means more than obeying meaningless rules about food. Respect the church leaders that work hard and sacrifice much for you, and keep praying for us. Jesus is the Good Shepherd who died for his sheep, and God rescued him from death so that we could live new lives of peace and blessing.

JAMES

1. Brothers and sisters around the world, your faith will help you endure any hard times that come your way. God will gladly increase your wisdom if you reach out to him without any doubt or ambivalence. Worldly wealth will burn up like a flower in the sun, but if you are poor, God will lift you up. God is responsible for every beautiful and perfect thing in this world, and he would never put evil temptations in your path. In fact, he longs to bless you and help you avoid the traps that could destroy you. When you're angry and tempted to say something spiteful, take a deep

breath, and listen more than you speak. Say only the words God plants in your heart, and act on the lessons you learn from scripture. Your religious traditions don't mean much to God if you hurt others with words and refuse to help people in need.

2. Don't judge others by what they wear or how rich they are. Treat the homeless man on the street with the same respect you would show to an executive in a suit. Your possessions make you no better than anyone else. Some poor people are the wisest and most Spirit-filled people you'll ever meet, and some rich people are the very ones who oppress you. God longs for mercy to override his judgment of you, but he may remove that mercy if you refuse to forgive others. If your faith doesn't inspire you to lovingly lift others up, your faith is a dead thing that does the world no good. Even demons know God is real, but their actions don't reflect that. It is only through kind and courageous action that your belief will come to life, and you can truly become a friend of God.

3. Not everyone could handle being a teacher like me; we are judged more harshly than others. None of us are perfect, but if we can control our tongue, we can begin to control our actions. Boastful, angry words poison our spirits and spread destruction like a forest fire in the hearts of our loved ones. Don't be a hypocrite who sings God's praises one moment and curses your neighbor the next. A clean heart will only yield pure, life-giving words. Those with selfish, bitter hearts often brag about their intelligence, but those with God's wisdom show it through their humble, peaceful, and friendly attitudes. True wisdom frees us from prejudice

and inspires us to bless others.

4. If **we** all would just set aside our selfish, worldly desires, all the fighting and wars would stop. When we turn to God with pure motives, he doesn't hesitate to bless us. Stop resisting the Father that loves you, and humble yourself before him. Let his grace be stronger than lesser things that tempt you. Let yourself cry honest tears before God, and he will allow those tears to wash you clean.

5. You rich people ignore the cries of your poor employees and hoard their wages for yourself. You exist to eat fancy food and enjoy expensive luxuries, but one day, you'll lose it all as this whole world returns to dust. Brothers and sisters, let's wait patiently for God to return and set all things right. In the meantime, treat each other with kindness and honesty. Pray to God in times of joy and pain, and help each other stay connected to the truth.

DAY FIVE - UNSTOPPABLE LOVE
1-2 PETER-1-3 JOHN-JUDE

BIG IDEA

The brother and two best friends of Jesus advise church members to share God's loving light with each other and hold tightly to the truth.

ADVICE FROM THE INNER CIRCLE

- **Stop worrying-** If you keep your eyes on Jesus, trials can't crush you. They only refine your spirit and make you stronger.
- **Honor his sacrifice-** Jesus gave up everything for you, so stop living in darkness like you were before you met him. Don't disrespect others with words or disrespect yourself with bodily passions.
- **Love fearlessly-** All the laws boil down to love, so show respect and dignity in all situations. Don't stop just because others might think of you as weird or different. Obedience helps you know Jesus even better.
- **Trust the truth-** The apostles witnessed Jesus' life, death, and resurrection with their own eyes, so they compel us not to take the Gospel lightly. The stories of Jesus are more than just legends or symbolic morality tales.
- **Worship while you wait-** Some grow impatient and curious about when Jesus is coming back, but God may wait until the message reaches many more people. Stop trying to predict his timing, and just focus on living fully.

- **Share the light-** Let your life reflect God's pure goodness, and don't be afraid to spread the truth with boldness and love. Jesus gave everything for us, so put the needs of others ahead of your own.

- **Avoid false teachers-** Some church leaders have selfish motives that cause them to distort the truth about God. Don't let these liars divide you.

HOW GOD SHOWS UP

Jesus chooses a few humble, imperfect men to learn from him during his life and offer inspired leadership to the early church. The brothers of Jesus, including Jude and James, become passionate advocates for faith along with the apostles. These witnesses passionately attest to the authenticity of Jesus' ministry, death, and victory over death. Jesus lifts the downtrodden, humbles the proud, and speaks the truth. These members of his inner circle encourage us to follow his example.

1 PETER

1. May the peace of Jesus be with all you Christians living as refugees in Asia. God restored our life by raising Jesus from death, and this gives us a hope that these unfair bouts of suffering cannot squash. God will allow these flames to refine you like gold, and you'll be rewarded when this life is over. Your joyful, loving worship is inspiring. Keep your eyes focused on eternity, and turn your eyes away from

temptations that could separate you from God. Christ gave his precious, perfect life for you, so don't take that sacrifice lightly. You are born again as children of God, so show that through your earnest love for others.

2. Stop all the lying, hypocrisy, jealousy, and disrespectful language. Crave God's wisdom like a baby craves his mother's milk. Jesus was like a precious gem the world discarded, but he is now the cornerstone of the church God is helping us build together. He pulled us out of the darkness and into the light of his mercy, so show some gratitude for that mercy. Don't waste your energy on bodily passions that fight for your soul's attention. Follow the laws of your land, and respect others, even when it's not easy. If someone harms or mistreats you, know that Jesus was insulted and tortured as well. He understands your pain, and he will enable you to endure anything without letting your heart be consumed by anger and revenge.

3. Beloved sisters, if any of you are married to unbelievers, convince them of the truth not with words but with your loving attitude and actions. The world will tell you that perfect hair, clothes, and jewelry make you beautiful, but if you have a gentle and courageous spirit, you are beautiful to God. Brothers, treat your wives with the respect they deserve as daughters of God. Love each other with attitudes of humility, peace, and kindness. If you want to truly enjoy your life, stay away from gossip and revenge. Who will be your enemy if you treat everyone with dignity? Those who mistreat you will be ashamed of themselves in the end, so you have no need to worry. The risen Christ has saved you.

4. You used to waste so much time with drunken parties, lust, and idol worship, and now your heathen friends make fun of you for setting those old habits aside. Just remember they will have to explain themselves before God one day, so don't let their insults discourage you from doing the right thing. If you love others earnestly, you'll be able to avoid all kinds of sins. God has blessed each of you with unique strengths, so allow those gifts to bless others. Don't be ashamed or surprised if others harm you because of your faith. Instead, just be proud to suffer alongside Christ, and trust him to judge those wicked bullies in the end.

5. I witnessed Christ's suffering with my own eyes and serve as an elder of his church. I ask you other leaders to care for your congregations like a gentle shepherd leads his flock. Approach them with a servant's heart, and let your life be a positive example for them to follow. Young people, humbly obey these leaders, and God will lift you up when the time is right. Leave your worries at the feet of your loving Father. The Devil may try to devour you, but your faith will equip you to win this fight. When the battle of this life is over, God will call you home to share in his perfect glory forever.

2 PETER

1. As a servant and apostle of Jesus, I pray that all of you will find the grace and peace that comes from knowing him. Our powerful God gives us every tool we need to fight the destructive temptations of this world. We must strengthen

our faith with good motives, wisdom, enduring discipline, and love. This will help us see the big picture and know Jesus even better. I know you know this, but our faith is not temporary. My life will probably end soon, but I'll continue reminding you to keep the faith until I'm gone. Remember, the life of Jesus isn't just a legend or a morality tale. Many of us witnessed his amazing life with our own eyes and heard God's voice proclaiming Jesus as his Son. Take our message seriously, and let the truth shine in your hearts.

2. Watch out for false teachers who spread lies about Jesus for their own financial gain. God sees every move they make and will judge them as he judged wicked-hearted people in the past. These arrogant deceivers show no respect for heavenly matters. They attack and insult anyone who disagrees with them like defensive, caged animals. Don't fall for their stupid statements and false promises. God's grace rescued you from the traps of this world, and for you to go right back to old patterns would be like a dog going back to his vomit.

3. Friends, keep your thoughts pure, and hold onto the truths of long-ago prophets. This age will be filled with self-serving, lustful mockers who say "If this Jesus guy was really coming back, he would have done it already." They ignore and disrespect our Creator, but they will not escape God's judgment in the end. Remember that a thousand years is like a day to God. We may be eager for Jesus to return quickly, but perhaps God is being patient with the human race, giving us plenty of time to wake up to the truth. He would love it if everyone turned away from sin so that he wouldn't have to destroy a single soul. When the end

days actually do come, destruction will come swiftly and unexpectedly like a thief in the night. God will create a new heaven and earth full of righteousness. As we wait, let's keep purity and peace in our hearts as we draw ever closer to the Father.

1 JOHN

1. Our living, promised Messiah existed before the world was made. We've seen him with our own eyes, and now we spread the word about the never-ending life he wants for us. We hope you will join in our joyful unity with God's Son. Jesus is purely goodness and light, so if we continue to stumble in the dark, thinking we don't really need him, we're fooling ourselves. We must confess our mistakes to him and eagerly accept his purifying grace.

2. When we mess up, our forgiving Savior advocates for us. When we turn from our sins toward a life of obedience, we learn to know and love God more perfectly. Share your Father's light by loving your brothers and sisters. If you know our Creator who forgives and strengthens us, teach others to find that same strength. Let your love for God extinguish your selfish desires and your attachment to this temporary world. Ignore the lies of people who try to lead you away from Jesus. Instead, let the Spirit speak to your heart and equip you with true wisdom and courage.

3. God loves us so much that he adopts us as his precious children. The world doesn't understand us because the

world doesn't understand our Father. Cain murdered his brother Abel out of the evil hatred in his heart, so we must reject all hatred from our hearts and treat everyone with life-giving love. Jesus sacrificed his life out of his love for you, so follow his example by loving others with sacrificial action. Open your hearts to people in need, and give portions of your time and treasure to make their lives better. Listen to your conscience, and let your love be more than just talk.

4. Many claim to have the Spirit, but whoever denies the divine humanity of Jesus is not really connected to God. The Spirit of truth assures us that God loves us so much that he sent his Son to rescue and forgive us. That's what love really means, and we should love each other like that to become one with God's heart. Let's continue to courageously spread the beautiful truth of Jesus, knowing his perfect love drives out all our fears. God loved us before we even knew how to love, so let's pay that unconditional favor forward.

5. Obedience to God's Law is not difficult if your heart knows how to love. If you know how to put the dignity of others ahead of your selfish desires, you can defeat any temptation in the world. The sacrifice of Jesus washes us clean and leads us to a full life that never ends. Let your knowledge of that truth give you courage. Speak to God with pure motives, and he'll honor your requests. Pray that your brothers and sisters will turn from their destructive sins and allow Jesus to lead them to safety. Watch out for deceivers, and let the one true God fill you with wisdom.

2 JOHN

1. To the sweet congregation I love so much, I hope our Savior gives you mercy and peace. You are beloved by all who cling to the truth. Obey God's commands by letting love be your highest priority. This is nothing new. Love was the most important law from the very beginning. We know that God lived among us as a human being, so don't let lying enemies of Jesus convince you otherwise. Stay far away from these deceivers. I have much more to tell you, but I will wait until I visit you. Seeing your faces again will make me so happy!

3 JOHN

1. My dear friend Gaius, I love you so much! I pray this letter finds you in good health that matches your awesome spirit. Our fellow brothers and sisters say you are incredibly faithful to the truth, and it makes me so happy to hear that. I love that you boldly reach out to strangers with kindness, and I know you'll do a great job teaching others to serve and please God. I know you'll equip them to spread the truth in new places with confidence. When I visit you, I'll confront that corrupt church leader Diotrephes. He refuses to provide a welcoming presence for those who need help, and he drives good people away from the church. I hope you'll avoid wicked examples like this and

surround yourself with good-hearted people. Until I see you in person, peace be with you.

JUDE

1. I pray that God will forgive and protect all who live in his love. Friends, I feel an urgent need to encourage you to hold onto your saving faith. Godless imposters have crept into our churches to justify sin and distort the truth of God's grace. Those who disrespect their bodies and act with selfish lust will earn God's anger. Even the most powerful angels recognize God as the only true Judge. These shameless rebels only care about themselves, and they constantly manipulate and blame others. Stay strong in God's love, and don't let liars divide you. Rescue each other from the tempting flames. Our glorious, eternal Jesus makes us better and happier than we could be on our own!

WEEK SIX REFLECTION
Church

DISCUSSION QUESTIONS

- What do you notice about the early church that is similar to the modern church? What has changed about the church in the past 2000 years?

- When Paul and the other apostles led people to Christ, how did they convince people that the resurrection was real? What attitude did they have when witnessing to others? What can you learn from this example as you communicate about your faith?

- Week Six speaks a great deal about the importance of the Holy Spirit. Why did God send the Holy Spirit into the world? How have you experienced his movement in your own life? How has the Holy Spirit affected your heart and decisions? What might you do to listen to the Spirit more actively in the future?

- Each letter to the early church has a slightly different perspective and purpose. What are some common themes that tie the letters together? Which letters or passages stand out as your favorites and why?

- According to the letters, how can a person's heart be transformed and saved? What role does the Law play in our life and salvation? What role does the Holy Spirit play in our life and salvation?

- After Paul's letters to the church, we see several brief letters written by James, Peter, John, and Jude. What do you know about each of these authors? What does each author seem to emphasize?

MUSIC MEDITATIONS

- **Romans-** Listen to "I Am New" by Jason Gray, and think about what Paul says about Jesus transforming our hearts and making us new.

- **1-2 Corinthians-** Paul advises the Corinthian church to heal their divisions through love. Listen to "Bleed the Same" by Mandisa, and reflect on how the modern church could benefit from the same lesson.

- **Galatians-** Paul encourages this church to choose internal transformation and grace over rigid enslavement to the Law. Listen closely to the second verse of "Lord I Need You" by Matt Maher to discover another beautiful and profound message about why we need grace.

- **Ephesians-** Listen to "Hold Us Together" by Matt Maher, and reflect on this letter's overarching lessons regarding love and unity.

- **Philippians-** This letter is one of my personal favorites because here Paul writes words of unshakable joy in the midst of a dark, uncertain time. Listen to "Joy" by For King and Country, and let yourself feel that same infectious energy as you smile and dance along.

- **Colossians-** In this letter, Paul encourages the church to remember the beautiful sacrifice of Jesus and allow gratitude to motivate us toward loving action. Reflect on any similar messages you notice in "This is Amazing Grace" by Phil Wickham.

- **1-2 Thessalonians-** Listen to "Where I Belong" by Building 429, and reflect on how this persecuted church may have drawn encouragement from these words.

- **1-2 Timothy and Titus-** Listen to "Lead Me" by Sanctus Real, and consider Paul's advice to church leaders like Timothy and Titus.

- **Philemon-** As a former slave becomes a beloved family member in this story, think about the similar transformation referenced within "No Longer Slaves" by Bethel Music.

- **Hebrews-** Listen to "We Will Not Be Shaken" by Bethel Music, and consider what this book says about unshakable faith.

- **James-** Listen to "Do Something" by Matthew West, and consider what this letter says about demonstrating faith through action.

- **1-2 Peter-** Peter speaks of struggle as a fire that refines and purifies us, and "Survivor" by Zach Williams speaks of the beautiful redemption that can happen once we are lifted from the fire.

- **1-2-3 John-** This apostle includes beautiful words about what it means to live in God's loving light. Listen to "In the Light" by DC Talk to consider that advice.

- **Jude-** This brief letter encourages Christians to let God's love inspire them toward positive decisions. Consider any similar messages within "Live Like You're Loved" by Hawk Nelson.

APPLICATION IDEAS

- The early church grew dramatically when its members allowed the Holy Spirit to enter their hearts and affect their actions. They immediately and enthusiastically healed, gave, and preached to the greatest extent they could. How can you inject a bit of that boldness and authentic energy into your own life and into your own church?

- Paul gave his testimony of transformation to anyone who would listen. A personal testimony can help believers connect to others and humbly show how God can change a person's direction in life. Write down the story of your personal internal shift, and practice saying it out loud. If you are prepared to share your story, the Lord will probably give you an opportunity to share it.

- As members of Christ's body, each of us has a different set of talents and gifts that we can use to benefit the whole church. Determine which of your gifts and talents could be utilized within the church, and talk to your church's leadership team about volunteer opportunities that would fit your personal strengths.

- The letters talk again and again about avoiding divisive people and false prophets. How can you respectfully speak out against people who divide the church and spread lies about Christianity? Brainstorm small and large ways to let the world know the truth about Jesus and his plan for our lives.

- The most important rule for our lives is love. Brainstorm the people in your life who are most difficult to love. Pray sincerely for the well-being of each person on that list. The next time you have the opportunity to interact with one of these folks, show him or her an attitude of love and respect.

WEEK SEVEN

Heaven

REVELATION AND REVIEW

DAY ONE - THE BIG PICTURE
REVELATION 1-7

BIG IDEA

Jesus reminds seven Asian churches that even when chaos overwhelms the earth in the last days, God's goodness will overshadow every scary circumstance.

LESSONS FOR THE SEVEN CHURCHES

- **Ephesus-** Don't let adversity divide you or cause you to turn cynical. Trust God to strengthen your hearts and your community. He is bigger than any harmful force you will ever face.

- **Smyrna-** You are not alone. Enemies have overwhelmed and persecuted you, but God loves you and will not let your story end in failure. He will protect faithful children like you when it's time to judge the earth.

- **Pergamum-** Regardless of the wicked culture around you, please remember to respect God, each other, and yourselves. Respect God by worshiping him alone. Respect others through words and actions. Respect yourself by keeping your body healthy and pure.

- **Thyatira-** Love does not equal complacency. We can offer warmth and acceptance to others while also holding tightly to our faith and to the moral guidance we receive from the Holy Spirit.

- **Sardis-** You may look strong and have a great reputation, but that means nothing if your hearts are dead. God sees right through your masks of strength and wealth. You cannot hide your true character from him.

- **Philadelphia-** Since you follow God obediently and patiently, he will create new opportunities for you and will enable you to overcome enemies.
- **Laodicea-** Your nominal, lukewarm faith means nothing to God. A genuine relationship with God includes a deep and passionate desire to follow him.

HOW GOD SHOWS UP

The overwhelmingly glorious Savior shows up on John's island to reveal amazing truths about God and about the future. He shows individualized love for each congregation by offering personalized messages of guidance, hope, and accountability. Jesus begins to reveal how the last days of this earthly age will unfold. Although human leaders will usher in an overwhelming age of war, famine, and disease, God offers a joyful and peaceful eternal future to anyone who accepts his grace.

REVELATION PART 1

1. This is a true story of a series of visions Jesus himself revealed to me not long ago. Those who understand and obey these words will be blessed because one day, all these visions will actually happen. I hope the grace of our risen

Savior will bless all you brothers and sisters in the seven Asian churches. He loves us and gave his life to free us from our mistakes. Let's glorify our powerful King forever! Eventually, everyone including Jesus' murderers will see him appear in the sky, and they'll acknowledge that he is the beginning and end of all things. Like many of you, I have endured great suffering, and our enemies exiled me to this island for speaking God's truth. One day, as I sat alone on this beach, Jesus appeared before me with white hair, blazing eyes, smooth bronze skin, and a face that shone so brightly I couldn't look directly at him. I fell at his feet as his voice trumpeted "Don't be afraid, John. I am the one death could not hold down. Write down every mysterious thing you see today, and send the book to the seven churches of Asia.

2. "Tell the Ephesians I notice their patience and hard work. They have stood up to wicked liars, and they do not give up in the face of adversity. Unfortunately, these taxing trials have chipped away at their love for me, and I want to turn them back to my saving presence. Tell the Smyrna congregation I see that they are beaten down by hurtful rumors, financial stresses, and the imprisonment of many of their members. They may feel alone, but I will never abandon them. I long to erase their fears and reward them with life no enemy can destroy. I know the Pergamum church is in an incredibly corrupt area and must withstand impossible temptations. Regardless, I must encourage them not to give up the fight. Some of them are falling into idolatry and sexual sin, and they must turn away from these self-destructive choices. I want the Thyatira congregation to know I

appreciate their loving, patient service to others, but some of them need to wake up to the evil that is infiltrating their community. They are allowing the corrupt false prophetess Jezebel to lead them into sexual corruption and idol worship, and that's simply not acceptable. If they hold tight to goodness, I will strengthen them and lead them to victory.

3. "The Sardis church has a great reputation and feels invincible, but I see that most of them are spiritually dead and unworthy to walk beside me in heaven. I hope they wake up and turn from their wicked pride. Tell the faithful Philadelphia church that I open doors no one can close. I have lifted them up, and their enemies will not be able to tear them down. The Lord Almighty defends and protects his enduring children. The lukewarm Laodicean congregation leans on their wealth and lacks any measure of passion or commitment to the faith. Their apathy disgusts me, and I wish they would make up their minds whether or not they really want to be in my family. I'm knocking on the door of their hearts, and they refuse to answer."

4. Jesus whisked me up into God's glorious throne room to show me the future. I was overwhelmed by the Holy Spirit as I saw the impossibly beautiful, dazzling face of my Creator. A rainbow glowed around the throne with colors earthly eyes can't see, and beyond that was an expansive sea as smooth and clear as glass. Two dozen elders threw their crowns at God's feet as they saw a thunderous lightning storm emanating from his presence. Four mysterious and powerful winged creatures sang this never-ending worship song: "Our impossibly mighty, amazing God has existed forever and gave life to everything that exists. He will always

deserve every ounce glory and gratitude we can muster."

5.   The beautiful Father held out a scroll containing mysterious prophecies that will unfold at the end of this earthly age. I wept as I realized no human or angel would ever be worthy to open the scroll, but one of the elders called my attention to the glorious Lamb standing in the center of the room, ready to accept the scroll. This Lamb came to earth to spread God's presence throughout the world, and he was killed for the world's sake. Millions of angels and every creature on earth bowed in passionate worship before the Lamb, and the massive chorus sang "Jesus, only you are worthy to look inside this scroll and set the future in motion. Your sacrifice brought the entire world back to God, and only you are worthy to receive anything good. Our words could never glorify you enough, and we'll praise your name forever!"

6.   I saw Jesus open the first four seals of the scroll and saw four horses representing the final years of this earthly age. I saw a white horse carrying a world conqueror with an arrowless bow. This leader gained power by promising peace to the world and unifying the nations under his false sense of security. A red horse followed, devastating the world with widespread war, murder, and conflict. A black horse signaled a time of economic crisis and famine that festered in the war-torn world. The fourth and final horse looked deathly pale and signaled the death of a quarter of humanity as a result of the chaotic mixture of disease, war, famine, and animal attacks. My heart hurt to witness this widespread devastation, but I breathed a sigh of relief as Jesus opened the fifth scroll seal. The good-hearted martyrs

of the past rose up and shouted "Holy God, we know you will bring justice on our wicked enemies who harmed and killed us. Only you can judge the world and set things right!" Just then, the powerful Lamb broke the sixth seal and unleashed a terrifying earthquake on the earth. The sky darkened, and the moon turned red. The stars fell, and the mountains moved. Every wealthy, prideful ruler hid under rocks, knowing none of them could ever stand up to the powerful God who defends his children.

7.   In the wake of the earthquake, everything went silent as angels held back the wind and protected the earth from further harm. God's angels moved through the earth marking the foreheads of 144,000 Jewish Christians who would be protected from all future plagues. I then saw the most enormous crowd I've ever seen representing every race and nation on earth. The crowd shouted "King Jesus saved our lives, and all the glory, power, and wisdom of the earth belong to him alone. He deserves our never-ending thanks!" The angel told me "This great multitude represents all the people through the ages who have been saved by the grace of Jesus. His sacrifice has purified their hearts, and their joyful worship will never end. They will live under God's perfect protection forever. They will never again experience hunger, pain, or sadness. The amazing Shepherd will guide them toward a full, happy life that no one on earth can imagine."

DAY TWO - THE END OF THE WORLD
REVELATION 8-16

BIG IDEA

As the world begins to crumble under the weight of evil forces, God rises up to protect his people from pain, disaster, and deception.

BEAUTY WITHIN THE TRIBULATION

- **God hears our prayers-** The seventh seal judgments are released with the prayers of God's people in mind. God notices when people abuse or persecute us, and in the end, he comes to our defense and sets all injustices right.

- **Satan's worst cannot touch us-** God cannot force us to accept his protection, but he longs to save any imperfect person willing to accept his invitation of grace. Children of God will be shielded from every evil and hurt that overwhelms those last days.

- **Evil will not win-** Satan may seem like an overwhelming, bloodthirsty dragon, but he is no match for the Creator of the universe. God is bigger and more glorious than anyone or anything. Satan may dish out terrible evils on earth for a time, but God has already written a victorious end to the world's story.

- **Plenty of warnings-** As Jerusalem unravels in those final years, two unshakable prophets perform miracles and persuade people to join God's family. Even those with desperately corrupt hearts have an opportunity to hear the truth because our loving

God longs for all people to choose his protection.

- **We won't be fooled-** Satan lifts up an unholy dictator and a false prophet in the last days, and these two trick many people into worshipping them and trusting them to save the world. However, God helps us identify these prideful, crafty leaders, so that none of his children will fall for their traps.

HOW GOD SHOWS UP

No evil force can overpower the God who breathed life into everything. God is bigger and stronger than any monster or disaster. Even though some humans and angels have chosen the path of pain and destruction, the worst evils in this universe will not overwhelm those who give their hearts to the Father. God gives us countless opportunities to turn to him, but he will not destroy our free will by forcing us to accept his grace and protection.

REVELATION PART 2

8. As Jesus broke the seventh seal, heaven went silent as seven angels lined up with trumpets signifying what would come next. I held my breath and waited in anticipation. Another angel approached the altar and brought all the prayers of God's children. With those prayers in mind, the angel unleashed a great lightning storm and earthquake to judge those who had repeatedly rejected God and harmed his people. The first four angels blew their trumpets, and the earth was devastated by a series of natural disasters.

Hailstorms and uncontrollable forest fires destroyed a third of the world's plants. Two giant meteors crashed into the ocean, killing a third of the ocean animals and contaminating a third of the world's fresh water supply. The terrible impact of these meteors filled the sky with residue so thick that the sun, moon, and stars seemed to grow much dimmer. As I observed this incredible devastation, an angel shouted "These plagues against God's enemies have been terrifying so far, but beware! What's coming next is even worse!"

9. When the fifth trumpet was blown, I saw Satan, the angel who long ago was exiled from heaven. This evil, bloodthirsty serpent unlocked the doors of hell and released a multitude of his most terrifying demons on the earth. Smoke poured out of hell and completely darkened the sky. The first swarm of murderous demons were like tiny, battle-ready horses with scorpion stingers and razor-sharp teeth. Satan allowed these insect-sized minions to swarm those who continued to ignore God's power. God desperately wanted to save these people from their pain, but they refused to accept the Lord's protection. The demons tortured the people for five months until they wished they were dead, giving them a small taste of the eternal torture in store for them if they continued to trust Satan over the Creator. As the sixth trumpet blew, Satan released an army of 200 million much larger demons to brutally murder a third of those who had just endured five months of torture. This second round of demons had breastplates the color of fire and rode horses with lion heads that destroyed people with smoke and flames from their mouths. The horses had venomous snakes spouting from their tails which bit and poisoned

anyone within range. Even in the aftermath of Satan's disgusting massacre of his followers, the survivors still refused
to turn to God. Their hearts remained stubbornly devoted
to their lifeless, homemade idols. They continued to destroy
themselves with sexual sin and continued to destroy each
other with theft and murder.

10. As I pondered the horrifying destruction I had just witnessed, God offered me a profound image of hope just
when I needed it most. I saw a beautiful angel emerge from
heaven with a robe of clouds and a halo of rainbows. His
skin shone like the sun and overwhelmed my senses. I saw
him place one foot on the earth and one foot on the ocean
as if to say "I know what you have seen so far looks horrible
and bleak. As you saw Satan torturing humanity and people
refusing to accept God's protection, it probably felt like evil
forces were winning this war. Just take a deep breath. I want
you to know the Creator of all things is still in charge here."
God roared a victory cry so loud that the sound reverber-
ated throughout the earth. As the sky echoed a seven-gun
salute, an angel whispered in my ear, asking me to stop
writing and simply listen to God's next message, which contained beautiful mysteries I wasn't allowed to write down.
My human words couldn't have done them justice anyway.
The angel straddled the earth in his powerful stance and
held the scroll whose seven seals had been broken. The
scroll lay open in his palms, and he said "God has already
written the end of this story, and none of this is a surprise
to him. These events may seem sour and dismal now, but
after the destruction is over, what comes after will be the
sweetest thing you've ever tasted. Don't lose heart, John! I

promise goodness will win! Help us proclaim that amazing truth throughout the world. Help us enrich the tired and devastated people with the hope they need so desperately."

11. God told me "For three and a half years, Jerusalem will be trampled and torn apart by godless people. In the midst of this wicked city, I will send two witnesses to proudly proclaim my message without holding back. They will speak profound words of peace in this time of sin and confusion. They will spread my light in this time of darkness. Many will try to silence them, but I will equip them to protect themselves from any evil that tries to destroy them." I saw the witnesses breathing fire to destroy would-be-assassins, and I watched as they sent a series of plagues on Jerusalem in an attempt to gain the people's respect and attention. When their mission was complete, the Antichrist killed these two men and left their bodies to rot in the streets. The wicked people of Jerusalem celebrated and congratulated themselves, thinking they had silenced God's message of hope. Three days later, the corpses rose to life, and the unstoppable witnesses were whisked up to heaven as an earthquake rattled Jerusalem. Only then did the onlookers praise the mighty, insurmountable God these witnesses had proclaimed. As the seventh trumpet blew, I heard the choir of elder angels singing "Our powerful Messiah existed before time began and will rule the world forever! Thank you for remaining in control! Satan's followers seethe in anger as God rewards those who love him and judges everyone else. Those who destroy God's beautiful creation will not escape." As the song ended, God unleashed his power through a heavy thunderstorm punctuated by

massive hail and an earthquake.

12. Next, I saw a mysterious vision of Jesus' pregnant mother getting ready to give birth to him. Satan emerged as a fearsome dragon hovering over Mary. In the midst of her labor pains, he licked his chops and threatened to consume her child once he was born. Despite the dragon's best efforts, God protected Mary and her child, guarding her in the wilderness, and lifting Jesus up to the heavenly throne room. The dragon recruited a third of the angels to declare war on God and his loyal angel armies. Satan could not prevail over God, and he and his demons were thrown out of heaven. The souls in heaven erupted into a celebration song, declaring "Our King has saved us all and has shown his incredible power over that prideful serpent. We defeated him by washing ourselves in God's grace, by never doubting the truth, and by willingly and unselfishly joining in this noble fight. We rejoice that Satan is finally locked out of heaven, but those who remain on earth should be on guard as he flails around like a caged animal. The bloodthirsty dragon knows his time is almost over, so he will stop at nothing to spread wickedness and destruction in the meantime. Fortunately, God will faithfully protect his children from Satan's murderous grasp. He cannot and will not win."

13. As Satan was thrown from heaven, I saw him empower two terrifying beasts to deceive and rule the world during this final earthly age. The first beast was a counterfeit Messiah and a crafty predator who rose as a worldwide political leader, gaining authority and influence over the people. This persuasive Antichrist claimed to be more powerful

than God and convinced the world to worship him. The second beast was a false prophet that Satan equipped to work impressive miracles and deceive the people into worshipping the Antichrist. This false prophet looked as harmless as a lamb but spoke with the violent assertiveness of the great Dragon himself. Together, the Antichrist and his false prophet recruited all nations to unify under one worldwide government and religion designed to further Satan's purposes. Under this final dictatorship, citizens were required to tattoo their loyalty to the Antichrist on their foreheads in order to buy food.

14. I saw Jesus on a mountaintop with the heavenly beings and the 144,000 protected followers standing behind him. I could see that these good-hearted followers trusted Jesus with all their hearts. They kept their bodies pure and always told the truth. This massive choir of believers sang a new worship song at the top of their voices. An angel loudly announced "Our God is so good, and it is finally time for him to bring true justice to the earth. Let's worship the One who made the whole universe with his bare hands! The Antichrist persuaded the world to follow him, but now his wicked kingdom will crumble. Those who have pledged their loyalty to this dictator will feel the full strength of God's anger. The fires of hell will torture them and separate them from God's presence forever. Those who have worked hard to serve God can now enjoy a much deserved rest as evil is destroyed once and for all! Harvest time has finally come! The fruit is finally ripe for picking, and it's time to separate the sweet grapes from the sour, rotten ones."

15. I saw a sea of flames and broken glass, and as far as my eyes

could see, a multitude of God's children stood determined on the shore, preparing to bring the Antichrist down. The crowd sang "Glorious King, you do wonderful things, and you allow all things to work together for your good purposes. We can't help but stand in awe of you. We can't help but worship you with everything in us. The whole world can see your greatness at last, and no one can deny your power." I saw seven angels reach for seven golden bowls containing the final expression of God's anger on his enemies.

16. One after another, the angels poured out the seven bowls on the wicked worshippers of the Antichrist. These people broke out in agonizing sores and went thirsty as the world's water supply turned to blood. An angel declared "These murderers deserve everything our eternal God is sending their way. They spilled the blood of God's children, so now they only get blood to drink." God turned up the heat of the sun, and everyone in the Antichrist's kingdom cursed God because of their pain. No matter how God proved his sovereign power, they refused to turn from their selfish, destructive ways. Ugly demons emerged from the unholy trinity (Satan, the Antichrist, and the false prophet) to perform miracles and gather the world's armies to battle God. As the army gathered in Babylon, God destroyed the unholy city with an unmatched earthquake that flattened every mountain on earth and caused all islands to crumble into the sea. God's enemies cursed the Creator as hundred-pound hailstones fell from the sky and crushed them.

DAY THREE - THE START OF ETERNITY
REVELATION 17-22

BIG IDEA

God puts an end to evil, and all that's left is pure beauty and eternal goodness.

WHAT WE KNOW ABOUT HEAVEN

- **No room for evil-** When the evil city of Babylon falls, the sins of pride, lust, greed, and anger lose their hold on humanity. The angels celebrate as the good Father overcomes every temptation that holds back his children.

- **Assured victory-** John watches with joy and awe as Jesus singlehandedly defeats the armies of hell and ends the reign of Satan himself. Every good person who suffered on earth returns to an eternal life of goodness and glory.

- **Overwhelming beauty-** John describes his experience of heaven, knowing earthly words could never do it justice. The whole city is filled with perfect structures, a glittering foundation, and a rainbow of colors too stunning for human eyes to see. John's knees buckle at the impossibly breathtaking sight.

- **God's loving presence-** God's love fills the whole place with light and beauty. All hearts fill with the security and freedom of knowing that their new home is protected on all sides by God's impenetrable power.

- **Unbridled joy-** John and the angels cannot contain their happiness as the reality of this perfect, beautiful place settles in. The multitude worships with giddy smiles and unrestrained singing as they finally see God's unfiltered beauty.
- **Perfect peace-** The battle is over, and it's time to enjoy perfect rest without fret or worry. God has ushered in the happy ending, and he is in control.
- **Free admission-** God doesn't care how broken and imperfect we are. He loves us anyway and chose to suffer so that our forgiveness would be guaranteed. All he asks in return is our acceptance and gratitude for his priceless gift.

HOW GOD SHOWS UP

Just when evil seems to have swallowed up the earth, Jesus arrives to defeat darkness once and for all. When good finally wins, the dazzling glory of God can now be seen by human eyes. At last, we can see that our God is more loving, more powerful, and more beautiful than we could have ever imagined. Finally, we get to experience him as he really is, and he invites us to rest in his perfect presence forever.

REVELATION PART 3

17. One of the angels pulled me aside and explained "In the final days of this earth, the city of Babylon will be like a wealthy prostitute that pleasures all the kings of the earth.

The Antichrist will turn his capital city into a thriving metropolis of corruption. She'll dress in fancy clothes and expensive jewelry, but her heart will be filthy. She'll get drunk on the blood of innocent people, and she'll thrive when God's children suffer. The Antichrist will die and come back to life in Babylon. He will proclaim her as the capital city of the whole world, and the ten kings ruling under him will unify in their fight against God and his followers. Babylon will be built up by powerful men, but those same men will rob, strip, abuse, and abandon her in the end."

18. A beautiful, mighty angel emerged from heaven with an air of uncontained excitement and the most infectious smile I've ever seen. His glory lit up the whole world as he joyfully announced "She's gone! Babylon has fallen! She proudly helped wicked, powerful men get richer, and she destroyed the hearts of her citizens with her pervasive culture of lust and selfishness. People of Babylon, wake up! Your city was overrun with evil, and you don't have to tolerate that foolishness anymore. Her power and luxury have vanished, and we can finally see her as the heartless troll that she is. Kings and tycoons who benefitted from Babylon's oppressive system weep as their fortunes go up in flames along with her. Let's celebrate as God throws bloodthirsty Babylon into the sea like a rock!"

19. All the people of heaven released a thundering victory yell and exclaimed "Thank you, glorious, powerful Savior! Your justice has won at last! Babylon was corrupting the earth and destroying the lives of innocent people, and now you have rightfully burned her to the ground. We cannot

contain our gratitude and happiness as we worship your impossible greatness. Finally, the time has come for the ultimate wedding feast. It's time for Jesus to return and unite with his beloved people!" My knees gave out, and I blinked back tears of joy as heaven opened to reveal the most beautiful and comforting sight I've ever seen. I saw Jesus on a white horse ready to make his victory complete. In his eyes, I saw the purest justice and the deepest love. His robe was stained with the blood he sacrificed to save our lives. The armies of heaven followed him as we gathered for the victory feast. The Antichrist and his kings tried to hold Jesus back, but they didn't stand a chance. Jesus single-handedly destroyed the armies of hell and threw the Antichrist and his false prophet into the flames that would contain and punish them forever.

20. An angel emerged from heaven and seized Satan. He placed heavy chains on the evil dragon and threw him into the abyss for a thousand years. The world finally felt relief from his deception and destruction. God lifted up the souls of all people who ever gave their lives proclaiming God's beautiful truths. These brave martyrs never gave into the threats or temptations of the Antichrist. God crowned them as kings and queens, and they enjoyed a beautiful millennium of fellowship with God. At the end of Satan's thousand-year imprisonment, he was let loose once more to test hearts around the world and gather his corrupt followers for a final epic battle against God and his people. Satan's army was more numerous than grains of sand on the beach, but they were no match for our infinitely powerful God. Heavenly fire struck the army down, and good decidedly triumphed

over evil once and for all. The great deceiver Satan was thrown in the eternal lake of fire, never to be seen again. I saw God sitting on a dazzling white throne as heaven and earth as we know it disappeared. Every soul that ever existed rose to life, and death had no more power or sting. God judged all souls according to whether their hearts and actions aligned with his good heart.

21. When the first heaven and earth dissolved, I saw an impossibly beautiful city emerge. God's thundering voice proclaimed "I will finally welcome human beings into my house and live with them forever. Under my protection, you will never again experience sorrow, pain, disappointment, or death. All evil and destructive forces are gone, never to return. Only good remains. I am making all things even more beautiful, glorious, and unspoiled than they were in the very beginning. I am the beginning and end of all things, and you can trust every word I say. I offer all thirsty people life-giving water for free. I am your Father who pulls you into my victory. You are my children, and I will protect you from evil by preventing corrupt murderers, liars, cowards, and traitors from entering this perfect place." An angel carried me to the top of a high mountain where I could see the entire heavenly city, sparkling with the glory of God. Twelve mighty angels guarded the perfectly square gate. The impossibly high city walls were made of strawberry-red jasper and iridescent pearl. The city buildings were made of pure gold and the streets were like clear, untouched glass. An array of glittering gemstones comprised the city foundation, and my senses were flooded with a beautiful combination of the clearest turquoise, the deepest red, the

coolest purple, the warmest yellow, and the most delicious green. The presence of God himself permeated every inch of the city with his glorious light, and the children of God lived in perfect joy and freedom in this open, welcoming place.

22. I saw the crystal blue river of life flowing out of the throne of God and nourishing the city. The life-giving tree bore perfect fruit every month and had leaves with the power to heal and prevent any illness or injury. No flaw or curse could ever spoil this place. All my worries and troubles disappeared, and all I could do was worship my Creator with unbridled joy. I fell to my knees, completely overwhelmed by God's beauty and goodness. The angel said "Every vision you saw represents the future that will unfold at the end of the world. Trust what the Spirit has revealed to you, and spread these truths to God's children everywhere. Those who believe and obey these words will find the deepest kind of hope and happiness." Then Jesus himself looked at me and said "John, my sweet friend, I am the bright morning star. I was there in the beginning, and I'll be there at the end of all things. I'm coming back to save the human race and destroy evil once and for all. I will bless my people beyond their wildest dreams. I long to purify the hearts of those who choose to eat my life-giving fruit, but those who chose to remain soaked in evil will not enter the perfect city you just witnessed. I am eager to welcome anyone who accepts my priceless gift of life." And then Jesus' dazzling form disappeared from my sight and left me sitting here on this beach, awestruck by what I had seen and heard. Let all who hear these mysterious prophecies accept them as

the truth and not attempt to add or take away from their fierce power and beauty. The end of this age will be overwhelmingly terrifying at first, but the battle will give way to pure, perfect beauty beyond our wildest imagination. No matter what we face between now and then, our story has a happy ending. Good will win! The grace of Jesus and the love of God will conquer all!

DAY FOUR - WE NEEDED GRACE
A LOOK BACK AT THE OLD TESTAMENT

BIG IDEA

God made a perfect, beautiful world, and people repeatedly chose to turn from God and disrespect each other.

LESSONS FROM WEEKS 1-4

- **Week One-** From the very beginning, humans generally get it wrong, but God lifts up the few who trust him. People like Noah, Abraham, Jacob, Joseph, and Moses do amazing things through their faith, even though none of them are flawless. When the enslaved Israelites need rescuing, God makes it happen and leads them to a land of prosperity and freedom.

- **Week Two-** The newly freed people turn away from their Deliverer and begin following foreign idols. God gives them countless chances to change and even lifts up great kings like David and Solomon to lead the way. Unfortunately, the nation runs so far from God that they lose his protection and experience widespread destruction. Fortunately, God never gives up on his people and delights in bringing them back home a few generations after exile.

- **Week Three-** The historical narrative pauses to focus on deep faith lessons various individuals learn from God before the birth of Christ. The story of Job explores difficult questions about earthly struggle, while Psalms records a wide variety of worship songs that praise God in all circumstances. Solomon's writings explore insightful, faith-filled perspectives on a wide variety of topics.

- **Week Four-** As Israel and Judah destroy themselves with sin, a number of prophets reveal God's glory to the doubters and try to inspire them to turn back to their Father. God uses miracles, visions, and bold statements to get the people's attention, and when that doesn't work, he removes his protection for a time to show the fallen people just how much they need him.

HOW GOD SHOWS UP

As soon as human beings begin replacing God's will with their own plans, the Lord continually reaches out to try to pull them back. He rescues them from slavery, and he protects them as they establish a new nation. When the people reject God's protection and guidance, God sends prophets and miracles to encourage the people to return to him and avoid disaster. Many refuse to listen, but those who obey experience the awesome power and protection of the loving Father.

OLD TESTAMENT REVIEW

If you have read every daily reading up until this point, you have officially familiarized yourself with every single chapter of the

Bible. All 66 books in a little over a month. That's pretty cool! Congrats! Go ahead and take a moment to do a little happy dance if the Spirit moves you. I'd be happy to wait.

Now it's time to take this spiritual quest one step forward. Today, your daily reading will look a little different. In a moment, I will encourage you to put this book down, and pick up your preferred translation of the Bible. If you don't own a Bible, that's perfectly fine. You can explore many translations for free through apps like YouVersion and through websites like www.biblegateway.com. My personal favorite Bible versions are the Good News Bible and the Common English Bible, but I encourage you to try out a few, and find a translation that you find compelling and easy-to-read.

Today, I offer you three short Bible-reading challenges to help you delve into your new Bible translation thoughtfully. You can choose to spend ten minutes exploring each challenge or thirty minutes exploring just one of these three areas. It's totally up to you. My main objective here is to end your journey through this book by helping you start a new one. Through these final challenges, I hope you decide to continue exploring the Bible regularly. You can start by setting aside daily time to communicate with God and meditate on his deep, eternal truths.

Challenge #1- Pick a story

Think back through the Old Testament readings and reflections, and try to remember the characters and stories you found the most compelling or relatable. Flip back through this book to help you find where your favorite story is located. Many of the readings in Weeks One and Two will fall into this category, as well as a few of the shorter books in Week Four (i.e. Jonah and Daniel). If you're having trouble narrowing it down, here are a few of my personal favorites:

- **Noah and the Ark-** This story can be found is Genesis chapters 6-9. This may be a good choice if you are inspired by the faith it must have taken for Noah to build a big boat long before any rainclouds appeared in the sky.
- **Moses and the Burning Bush-** Explore Moses' origin story as well as his initial conversation with God by reading Exodus chapters 1-4. This may be a good passage for you if you can relate to Moses' anxiety over leaving his comfort zone and becoming a leader.
- **Grandma Ruth-** Read all four chapters of Ruth to explore the story of King David's great-grandmother whose selfless love for family leads her to the town of her future husband.
- **David's Rise from Obscurity-** Read 1 Samuel 16-18 to see how God took an unknown shepherd boy and helped him become a prominent military officer in King Saul's army.
- **Jonah and the Whale-** Read all four chapters of Jonah to dive into a story of this runaway prophet who cannot seem to avoid God's call. Consider reading this if you need a reminder that God notices and cares about you, even when you try to hide from him.

Once you read your preferred story, take a moment to think about why you chose this particular story. Consider whether you relate to any of the characters or situations in the story, and notice whether the lessons within the story might help you gain perspective with whatever you're currently facing. Notice how God shows up for the main character in the story, and think about asking God to show up for you in a similar way.

Challenge #2- Pick a wisdom passage

Consider the portions of Week Three that struck you the most. Flip through the readings from that week to remember which lessons felt the most meaningful or helpful to you. If you're in a season of struggle, maybe you'd find validation within Job's story. If you really connect to God through worship music, pick a psalm. If you are searching for general wisdom regarding life, work, love, and family, I'm sure one of Solomon's writings could speak insight into that area for you. Here are a few ideas:

- **God in the Storm**- Job 38-42 explores how God's response to Job's time of struggle. This may be a great passage if you need a reminder that God is bigger than your pain.
- **The Lord is my Shepherd**- Psalm 23 is a timeless and beautiful passage about how God tenderly loves and protects us when we feel vulnerable and weak.
- **The Woman I Want to Be**- When I need God's advice on how I can be more balanced and more effective as a wife, mom, student, and therapist, I typically turn to Proverbs 31

for a practical, action-oriented perspective.

- **The Beauty of Intimacy-** Any passage within the eight chapters of Song of Songs will give a beautiful picture of a loving and intimate relationship between two people committed to God and each other. This may be a good book to explore if you need advice on deepening your relationship with your spouse or significant other.

Determine one lesson that stood out to you the most within this reading. Meditate on your favorite verse to consider how those words might help you. Consider writing down your takeaway message on a sticky note or index card, so you can be reminded of this lesson throughout your day.

Challenge #3- Pick a prophet

God chose a wide variety of people to courageously speak the truth and persuade the corrupted people to change their ways. Flip through the Week Four readings to determine the prophet or passage that stood out to you the most. Perhaps there was a wake-up call within the text that you needed to hear, or perhaps you were moved by a particular miracle God used to gain his people's attention. If nothing's standing out right away, I've included a few compelling passages below to help you brainstorm:

- **Jeremiah's Uncertainty-** Jeremiah 1 gives a vulnerable and compelling account of what it can be like to feel unworthy of God's calling. You might choose this passage if you feel like God is pushing you toward a project or ministry that falls outside your comfort zone.

- **Dry Bones**- Ezekiel 37 would be a great choice if you are wondering what it might look and feel like for God to transform you and bring you to life.
- **Hosea and Gomer**- Hosea was instructed to marry a woman who was always messing up and pushing him away. Read Hosea 14 if you need a reminder that God loves you no matter how imperfect you are.
- **Powerful Hope**- The short books of Habakkuk and Zephaniah both offer compelling images of a mighty Father who rescues his people even when circumstances feel hopeless.

After you read your favorite prophecy passage, consider what God was trying to communicate with his people through that prophet, and think about how you might benefit from that same wake-up call.

DAY FIVE - GRACE CAME DOWN
A LOOK BACK AT THE NEW TESTAMENT

BIG IDEA

God sent his Son to earth to rescue our hearts and offer us love that never ends.

LESSONS FROM WEEKS 5-7

- **Week Five-** Jesus may have looked like an average working class guy, but his revolutionary words and miraculous actions proved he was the long-awaited Savior that God had promised long before. This extraordinary Son of God reached out to sinners and outcasts, setting a powerful example for the love he expects us to show each other. After several years of ministry, Jesus sacrificed his own life so that we could be forgiven and freed from our mistakes. When death could not hold Jesus down, many people were inspired to believe in him and accept the new life of grace that he offers.

- **Week Six-** The early church experienced rapid growth throughout many nations thanks to leaders like Paul, James, Peter, John, and Jude. These men wrote a number of letters to these budding congregations to inspire them to stay connected to the Holy Spirit, stay unified with each other, and hold fast to the truth. These letters also contain priceless words of wisdom that reveal the transformative power of God's grace and faith-filled action.

- **Week Seven-** The risen Jesus appears to his dear friend John and offers him a series of visions designed to motivate and inspire seven struggling churches. Jesus wants these churches to know that they're not alone in their struggles, and even when the world falls apart someday, our lives will not end in darkness. These beautiful, symbolic visions help us see that the end of this earthly age will actually usher in an overwhelmingly beautiful beginning. Jesus gives John a powerful glimpse of the eternal home we will share with God when this life is over.

HOW GOD SHOWS UP

God loves us so much that he refuses to watch us self-destruct from a distance. He draws near to us by becoming human, and he makes it clear that he unconditionally loves even the smallest among us. He offers us forgiveness, freedom, and new life without asking anything in return. Our powerful Creator puts himself through unspeakable pain so that we never have to endure that same pain. He lifts us up from the hell we created for ourselves and invites us to live in his perfect presence forever.

NEW TESTAMENT REVIEW

Congratulations on completing this journey through the Bible and making it to our final daily reading. Thank you so much for trusting me to guide you through scripture. I hope this was a helpful and transformative learning experience for you.

Today, we will explore three final Bible-reading challenges that will help you explore the overarching sections of the New Testament. Like yesterday, you might choose to explore each challenge for ten minutes apiece or dive into just one of these areas for thirty minutes. Regardless, I hope that today's passages help you further deepen your understanding of the life of Jesus and his guidance for the early church. Most of all, I hope that when you wake up tomorrow, you continue setting aside daily time to read scripture, so you can get to know our amazing Father even better.

Challenge #1- Pick a gospel passage

Reflect on which gospel is your favorite and why. Flip through the Week Five daily readings to rediscover your favorite passages within your preferred gospel. Try to pinpoint a chapter or two that you'd like to read in its entirety. Perhaps you are incredibly touched by one of Jesus' healings or one of his sermons. Maybe you'd like to explore the deep sacrifices Jesus made before his death, or perhaps you'd like to read about how he rose three days later. There are so many inspiring passages within these four books, but here are a few of my favorites:

- **Sermon on the Mount-** This revolutionary speech found in Matthew 5-7 flies in the face of many common beliefs supported by the Jewish leaders at that time. While the religious leaders valued wealth, status, and perfect adherence to the

Law, Jesus valued humility, authenticity, and vulnerable faith.

- **Healing with Boldness**- Mark 2-5 describes many examples of Jesus reaching out to hurting people the world had forgotten. He repeatedly shows kindness through his miraculous actions, even when those actions go against the rigid laws laid out by the pharisees.

- **Loving the Lost**- Read Luke 15 if you'd like to read three parables that beautifully express how deeply our Father loves us. In these stories of a lost coin, a lost sheep, and a runaway son, we see that God reaches out to embrace us even when we feel insignificant and undeserving.

- **Last Supper**- In John 13-17 the Messiah's best friend takes us behind the scenes to hear Jesus' final dinner conversation with his inner circle.

Once you read your preferred story from Jesus' life, take a moment to think about why you chose this particular story. Consider how Jesus demonstrates love and goodness through this passage. Take a moment to simply thank Jesus for being awesome. Think about how you might learn from his example to improve your own attitude and interactions with others.

Challenge #2- Pick a church letter

Each letter has a slightly different combination of lessons designed to help the early church follow the example of Jesus, so flip through the readings from Week Six to determine which letter or passage struck you the most. If you need a little guidance narrowing down one passage to read, consider these ideas:

- **Nothing Can Separate Us**- Romans 8 is chock full of powerful insights about God's unconditional love and goodness. This passage emphasizes that all circumstances work together for our good, and we can't do anything that would make our Father quit loving us.
- **All About Love**- If you've ever been to a wedding, you've probably heard the beautiful description of love from 1 Corinthians 13. If you want to explore what it really means to love others, read this passage slowly, and assess how well these qualities of love show up in your relationships.
- **Fruits of the Spirit**- Read Galatians 5 if you're wondering how the Holy Spirit might transform our hearts and inspire us to live differently.
- **Unstoppable Joy**- All four chapters of Phillipians are full of infectious happiness that does not depend on earthly circumstances. I'd encourage you to read this letter if you need a mood boost or a perspective shift.
- **Transformative Faith**- Hebrews 11-13 discusses what it means to have unshakable faith. This passage reviews many inspiring Old Testament stories of faith and emphasizes that when we trust God, we can do great things.

After you read your favorite Week Six passage, determine one lesson that you found particularly helpful. Meditate on your favorite verse within the passage, and ask God to help you draw new meaning from it. Consider writing down that verse on a sticky note or index card, so you can be reminded of this lesson throughout the day.

Challenge #3- Pick a Revelation passage

This book is full of complex passages, mysterious prophecies, and symbolic imagery that have sparked countless debates among pastors and Bible scholars. For years, I was intimidated and confused by many of these passages myself, so I usually avoided them. If you've ever felt the same way, I hope that the Week Seven readings helped Revelation feel more approachable and less intimidating. I invite you to choose one portion of Revelation to read in its entirety. A few ideas include:

- **The Seven Churches-** If you'd like to take a closer look at Jesus' individualized messages for the seven Asian churches, read Revelation 2-3. It's interesting how the early church mirrors some of the strengths and challenges we experience in our modern congregations. Consider which of the seven churches you identify with the most, and reflect on what you might learn from Jesus' message to them.

- **Throne Room-** Revelation 4 offers a beautiful and detailed description of the heavenly throne room. Allow yourself to read this passage slowly to try to visualize this awesome sight. Imagine yourself standing with awe and worship in that place.

- **Fall of the Dragon-** Revelation 12 reminds me of many

of the fairy tales and epic stories I read as a kid. God is the unstoppable hero, and Satan is the fearsome dragon. Read this chapter if you appreciate colorful depictions of good conquering evil.

- **Glimpse of Heaven-** There are few pieces of literature more beautiful or profound than Revelation 21-22. If you have experienced the loss of a loved one, you might find comfort in this passage, knowing he or she is experiencing perfect beauty and joy in God's presence.

Pray for God to open your eyes to the deeper insights within the passage you chose. Whether you agree with my interpretation or discover a totally different perspective, I hope that your reading time helps you see God and heaven more clearly.

WEEK SEVEN REFLECTION
Heaven

DISCUSSION QUESTIONS

- When God gave John a glimpse of eternity, how do you think that experience changed his perspective? How might this vision help us combat worry or muster up hope?

- Chapters two and three of John's letter address each of the seven Asian churches. Which church do you relate to the most and why? What was Jesus' advice to that church?

- Read the fourth chapter of Revelation in its entirety, and picture the throne room of God. What feelings arise in your heart as you try to picture the throne room?

- How is God's power revealed through John's vision? How can his love and mercy be seen?

- What does Revelation reveal about the nature of Satan? How will Satan be evident in the heart of the Antichrist? How is Satan's presence evident in the world today?

- When Jesus locks Satan in the abyss for 1,000 years, how will the world be different during that time?

- What does Revelation 21-22 reveal about the "new heaven and new earth?" What are you most excited about experiencing there?

- When going through the Old and New Testament reading challenges, which Bible passages did you choose to read? Why did you choose these passages, and what did you learn during your reading time? What Bible translation did you use, and what made you choose that translation?

MUSIC MEDITATIONS

- **Revelation part 1-** When John gets his first glimpses of heaven, he watches in awe as a great crowd worships the beautiful Creator with great passion. Close your eyes, listen to "Revelation Song" by Kari Jobe, and try to picture that scene.

- **Revelation part 2-** It is difficult to read about the final days of tribulation, but as John witnesses these events, God encourages him to remember that God's children will be protected from harm, and this ugly battle won't last forever. Where do you see similar messages of hope in "Eye of the Storm" by Ryan Stevenson or "It is Well" by Bethel Music?

- **Revelation part 3-** Many artists have written beautiful songs about the perfect beauty, joy, and peace that awaits us in heaven. Some of my favorites include "Forever" by Kari Jobe, "I Can Only Imagine" by Mercy Me, and "Heaven Song" by Phil Wickham. How do each of these songs highlight different, beautiful characteristics of our eternal home?

APPLICATION IDEAS

- Take some time to let go of your earthly worries today. You may choose to take a bubble bath, listen to music, go on a run, or practice any other healthy skill that helps you unwind. In light of eternity, these stresses do not deserve a permanent home in your brain.

- Although Satan's days are numbered, he will try to wreck as much havoc as he can for now. What are the most prominent ways that Satan wreaks havoc in your circle of influence? How can you start recognizing those struggles and battling them more confidently?

- Make a list of people in your life who you would like to spend time with in heaven. Pray sincerely that God will reveal himself to each of these loved ones in new ways.

ACKNOWLEDGMENTS

This book would not exist without the support of a number of individuals. Whether you walked with me every step of this journey or simply gave me a boost along the way, I'd like to thank you for being a part of my life and helping bring this book to life.

Topping the list is the God responsible for all good and beautiful things in this world including my children, music, sunrises, puppies, and coffee. He loves me enough to save me from my mistakes, and he guides me each day to become a better version of myself. He planted the initial ideas for this book in my mind seven years ago and has gently nudged me many times over the years to revisit it.

Kevin, you are my first and last love. You're my very best friend, an awesome dad to our boys, and the person who makes me take breaks when I turn into a crazy, anxious perfectionist. You took on extra parenting time to give me writing time, and you listened patiently when I rambled endlessly about whether this book would ever get done. You offered me priceless encouragement and feedback whenever I was stuck, and I absolutely couldn't have done it without you.

Caleb, my brilliant and hilarious kindergartener, I am incredibly thankful that God allowed me to bring you into this world. Your courage pushes me to expand my comfort zone, and your endless curiosity causes me to see the world with fresh eyes every day. I love you, buddy!

Bennett, my sweet angel and toddler tornado, I honestly don't know what I would do without you. Your belly laugh fills me with giddy joy, and your squishy hugs calm my restless heart. I adore you, and I am unbelievably blessed that I was chosen and trusted to be your mom.

A huge thank you to my grandparents, Betty Brumett, Jude Brumett, Alice Robison, and John Robison. Even though each of you have moved on from this life, you continue to inspire me to be the best person I can be. You raised my parents to be the amazing people they are, and you taught me what it means to live for God and others.

To my parents Rick and D'Ann Brumett, thank you for encouraging me and offering priceless feedback that shaped each draft of this work. Thanks for introducing me to God and encouraging me to live according to his guidance and grace. You are my heroes, and I want to be like you when I grow up.

To my little brother, Matt Brumett, you have always been my biggest cheerleader in every area of my life. Your positivity has encouraged me forward with this project, and you've offered brilliant suggestions about how to better reach youngsters like you. Autumn, thank you so much for taking care of my goofy brother. Our family is better with you in it.

Thanks to all the Brumetts, Robisons, Nortons, and Rutherfords who knew and loved me when I was a shy, nerdy kid. Thank you for supporting me and embracing my boys as part of our family. A special thank you to Judie Brumett for helping shape me into the history nerd that I am.

To the best in-laws a gal could ask for: Peggy, Larry, Chris, Sarah, David, and Julia Rotert, as well as all the Shaws, Mensings, and Roterts in our extended family. I admire each of you, and I feel lucky to be a part of this crazy, awesome family.

To my sweet nieces and nephews: Abigail, Kylie, Eric, Benjamin, Haylee, and Piper Rotert. Few things make me happier than watching you kids grow up together and watching each of you develop into strong, amazing individuals. I love you guys!

Heather Underwood and Machelle Minter, thank you for being my besties and soul sisters. So glad we've grown from kids to full blown moms together.

Kristy Ladd Culp and Allison Mabe, thank you for encouraging me forward with this project and for offering priceless feedback about things I don't understand like marketing and design. I am so lucky to know you ladies.

Vanessa Mendozzi, thank you for helping make the cover and interior layout of this book beautiful. As far as I'm concerned, you're the best designer in the business, and I feel honored to be collaborating with you.

I want to thank our leaders and friends at Liberty United Methodist Church (Liberty, MO), Trinity United Methodist Church (Lincoln, NE), and Heritage Church (Van Buren, AR). You have walked by us through many of life's tests, inspired us to do our best, and always helped us feel loved.

Thanks to the many work friends, school friends, mom friends, old friends, and new friends near and far who have added so much support, fun memories, and interesting conversation to our lives over the years. Even if you haven't specifically seen your name in these pages, please know that my life is better with you in it, and I am incredibly thankful to know each of you.

Finally, thanks to you for picking up this book and trusting me to lead you on this journey.

www.ingramcontent.com/pod-product-compliance
Lightning Source LLC
Chambersburg PA
CBHW021131090426
42740CB00008B/745